PETER J. PARISH A Londoner by birth, and a
graduate of the University of London, Peter J. Parish
taught American history for twenty-five years in
Scotland, first at the University of Glasgow, and
then as Bonar Professor of Modern History at the
University of Dundee. From 1983 to 1992, he was
Director of the Institute of United States Studies,
University of London. A former chairman of the
British Association for American Studies, he has
lectured at a number of American universities and
colleges. He has written extensively on the era of the
American Civil War and on slavery; his books
include *The American Civil War* (1975) and *Slavery:
History and Historians* (1989).

ABRAHAM LINCOLN

Speeches and Letters

Edited by
Peter J. Parish

Consultant Editor for this volume
Christopher Bigsby
University of East Anglia

J.M. Dent
London
Charles E. Tuttle
Rutland, Vermont
EVERYMAN'S LIBRARY

Selection, introduction and other apparatus
© J.M. Dent 1993

Speeches and Letters first published in Everyman in
1907

This selection first published in Everyman in 1993

All rights reserved

Typeset by Deltatype Ltd, Ellesmere Port, Cheshire

Printed in Great Britain by
The Guernsey Press Co., Ltd, Guernsey, C.I.
for
J.M. Dent
Orion Publishing Group
Orion House
5 Upper St Martin's Lane
London WC2H 9EA
and
Charles E. Tuttle Co., Inc.
28 South Main Street
Rutland, Vermont
05701 USA

ISBN 0 460 87146 3

Everyman's Library
Reg. US Patent Office

CONTENTS

Introduction by Peter J. Parish   vii
Suggestions for Further Reading   xvii

Chapter 1
The Young Lincoln: Politics, Law and Love, 1832–42   3

Chapter 2
Congressman, Husband and Father, 1843–52   31

Chapter 3
Kansas-Nebraska and the Return to Active Politics, 1854–7   55

Chapter 4
The Debates with Stephen A. Douglas, 1858   78

Chapter 5
The Making of the First Republican President, 1859–61   126

Chapter 6
Going to War, 1861   160

Chapter 7
Battlefield Setbacks and the
    Politics of Emancipation, 1862–3   195

Chapter 8
A President in His Prime, 1863   236

Chapter 9
Triumph and Tragedy, 1864–5   272

Chronology of Lincoln's Life   295

INTRODUCTION

The historical Lincoln stands at the meeting-place of at least three of the great myths which sustain Americans' sense of their national past. First, he exemplifies the log-cabin-to-White-House story of the poor boy from the frontier who could rise to the highest office in the land. Secondly, he is the savior of the Union in its time of supreme trial, who became martyr as well as hero when he gave his life to the cause in its moment of final triumph. Thirdly, he is the great emancipator, who struck the shackles from four million slaves, and thus removed the ugliest stain on the image of the American republic. As good myths should, all three contain a healthy measure of historical truth – simplified and dramatized, but truth none the less. By association with these three myths, Lincoln became the symbolic champion of American liberty and democracy, and in the process emerged as the personal embodiment of the American national identity.

Lincoln's writings and speeches speak clearly to all these themes. The body of his writings is much smaller than that of many of the great names of American history. This is no doubt a reflection of both his humble origins and the comparative brevity of his public life, at least on the national stage. The contrast between Lincoln and Jefferson, for example, could scarcely be greater. Lincoln's mind, and his use of language, were not shaped by formal education, fine libraries and familiarity with the world of culture and learning on both sides of the Atlantic. His father was almost illiterate, he had barely a year of schooling himself, he never traveled beyond the United States, and he knew nothing of foreign languages. His prose style was shaped as much by the newspapers and his law books, as by Shakespeare and the Bible.

Whatever he may have lost, Lincoln almost certainly gained something from the avoidance of a conventional education. In contrast to the pomposity and prolixity of much Victorian rhetoric on both sides of the Atlantic, Lincoln wrote and spoke in a much more direct, uncluttered, lucid style. There were times, of course, when his prose was clumsy and labored, and his grasp of grammar and syntax was not always secure. However, his finest writings are marked by their simplicity, purity, grace and balance – as, for example, in the sentence from his 1862 message to Congress: 'we shall nobly save, or meanly lose, the last, best hope of earth.' Similarly, almost three-quarters of the words in the Gettysburg Address contain only one syllable.

In some of his letters, he achieved a variety of effects by the same simple means. His self-deprecating humor emerges from his reassuring reply to an actor who had apologized for the leaking to the press of an earlier private letter: 'I have endured a great deal of ridicule without much malice; and have received a great deal of kindness not quite free from ridicule. I am used to it.' But he could be severe, or even harsh, with equal effect, as for example in his letter to a group of discontented Democrats from his own state: 'You say you will not fight to free Negroes. Some of them seem willing to fight for you; but no matter.' In very different vein, he could show compassion and deep humanity when writing to the afflicted or bereaved. In a letter to the daughter of a friend, recently killed in battle, he wrote:

> In this sad world of ours, sorrow comes to all; and, to the young, it comes with bitterest agony, because it takes them unawares. The older have learned to ever expect it . . . Perfect relief is not possible, except with time. You cannot now realize that you will ever feel better. Is not this so? And yet it is a mistake. You are sure to be happy again. To know this, which is certainly true, will make you some less miserable now.

The most remarkable feature of the president's letters is their intensely personal quality. Written by a man grossly overburdened by the cares of wartime leadership, they are still unmistakably his own, and not the product of an impersonal bureaucracy, or of a White House staff practising the arts of public relations and media manipulation. This is not to deny that Lincoln was keenly interested in the shaping and promotion of his own image. But his letters reveal much about Lincoln the man, and the times in which he lived.

*

There is no need to romanticize Lincoln's humble beginnings, although the attempt has often been made. The truth is plain enough – 'the short and simple annals of the poor' was his own description. Born in 1809 in a cabin in the slave state of Kentucky, he moved with his family first to another location in Kentucky, then into Indiana, and later on to Illinois – all by the time he had reached the age of twenty-one. The hasty construction of a crude family home, the clearing of the surrounding land, the cultivation of corn and other crops to support the family at basic subsistence level, and then another move and the beginning of the whole process yet again – all of this mirrored the frontier experience of many pioneer families. So too did the hardships and setbacks, and the all-too-common encounters with sickness and death. Lincoln's mother died when he was only nine years old, his sister died in childbirth, and several other family members, friends and neighbors succumbed to the diseases which swept through the region from time to time. (Later, two of Lincoln's four sons were to die in childhood, and a third at the age of eighteen.)

As a young man in Illinois, Lincoln made his way as store-keeper, postmaster, surveyor, and jack-of-all-trades. In the process, he made himself into something of a local 'character'. The window which opened up wider horizons to him was provided by law and politics. Illinois had been a state for scarcely twenty years, and the way ahead was not yet barred against an intelligent young man, with plenty of ambition but no formal qualifications. Eight years in the state legislature sharpened his political skills, but he made little mark during a single two-year term, from 1847 to 1849, in the House of Representatives in Washington.

For the next dozen years, he held no public office whatsoever until he entered the White House in March 1861. But he never abandoned politics, and the Kansas-Nebraska crisis in 1854 brought him back into active participation. Moving with charac-teristic prudence, he made himself a key figure in the evolution of the new anti-slavery Republican party in Illinois. In the campaign for a Senate seat in 1858, his debates with Stephen A. Douglas, one of the great stars of American politics in the 1850s, gave him fresh prominence on the national stage. Ironically, his per-formance did not win him the Senate seat, which probably represented the very height of his political ambition, but it propelled him towards nomination as the Republican candidate for the presidency two years later, in 1860. It was his election as the first president of this new party, drawing support exclusively from the North, which sparked the secession of seven Southern states and then the outbreak of civil war.

By any standard, Abraham Lincoln would seem to have been one of the least qualified and least experienced men ever to become president of the United States – let alone to become war leader. With minimal formal education, no administrative experience, the briefest involvement on the national political stage, and no military training or expertise beyond eighty days' service in the militia almost thirty years earlier, Lincoln's destiny was to preside for four years over the life-and-death struggle to save the Union. It is small wonder that many Americans, even including some members of his own cabinet, believed in 1861 that he was simply not up to the job. Some persisted in that belief until the end of his life. In sharp contrast, the ultimate triumph of the Union cause, the emancipation of the slaves, and Lincoln's assassination in the hour of victory, encouraged those blessed with hindsight to elevate this most human of American presidents to demi-god status. The truth lies somewhere in the broad area in between.

Whatever the limitations of his earlier experience, Lincoln developed out of it not only the skills of a master politician, but also a set of ideals, principles and values which shaped his presidency. In his passionate belief in both liberty and Union, he saw, not an inevitable tension between the two, but a mutually supportive relationship in which the latter was the guardian and promoter of the former. It is against this background that some understanding may be sought of Lincoln's attitude towards the South's peculiar institution of racial slavery, which mocked American pretensions to be the standard-bearer of liberty and democracy.

During his active political life, Lincoln consistently denounced slavery as a moral wrong. When, in the 1850s, he championed the cause of 'free soil' – that is, the policy of preventing any further extension of slavery into the western territories – he constantly linked the restriction of slavery to its inherent moral unacceptability. In December 1860, shortly after his election, he wrote to Alexander Stephens of Georgia (the future vice-president of the Confederate States) in words very close to those used a few months later in his inaugural address: 'You think slavery is *right* and ought to be extended; while we think it is *wrong* and ought to be restricted ... It certainly is the only substantial difference between us.'

If Lincoln was so convinced that slavery was wrong, why did he not join the campaign for its immediate and total abolition? The answer no doubt lies partly in Lincoln's nature: as a highly political animal, he was sensitive to political realities, and sought solutions through political action. In thirty years of moral crusading before the Civil War, the abolitionists had succeeded in putting the slavery issue on the national agenda, but had completely failed to rouse the bulk of Northern opinion in support of their cause. For his part, Lincoln argued that a policy of geographical restriction would put slavery on the road to 'ultimate extinction', although he did not commit himself on the question of how long the process would take.

He was well aware that, although an increasing proportion of his fellow-Northerners opposed slavery, and deplored its existence in the South, only a small minority were prepared to contemplate direct action to eradicate it. For the great majority of Northerners, slavery became a problem requiring such action only when it threatened their interests or obstructed their future prospects – for example, if it impeded the settlement of the west by Northern farmers and Northern free white labor.

There were other reasons, too, why Lincoln's anti-slavery stance fell far short of outright abolitionism. He accepted the conventional wisdom, shared by all engaged in mainstream politics, that the Constitution ruled out federal interference in the domestic institutions of the states. In 1845, he noted the irony of a situation which required acceptance of slavery where it already existed in the name of defending the rights and liberties of the Southern states and their citizens. Even as president, he drew a clear distinction between his own personal wish that slavery might be brought to an end, and his public duty to respect the Constitution and enforce the laws.

Behind the problem of slavery lay the question of race. Virtually all white Americans, in North as well as South (and including Lincoln himself), accepted the prevailing view, backed by the scientific wisdom of the day, that there were superior and inferior races, and that blacks were inherently inferior to whites. What may well strike the late twentieth-century ear as Lincoln's equivocations and evasions on matters of race have to be understood (if not always excused) in the context of the climate of opinion of his day. Whether in the struggle with Stephen A. Douglas for a Senate seat in 1858, or in the presidential contests of 1860 and 1864, Lincoln and his fellow-Republicans had to withstand blatantly racist propaganda from their Democratic opponents, eager to exploit fears of racial amalgamation.

As president leading the resistance to the attempt of the slave South to disrupt the Union, Lincoln faced a number of dilemmas. From the outset, he insisted that the purpose of the war was to save the Union, but other questions forced themselves upon him. Did the war enable him to act constitutionally against slavery in ways denied to him in normal circumstances? Did it make sense to fight the South without attacking its peculiar institution? Should emancipation be added to salvation of the Union as a war aim? In addressing these formidable questions, Lincoln confronted a daunting problem in practical politics. Once convinced – as he surely was by the summer of 1862 – that an emancipation policy was morally right, in the national interest, and militarily ex-pedient, how was he to explain it and implement it in face of a Northern majority which remained deeply suspicious, if not actively hostile?

Lincoln's answer was to adopt a very low-key approach. Where appeals to conscience or principle were not enough, he argued that emancipation was in the interest of white, as well as black, Americans. He sought at every stage to soothe racial prejudice and to allay fears about the consequences of emancipation. He went through the motions, at least, of experimenting with various compromise solutions, including gradual emancipation and even colonization of the freed slaves abroad, if only to convince his critics that he had considered every possibility. He waited as long as possible before committing himself irrevocably to any one policy. He denied himself dramatic gestures or high-flown rhetoric; even the Emancipation Proclamations themselves are very prosaic legal documents – 'with all the moral grandeur of a bill of lading', as one historian has put it. Because the Proclama-tions declared free only those slaves living in areas still under Confederate control, many critics derided them as an empty gesture. In reality, however, for Lincoln and for the Union cause, they marked a point of no return. If the North won the war and the Union was saved, slavery was surely doomed.

Having accepted a new commitment, the president acted upon

it. He supported the recruitment of black troops, about which he had earlier harbored grave doubts; to put weapons in the hands of blacks to fight against whites was clearly a revolutionary act, by the standards of the mid-nineteenth century. He became the first president ever to receive blacks in the White House. He put his full weight behind the Thirteenth Amendment to the Constitution, which abolished slavery once and for all throughout the United States. His pragmatic, piecemeal approach secured the emancipation of the slaves, which no one could have expected a few years earlier; but it neglected or postponed serious consideration of many of the problems which freedom would bring with it for the former slaves.

Lincoln's handling of the crucial issue of emancipation was typical of his presidential style. He preferred to deal with the specific rather than the general, with people rather than with institutions. He made no attempt to dominate Congress, but had a close relationship with many individual congressmen. His cabinet scarcely operated as a unit, but the president got the best out of its ablest (and often most intractable) members. He was an unsystematic and haphazard administrator, but usually had his way when it really mattered. Until 1864, he had no clear high command structure to develop and implement his grand strategy; but he had a direct and personal relationship with many individual generals, and increasing confidence in his own judgement in military matters. He delivered remarkably few public addresses during the war; but the White House corridors were crowded with callers waiting to see him, and he clearly thought it worthwhile to devote many long hours to them.

One of the president's most important tasks was to promote and sustain popular support for a war which proved to be much longer and immeasurably more costly than anyone had foreseen in 1861. In pursuit of this goal, he appealed for loyalty to the Union, encouraged his fellow-citizens to see how their hopes and ambitions depended on its survival, and defined the issues at stake in the conflict in terms which millions of Americans could understand. He sought to placate opponents, and to relieve warweariness and frustration. Not all opposition could be won over, and the other side of Lincoln's policy required the containment of dissent. He authorized large numbers of arbitrary arrests but, in characteristic style, showed flexibility, pragmatism and humanity in execution of this policy and mitigation of its effects, whatever dangerous precedents he may have been setting for the future.

On the whole, the war – and a civil war at that – was conducted with remarkably little infringement of civil liberties and individual rights. As far as possible, Lincoln preferred to operate through the normal political processes. In fact, the continuation of party politics and electoral competition made a significant contribution to the Union war effort, by providing a mechanism for both the expression of opposing views and the containment of discontent. In 1864 the vigorous conduct of a presidential election campaign in the middle of a civil war testified to the robust condition of American political democracy. Lincoln became the first president since 1832 to be re-elected for a second term.

One of the keys to Lincoln's performance as president and war leader lies in his ability to operate at several levels at the same time. He could ponder electoral as well as military strategy, haggle over a political appointment, outmaneuver a political opponent, encourage or chastise a general in the field, pardon a soldier sentenced to death for sleeping on duty – and all without losing sight of basic principles and ultimate objectives. He also showed extraordinary strength of will and pertinacity, in the face of frequent setbacks on the field of battle and ever-increasing casualty lists. The humane and humorous Lincoln was also the stern and relentless Lincoln. The lined and ravaged face revealed in photographs taken in the last few months of his life suggests something of the agony of four years of wartime leadership.

Lincoln presided over a huge, and ultimately successful, struggle to save the Union, defend the values of the 'free labor' society of the North, and reaffirm the American commitment to liberty. But in striving to achieve these goals, he helped to re-define, and even transform, them. As the new apostle of American nationalism, Lincoln hastened the transition from the loose-limbed union of ante-bellum America into a new, more tightly integrated nation, with enhanced powers and new moral commitments. The very word 'Union' was increasingly supplanted by 'nation' or 'national' during the war years. (A comparison between Lincoln's First Inaugural Address in March 1861 and the Gettysburg Address of November 1863 is instructive on this point.)

As the spokesman of the Republican free-labour ideology,

Lincoln lost no chance, even in the darkest moments of the war, to draw attention to continuing economic expansion and development. He stressed the importance of the 'right to rise' which offered every American the opportunity to improve his lot and achieve economic independence by his own efforts. Understandably, he did not indulge in speculation about the future prospects of the 'right to rise' in the urban-industrial, big-business America which was to come.

As the champion of American liberty, he expanded its scope to embrace the freed slaves, although he could not provide adequate guarantees of their newly-won freedom. Borrowing from the two concepts of liberty defined by Isaiah Berlin, James McPherson has depicted Lincoln as a key figure in the transition from a negative to a positive idea of liberty. From the Revolution to the Civil War, American freedom had been defined mainly in the negative sense of freedom from the intrusions of government power. The Emancipation Proclamations and the Thirteenth, Fourteenth and Fifteenth Amendments to the Constitution, passed between 1865 and 1870, signaled a shift to the positive use of government power as the promoter and protector of liberty, whether to free the slaves or to guarantee the civil rights of all American citizens.

In the 1920s, the distinguished medievalist, David Knowles, wrote a short book on the American Civil War. In his preface, he expressed his admiration for Lincoln as 'the man who, above all others in modern times, has gone far to solve the deep moral problems underlying the exercise of power over others'. It is a just tribute, amply supported by the evidence of many of Lincoln's major speeches and state papers. However, there is at least as much evidence from his letters and speeches to show that he was also a politician to his fingertips. Indeed, it took all the skills of the adroit and ambitious politician, as well as participation in one of the great events of modern history, to provide the moral statesman with a stage on which to achieve his true stature.

SUGGESTIONS FOR FURTHER READING

Few figures in history have attracted as much attention from biographers and historians as Abraham Lincoln. However, there are few modern biographies of real quality; much of the best work on Lincoln has dealt with particular aspects of his life and times.

Biographies

Stephen B. Oates, *With Malice toward None: The Life of Abraham Lincoln* (New York, 1976; London, 1977). The fullest and most reliable modern biography.

Benjamin P. Thomas, *Abraham Lincoln: A Biography* (New York, 1952; London, 1953). An older study, long regarded as the best single-volume biography.

Particular Aspects of Lincoln's Life and Political Career

Don E. Fehrenbacher, *Lincoln in Text and Context: Collected Essays* (Stanford, Ca, 1987). Wise and wide-ranging essays by a leading Lincoln scholar.

Stephen B. Oates, *Abraham Lincoln: The Man behind the Myths* (New York, 1984). Reflections, and second thoughts, from a leading Lincoln biographer.

James M. McPherson, *Abraham Lincoln and the Second American Revolution* (New York, 1991). A probing examination of Lincoln's ideas and policies, and of the meaning of the Civil War.

Charles B. Strozier, *Lincoln's Quest for Union: Public and Private Meanings* (New York, 1982; Urbana, Ill., 1987). Much the best of the psycho-historical studies of Lincoln's personality and pre-presidential career.

Jean H. Baker, *Mary Todd Lincoln: A Biography* (New York, 1987). A revealing biography of Mrs Lincoln which sheds much light on her husband.

The Civil War

James M. McPherson, *Battle Cry of Freedom: The Civil War Era* (New York, 1988).

Peter J. Parish, *The American Civil War* (London & New York, 1975). Two large-scale interpretative histories of the Civil War period, which focus particularly on the four years of the war itself.

Bruce Levine, *Half Slave and Half Free: The Roots of Civil War* (New York, 1992). A recent and readable brief study which portrays the Civil War as a clash between two widely diverging cultures.

Eric Foner, *Free Soil, Free Labor, Free Men: The Ideology of the Republican Party before the Civil War* (New York, 1970). Very influential study of the ideas and outlook of the party which put Lincoln in the White House.

SPEECHES AND LETTERS
OF
ABRAHAM LINCOLN

Chapter 1
The Young Lincoln:
Politics, Law and Love
1832–42

Predictably, there is only the scantiest written record of the early life of the son of illiterate parents on the American frontier in the early nineteenth century. Lincoln's own writings as a young man reflect his interest in law and politics, not least as vehicles for his own advancement. He was a very active Whig member of the Illinois state legislature for eight years, at a time when the Jacksonian Democrats were usually the more popular party in the state.

His early writings also show a concern for more fundamental political issues, as in his first major public address to the Young Men's Lyceum in 1838. This is also the period of Lincoln's first encounter with slavery; his description of happy, laughing slaves, shrugging off the misery of their condition, contrasts with his later, more considered, reflections on this incident and on the wider questions posed by slavery.

The early writings also offer tantalizing glimpses of Lincoln's personal and emotional life. The dry, self-deprecating humor, the quirky personal style, the curious mixture of bluntness and acuteness, earthiness and gentleness, the self-doubt and the bouts of depression, all contributed to a unique personality. Anxieties and inhibitions of various kinds bedeviled his relationships with women, and led, for example, to the two broken engagements, with Mary Owens and Mary Todd (whom he married eighteen months later). In his letter to Mrs Browning, the coarseness of Lincoln's comments on the generously built Mary Owens can still shock. On the other hand, his correspondence with his one close personal friend, Joshua Speed, reveals great sensitivity and deep personal agony, as he sometimes projects his own feelings and concerns on to his reactions to Speed's courtship and marriage. The afterthought at the end of an 1842 letter on legal business is characteristic of the man: 'Nothing new here, except my marrying, which to me is matter of profound wonder.'

Political announcement: communication to the Sangamo Journal *of Springfield, Illinois.*

9 March 1832

Fellow-Citizens: Having become a candidate for the honorable office of one of your representatives in the next General Assembly of this state, in accordance with an established custom, and the principles of true republicanism, it becomes my duty to make known to you – the people whom I propose to represent – my sentiments with regard to local affairs . . .

Upon the subject of education, not presuming to dictate any plan or system respecting it, I can only say that I view it as the most important subject which we as a people can be engaged in. That every man may receive at least a moderate education, and thereby be enabled to read the histories of his own and other countries, by which he may duly appreciate the value of our free institutions, appears to be an object of vital importance, even on this account alone, to say nothing of the advantages and satisfaction to be derived from all being able to read the scriptures and other works, both of a religious and moral nature, for themselves. For my part, I desire to see the time when education, and by its means morality, sobriety, enterprise, and industry, shall become much more general than at present, and should be gratified to have it in my power to contribute something to the advancement of any measure which might have a tendency to accelerate the happy period.

With regard to existing laws, some alterations are thought to be necessary. Many respectable men have suggested that our estray laws – the law respecting the issuing of executions, the road law, and some others – are deficient in their present form, and require alterations. But considering the great probability that the framers of those laws were wiser than myself, I should prefer not meddling with them, unless they were first attacked by others, in which case I should feel it both a privilege and a duty to take that stand, which in my view might tend most to the advancement of justice.

But, fellow-citizens, I shall conclude. Considering the great degree of modesty which should always attend youth, it is probable I have already been more presuming than becomes me. However, upon the subjects of which I have treated, I have spoken as I thought. I may be wrong in regard to any or all of them; but holding it a sound maxim, that it is better to be only sometimes right, than at all times wrong, so soon as I discover my opinions to be erroneous, I shall be ready to renounce them.

Every man is said to have his peculiar ambition. Whether it be true or not, I can say for one that I have no other so great as that of being truly esteemed of my fellow men, by rendering myself worthy of their esteem. How far I shall succeed in gratifying this ambition is yet to be developed. I am young and unknown to many of you. I was born and have ever remained in the most humble walks of life. I have no wealthy or popular relations to recommend me. My case is thrown exclusively upon the independent voters of this county, and if elected they will have conferred a favor upon me for which I shall be unremitting in my labors to compensate. But if the good people in their wisdom shall see fit to keep me in the background, I have been too familiar with disappointments to be very much chagrined.[1] Your friend and fellow-citizen

Letter from the postmaster of New Salem, Illinois, to a patron.
1 July 1834

Mr Spears: At your request I send you a receipt for the postage on your paper. I am somewhat surprised at your request. I will, however, comply with it. The law requires newspaper postage to be paid in advance and now that I have waited a full year you choose to wound my feelings by insinuating that unless you get a receipt I will probably make you pay it again. Respectfully

Received of George Spears in full for postage on the *Sangamo Journal* up to the first of July, 1834.

A. LINCOLN, P.M.

---

[1] Lincoln was not elected, but a promising political career was indicated by the fact that he received 277 of the 300 votes cast in the New Salem precinct, where he lived.

Statement of political principles: communicated to the Sangamo
Journal.

New Salem, 13 June 1836

To the Editor of the Journal:

In your paper of last Saturday I see a communication over the
signature of 'Many Voters,' in which the candidates who are
announced in the Journal are called upon to 'show their hands.'
Agreed. Here's mine!

I go for all sharing the privileges of the government who assist
in bearing its burdens. Consequently I go for admitting all whites
to the right of suffrage who pay taxes or bear arms (by no means
excluding females).

If elected, I shall consider the whole people of Sangamon my
constituents, as well those that oppose as those that support me.

While acting as their representative I shall be governed by their
will, on all subjects upon which I have the means of knowing what
their will is; and upon all others, I shall do what my own judgment
teaches me will best advance their interests. Whether elected or
not, I go for distributing the proceeds of the sales of the public
lands to the several states, to enable our state, in common with
others, to dig canals and construct railroads, without borrowing
money and paying interest on it.

If alive on the first Monday in November, I shall vote for Hugh
L. White[1] for President. Very respectfully

Letter to Robert Allen, a political opponent.

New Salem, 21 June 1836

Dear Col.: I am told that during my absence last week, you passed
through this place and stated publicly that you were in possession
of a fact or facts, which, if known to the public, would entirely
destroy the prospects of N. W. Edwards[2] and myself at the
ensuing election; but that, through favor to us, you should forbear
to divulge them.

No one has needed favors more than I, and generally, few have
been less unwilling to accept them; but in this case, favor to me
would be injustice to the public, and therefore I must beg your
pardon for declining it. That I once had the confidence of the

---

[1] United States Senator from Tennessee.
[2] Like Lincoln, a Whig candidate for the legislature.

people of Sangamon is sufficiently evident, and if I have since done anything, either by design or misadventure, which if known would subject me to a forfeiture of that confidence, he that knows of that thing and conceals it is a traitor to his country's interest.

I find myself wholly unable to form any conjecture of what fact or facts, real or supposed, you spoke; but my opinion of your veracity will not permit me for a moment to doubt that you at least believed what you said.

I am flattered with the personal regard you manifested for me, but I do hope that on more mature reflection you will view the public interest as a paramount consideration, and therefore determine to let the worst come.

I here assure you that the candid statement of facts on your part, however low it may sink me, shall never break the tie of personal friendship between us.

I wish an answer to this, and you are at liberty to publish both if you choose. Very respectfully

Letter to Mary S. Owens, to whom Lincoln had proposed marriage.

Springfield, 7 May 1837

Friend Mary: I have commenced two letters to send you before this, both of which displeased me before I got half done, and so I tore them up. The first I thought wasn't serious enough, and the second was on the other extreme. I shall send this, turn out as it may.

This thing of living in Springfield[1] is rather a dull business after all, at least it is to me. I am quite as lonesome here as I ever was anywhere in my life. I have been spoken to by but one woman since I've been here, and should not have been by her, if she could have avoided it. I've never been to church yet, nor probably shall not be soon. I stay away because I am conscious I should not know how to behave myself.

I am often thinking about what we said of your coming to live at Springfield. I am afraid you would not be satisfied. There is a great deal of flourishing about in carriages here, which it would be your doom to see without sharing in it. You would have to be poor without the means of hiding your poverty. Do you believe you

---

[1] Lincoln had moved to Springfield from New Salem on 15 April, and had started to practice law with John T. Stuart, an established lawyer.

could bear that patiently? Whatever woman may cast her lot with mine, should any ever do so, it is my intention to do all in my power to make her happy and contented; and there is nothing I can imagine that would make me more unhappy than to fail in the effort. I know I should be much happier with you than the way I am, provided I saw no signs of discontent in you. What you have said to me may have been in jest, or I may have misunderstood it. If so, then let it be forgotten; if otherwise, I much wish you would think seriously before you decide. For my part I have already decided. What I have said I will most positively abide by, provided you wish it. My opinion is that you had better not do it. You have not been accustomed to hardship, and it may be more severe than you now imagine. I know you are capable of thinking correctly on any subject; and if you deliberate maturely upon this, before you decide, then I am willing to abide your decision.

You must write me a good long letter after you get this. You have nothing else to do, and though it might not seem interesting to you, after you had written it, it would be a good deal of company to me in this 'busy wilderness.' Tell your sister I don't want to hear any more about selling out and moving. That gives me the hypo whenever I think of it. Yours, etc.

To Mary S. Owens: a second letter on marriage.

Springfield, 16 August 1837

Friend Mary: You will, no doubt, think it rather strange that I should write you a letter on the same day on which we parted; and I can only account for it by supposing that seeing you lately makes me think of you more than usual, while at our late meeting we had but few expressions of thoughts. You must know that I cannot see you or think of you, with entire indifference; and yet it may be that you are mistaken in regard to what my real feelings towards you are. If I knew you were not, I should not trouble you with this letter. Perhaps any other man would know enough without further information; but I consider it *my* peculiar right to plead ignorance, and your bounden duty to allow the plea. I want in all cases to do right, and most particularly so in all cases with women. I want at this particular time, more than anything else, to do right with you, and if I *knew* it would be doing right, as I rather suspect it would, to let you alone, I would do it. And for the purpose of making the matter as plain as possible, I now say that you can now drop the subject, dismiss your thoughts (if you ever had any) from me forever, and leave this letter unanswered, without calling forth one accusing murmur from me. And I will even go further and say that if it will add anything to your comfort or peace of mind to do so, it is my sincere wish that you should. Do not understand by this that I wish to cut your acquaintance. I mean no such thing. What I do wish is that our further acquaintance shall depend upon yourself. If such further acquaintance would contribute nothing to your happiness, I am sure it would not to mine. If you feel yourself in any degree bound to me, I am now willing to release you, provided you wish it; while on the other hand, I am willing and even anxious to bind you faster if I can be convinced that it will in any considerable degree add to your happiness. This, indeed, is the whole question with me. Nothing would make me more miserable than to believe you miserable – nothing more happy than to know you were so.

In what I have now said I think I cannot be misunderstood; and to make myself understood is the only object of this letter.

If it suits you best not to answer this – farewell – a long life and a merry one attend you. But if you conclude to write back, speak as plainly as I do. There can be neither harm nor danger in saying to me anything you think, just in the manner you think it.

My respects to your sister. Your friend

Address before the Young Men's Lyceum of Springfield, Illinois.
27 January 1838

... We find ourselves under the government of a system of political institutions, conducing more essentially to the ends of civil and religious liberty, than any of which the history of former times tells us. We, when mounting the stage of existence, found ourselves the legal inheritors of these fundamental blessings. We toiled not in the acquirement or establishment of them – they are a legacy bequeathed us, by a once hardy, brave and patriotic, but now lamented and departed race of ancestors. Theirs was the task (and nobly they performed it) to possess themselves, and through themselves, us, of this goodly land; and to uprear upon its hills and its valleys, a political edifice of liberty and equal rights; 'tis ours only to transmit these, the former unprofaned by the foot of an invader; the latter undecayed by the lapse of time ...

How, then, shall we perform it? At what point shall we expect the approach of danger? By what means shall we fortify against it? Shall we expect some transatlantic military giant, to step the ocean and crush us at a blow? Never! All the armies of Europe, Asia and Africa combined, with all the treasure of the earth (our own excepted) in their military chest; with a Buonaparte for a commander, could not by force take a drink from the Ohio, or make a track on the Blue Ridge, in a trial of a thousand years.

At what point then is the approach of danger to be expected? I answer, if it ever reach us, it must spring up amongst us. It cannot come from abroad. If destruction be our lot, we must ourselves be its author and finisher. As a nation of freemen, we must live through all time, or die by suicide.

I hope I am over wary; but if I am not, there is, even now, something of ill-omen amongst us. I mean the increasing disregard for law which pervades the country; the growing disposition to substitute the wild and furious passions, in lieu of the sober judgment of courts; and the worse than savage mobs, for the executive ministers of justice. This disposition is awfully fearful in any community; and that it now exists in ours, though grating to our feelings to admit, it would be a violation of truth, and an insult to our intelligence, to deny. Accounts of outrages committed by mobs form the every-day news of the times . . .

. . . We hope all dangers may be overcome; but to conclude that no danger may ever arise would itself be extremely dangerous. There are now, and will hereafter be, many causes, dangerous in their tendency, which have not existed heretofore; and which are not too insignificant to merit attention. That our government should have been maintained in its original form from its establishment until now, is not much to be wondered at. It had many props to support it through that period, which are now decayed and crumbled away. Through that period, it was felt by all to be an undecided experiment; now it is understood to be a successful one. Then, all that sought celebrity and fame, and distinction, expected to find them in the success of that experiment. Their all was staked upon it: — their destiny was inseparably linked with it. Their ambition aspired to display to an admiring world, a practical demonstration of the truth of a proposition, which had hitherto been considered at best no better than problematical; namely, the capability of a people to govern themselves. If they succeeded, they were to be immortalized; their names were to be transferred to counties and cities, and rivers and mountains; and to be revered and sung, and toasted through all time. If they failed, they were to be called knaves and fools, and fanatics for a fleeting hour; then to sink and be forgotten. They succeeded. The experiment is successful; and thousands have won their deathless names in making it so. But the game is caught; and I believe it is true, that with the catching end the pleasures of the chase. This field of glory is harvested, and the crop is already appropriated. But new reapers will arise, and they, too, will seek a field. It is to deny what the history of the world tells us is true, to suppose that men of ambition and talents will not continue to spring up amongst us. And, when they do, they will as naturally seek the gratification of their ruling passions, as others have so done before them. The question, then, is can that gratification be found in supporting and maintaining an edifice that has been erected by others? Most certainly it cannot. Many great and good men sufficiently qualified for any task they should undertake, may ever be found, whose ambition would aspire to nothing beyond a seat in Congress, a gubernatorial or a presidential chair; but such belong not to the family of the lion, or the tribe of the eagle. What! think you these places would satisfy an Alexander, a Cæsar, or a Napoleon? Never! Towering genius disdains a beaten path. It seeks regions hitherto unexplored. It sees no distinction in adding story to story, upon the monuments of fame, erected to the memory of others. It denies that it is glory enough to serve under any chief. It scorns to tread in the footsteps of any predecessor, however illustrious. It thirsts and burns for distinction; and, if possible, it will have it, whether at the expense of emancipating slaves, or enslaving freemen. Is it unreasonable then to expect that some man possessed of the loftiest genius, coupled with ambition sufficient to push it to its utmost stretch, will at some time spring up among us? And when such a one does, it will require the people to be united with each other, attached to the government and laws, and generally intelligent, to successfully frustrate his designs.

Distinction will be his paramount object; and although he would as willingly, perhaps more so, acquire it by doing good as harm; that opportunity being past, and nothing left to be done in the way of building up, he would set boldly to the task of pulling down . . .

To Mrs Orville H. Browning:[1] *a letter about himself and Mary S. Owens.*

Springfield, 1 April 1838

Dear Madam: Without apologizing for being egotistical, I shall make the history of so much of my own life as has elapsed since I saw you the subject of this letter. And by the way, I now discover that in order to give a full and intelligible account of the things I have done and suffered *since* I saw you, I shall necessarily have to relate some that happened *before*.

It was, then, in the autumn of 1836, that a married lady of my acquaintance, and who was a great friend of mine, being about to pay a visit to her father and other relatives residing in Kentucky, proposed to me, that on her return she would bring a sister of hers with her, upon condition that I would engage to become her brother-in-law with all convenient dispatch. I, of course, accepted the proposal; for you know I could not have done otherwise, had I really been averse to it; but privately between you and me, I was most confoundedly well pleased with the project. I had seen the said sister some three years before, thought her intelligent and agreeable, and saw no good objection to plodding life through hand in hand with her. Time passed on, the lady took her journey and in due time returned, sister in company sure enough. This stomached me a little; for it appeared to me that her coming so readily showed that she was a trifle too willing; but on reflection it occurred to me that she might have been prevailed on by her married sister to come without anything concerning me ever having been mentioned to her; and so I concluded that if no other objection presented itself I would consent to waive this. All this occurred upon my *hearing* of her arrival in the neighborhood; for, be it remembered, I had not yet *seen* her, except about three years previous, as before mentioned.

In a few days we had an interview, and although I had seen her before, she did not look as my imagination had pictured her. I knew she was oversize, but she now appeared a fair match for Falstaff; I knew she was called an 'old maid,' and I felt no doubt of the truth of at least half of the appellation; but now, when I beheld her, I could not for my life avoid thinking of my mother; and this, not from withered features, for her skin was too full of fat to

---

[1] The wife of Orville H. Browning of Quincy, Illinois, a lawyer and Whig member of the Illinois legislature.

permit its contracting into wrinkles; but from her want of teeth, weather-beaten appearance in general, and from a kind of notion that ran in my head that *nothing* could have commenced at the size of infancy and reached her present bulk in less than thirty-five or forty years; and, in short, I was not [at] all pleased with her. But what could I do? I had told her sister that I would take her for better or for worse; and I made a point of honor and conscience in all things to stick to my word, especially if others had been induced to act on it, which in this case I doubted not they had, for I was now fairly convinced that no other man on earth would have her, and hence the conclusion that they were bent on holding me to my bargain. Well, thought I, I have said it, and, be consequences what they may, it shall not be my fault if I fail to do it. At once I determined to consider her my wife; and this done, all my powers of discovery were put to the rack in search of perfections in her, which might be fairly set off against her defects. I tried to imagine she was handsome, which, but for her unfortunate corpulency, was actually true. Exclusive of this, no woman that I have seen has a finer face. I also tried to convince myself that the mind was much more to be valued than the person; and in this she was not inferior, as I could discover, to any with whom I had been acquainted.

Shortly after this, without attempting to come to any positive understanding with her, I set out for Vandalia, where and when you first saw me. During my stay there I had letters from her which did not change my opinion of either her intellect or intention; but on the contrary, confirmed it in both.

All this while, although I was fixed 'firm as the surge repelling rock' in my resolution, I found I was continually repenting the rashness which had led me to make it. Through life I have been in no bondage, either real or imaginary, from the thraldom of which I so much desired to be free.

After my return home I saw nothing to change my opinion of her in any particular. She was the same and so was I. I now spent my time between planning how I might get along through life after my contemplated change of circumstances should have taken place; and how I might procrastinate the evil day for a time, which I really dreaded as much – perhaps more – than an Irishman does the halter.

After all my suffering upon this deeply interesting subject, here I am, wholly unexpectedly, completely out of the 'scrape'; and I now want to know if you can guess how I got out of it. Out clear in every sense of the term; no violation of word, honor, or conscience. I don't believe you can guess, and so I may as well tell you at once. As the lawyers say, it was done in the manner following, to wit. After I had delayed the matter as long as I thought I could in honor do, which by the way had brought me round into the last fall, I concluded I might as well bring it to a consummation without further delay; and so I mustered my resolution, and made the proposal to her direct; but, shocking to relate, she answered, No. At first I supposed she did it through an affectation of modesty, which I thought but ill became her, under the peculiar circumstances of her case; but on my renewal of the charge, I found she repelled it with greater firmness than before. I tried it again and again, but with the same success, or rather with the same want of success. I finally was forced to give it up, at which I very unexpectedly found myself mortified almost beyond endurance. I was mortified, it seemed to me, in a hundred different ways. My vanity was deeply wounded by the reflection that I had so long been too stupid to discover her intentions, and at the same time never doubting that I understood them perfectly; and also, that she whom I had taught myself to believe nobody else would have, had actually rejected me with all my fancied greatness; and to cap the whole, I then, for the first time, began to suspect that I was really a little in love with her. But let it all go. I'll try and outlive it. Others have been made fools of by the girls; but this can never be with truth said of me. I most emphatically, in this instance, made a fool of myself. I have now come to the conclusion never again to think of marrying; and for this reason: I can never be satisfied with anyone who would be blockhead enough to have me.

When you receive this, write me a long yarn about something to amuse me. Give my respects to Mr Browning. Your sincere friend

To William Butler, friend and political associate.

Vandalia, 1 February 1839

Friend Butler: Your letter enclosing one to Mr Baker[1] was received on yesterday evening. There is no necessity for any bad feeling between Baker and yourself. Your first letter to him was

[1] Edward D. Baker, Springfield lawyer and Whig member of the Illinois legislature.

written while you were in a state of high excitement, and therefore ought not to have been construed as an emanation of deliberate malice. Unfortunately, however, it reached Baker while he was writhing under a severe toothache, and therefore he at that time was incapable of exercising that patience and reflection which the case required. The note he sent you was written while in that state of feeling, and for that reason I think you ought not to pay any serious regard to it. It is always magnanimous to recant whatever we may have said in passion; and when you and Baker shall have done this, I am sure there will no difficulty be left between you. I write this without Baker's knowledge; and I do it because nothing would be more painful to me than to see a difficulty between two of my most particular friends . . .

No news here now. Your friend as ever

To John T. Stuart, Lincoln's law partner, now in Washington as a member of Congress.
                                        Springfield, 23 December 1839

Dear Stuart: Dr Henry will write you all the political news. I write this about some little matters of business. You recollect you told me you had drawn the Chicago Musick money and sent it to the claimants. A d——d hawk-billed yankee is here, besetting me at every turn I take, saying that Robt Kinzie never received the $80 to which he was entitled. Can you tell anything about the matter?

Again old Mr Wright, who lives up South Fork somewhere, is teasing me continually about some *deeds* which he says he left with you, but which I can find nothing of. Can you tell where they are?

The legislature is in session, and has suffered the Bank to forfeit its charter without *Benefit* of *Clergy*. There seems to be but very little disposition to resuscitate it. Whenever a letter comes from you to Mrs Stuart I carry it to her, and then I see Betty. She is a tolerably nice *fellow* now. Maybe I will write again when I get more time. Your friend as ever

P.S. The Democratic giant[1] is here; but he is not now worth talking about.

---

[1] Stephen A. Douglas, whom Stuart had narrowly defeated in the Congressional election.

Letter to William G. Anderson, a political opponent.
Lawrenceville, Illinois, 31 October 1840

Dear Sir: Your note of yesterday is received. In the difficulty between us, of which you speak, you say you think I was the aggressor. I do not think I was. You say my 'words imported insult.' I meant them as a fair set-off to your own statements, and not otherwise; and in that light alone I now wish you to understand them. You ask for my 'present feelings on the subject.' I entertain no unkind feeling to you, and none of any sort upon the subject, except a sincere regret that I permitted myself to get into such an altercation. Yours, etc.

To John T. Stuart.
Springfield, 20 January 1841

Dear Stuart: I have had no letter from you since you left. No matter for that. What I wish now is to speak of our post office. You know I desired Dr Henry[1] to have that place when you left; I now desire it more than ever. I have, within the last few days, been making a most discreditable exhibition of myself in the way of hypochondriaism and thereby got an impression that Dr Henry is necessary to my existence. Unless he gets that place he leaves Springfield. You therefore see how much I am interested in the matter.

We shall shortly forward you a petition in his favor signed by all or nearly all the Whig members of the Legislature, as well as other Whigs.

This, together with what you know of the Dr's position and merits, I sincerely hope will secure him the appointment. My heart is very much set upon it.

Pardon me for not writing more; I have not sufficient composure to write a long letter. As ever yours

From a letter to John T. Stuart.
Springfield, 23 January 1841

. . . For not giving you a general summary of news, you *must* pardon me; it is not in my power to do so. I am now the most

---

[1] Anson G. Henry, Springfield physician and Whig politician. On 1 January 1841 Lincoln's engagement to Mary Todd had been broken, leaving him afflicted with the deepest melancholia.

miserable man living. If what I feel were equally distributed to the whole human family, there would not be one cheerful face on the earth. Whether I shall ever be better I cannot tell; I awfully forebode I shall not. To remain as I am is impossible; I must die or be better, it appears to me. The matter you speak of on my account, you may attend to as you say, unless you shall hear of my condition forbidding it. I say this because I fear I shall be unable to attend to any business here, and a change of scene might help me. If I could be myself I would rather remain at home with Judge Logan. I can write no more. Your friend, as ever

To Mary Speed after a visit to the Speed home near Louisville, Kentucky, at the invitation of her brother Joshua, former Springfield store-keeper.
                        Bloomington, Illinois, 27 September 1841

My Friend: Having resolved to write to some of your mother's family, and not having the express permission of any one of them to do so, I have had some little difficulty in determining on which to inflict the task of reading what I now feel must be a most dull and silly letter; but when I remembered that you and I were something of cronies while I was at Farmington, and that, while there, I once was under the necessity of shutting you up in a room to prevent your committing an assault and battery upon me, I instantly decided that you should be the devoted one.

I assume that you have not heard from Joshua and myself since we left, because I think it doubtful whether he has written.

You remember there was some uneasiness about Joshua's health when we left. That little indisposition of his turned out to be nothing serious; and it was pretty nearly forgotten when we reached Springfield. We got on board the steamboat *Lebanon*, in the locks of the canal, about twelve o'clock m. of the day we left, and reached St Louis the next Monday at 8 p.m. Nothing of interest happened during the passage, except the vexatious delays occasioned by the sand-bars be thought interesting. By the way, a fine example was presented on board the boat for contemplating the effect of *condition* upon human happiness. A gentleman had purchased twelve Negroes in different parts of Kentucky and was taking them to a farm in the South. They were chained six and six together. A small iron clevis was around the left wrist of each, and this fastened to the main chain by a shorter one at a convenient distance from the others; so that the Negroes were strung together precisely like so many fish upon a trot-line. In this condition they were being separated forever from the scenes of their childhood, their friends, their fathers and mothers, and brothers and sisters, and many of them, from their wives and children, and going into perpetual slavery where the lash of the master is proverbially more ruthless and unrelenting than any other where; and yet amid all these distressing circumstances, as we would think them, they were the most cheerful and apparently happy creatures on board. One, whose offense for which he had been sold was an over-fondness for his wife, played the fiddle almost continually; and the others danced, sung, cracked jokes, and played various games with cards from day to day. How true it is that 'God tempers the wind to the shorn lamb,' or in other words, that He renders the worst of human conditions tolerable, while He permits the best to be nothing better than tolerable.

To return to the narrative. When we reached Springfield, I stayed but one day when I started on this tedious circuit where I now am. Do you remember my going to the city while I was in Kentucky to have a tooth extracted, and making a failure of it? Well, that same old tooth got to paining me so much that about a week since I had it torn out, bringing with it a bit of the jawbone; the consequence of which is that my mouth is now so sore that I can neither talk nor eat. I am literally 'subsisting on savory remembrances' – that is, being unable to eat, I am living upon the remembrance of the delicious dishes of peaches and cream we used to have at your house.

When we left, Miss Fanny Henning[1] was owing you a visit, as I understood. Has she paid it yet? If she has, are you not convinced that she is one of the sweetest girls in the world? There is but one thing about her, so far as I could perceive, that I would have otherwise than as it is. That is something of a tendency to melancholy. This, let it be observed, is a misfortune not a fault. Give her an assurance of my very highest regard, when *you* see her.

Is little Siss Davis at your house yet? If she is kiss her 'o'er and o'er again' for me.

Tell your mother that I have not got her 'present' with me; but that I intend to read it regularly when I return home. I doubt not

---

[1] Speed's future wife.

that it is really, as she says, the best cure for the 'blues' could one but take it according to the truth.

Give my respects to all your sisters (including 'Aunt Emma') and brothers. Tell Mrs Peay, of whose happy face I shall long retain a pleasant remembrance, that I have been trying to think of a name for her homestead, but as yet cannot satisfy myself with one. I shall be very happy to receive a line from you, soon after you receive this; and, in case you choose to favor me with one, address it to Charleston, Coles County, Illinois, as I shall be there about the time to receive it. Your sincere friend

To Joshua Speed, beset by doubts about his forthcoming marriage.

Springfield, [3? January 1842]

My dear Speed: Feeling, as you know I do, the deepest solicitude for the success of the enterprise you are engaged in, I adopt this as the last method I can invent to aid you, in case (which God forbid) you shall need any aid. I do not place what I am going to say on paper, because I can say it any better in that way than I could by word of mouth; but because, were I to say it orally, before we part, most likely you would forget it at the very time when it might do you some good. As I think it reasonable that you will feel very badly some time between this and the final consummation of your purpose, it is intended that you shall read this just at such a time.

Why I say it is reasonable that you will feel very badly yet, is because of *three special causes*, added to the *general one* which I shall mention.

The general cause is that you are *naturally of a nervous temperament*; and this I say from what I have seen of you personally, and what you have told me concerning your mother at various times, and concerning your brother William at the time his wife died.

The first special cause is *your exposure to bad weather* on your journey, which my experience clearly proves to be very severe on defective nerves.

The second is *the absence of all business and conversation of friends*, which might divert your mind and give it occasional rest from that *intensity* of thought, which will sometimes wear the sweetest idea threadbare and turn it to the bitterness of death.

The third is *the rapid and near approach of that crisis on which all your thoughts and feelings concentrate.*

If from all these causes you shall escape and go through triumphantly, without another 'twinge of the soul,' I shall be most happily, but most egregiously, deceived.

If, on the contrary, you shall, as I expect you will at some time, be agonized and distressed, let me, who have some reason to speak with judgment on such a subject, beseech you to ascribe it to the causes I have mentioned, and not to some false and ruinous suggestion of the Devil.

'But,' you will say, 'do not your causes apply to everyone engaged in a like undertaking?'

By no means. *The particular causes*, to a greater or less extent, perhaps do apply in all cases; but the *general one*, nervous debility, which is the key and conductor of all the particular ones, and without which *they* would be utterly harmless, though it *does* pertain to you, *does not* pertain to one in a thousand. It is out of this that the painful difference between you and the mass of the world springs.

I know what the painful point with you is, at all times when you are unhappy. It is an apprehension that you do not love her[1] as you should. What nonsense! How came you to court her? Was it because you thought she desired it; and that you had given her reason to expect it? If it was for that, why did not the same reason make you court Ann Todd, and at least twenty others of whom you can think, and to whom it would apply with greater force than to *her*? Did you court her for her wealth? Why, you knew she had none. But you say you *reasoned* yourself *into* it. What do you mean by that? Was it not that you found yourself unable to *reason* yourself *out* of it? Did you not think, and partly form the purpose, of courting her the first time you ever saw or heard of her? What had reason to do with it, at that early stage? There was nothing *at that time* for reason to work upon. Whether she was moral, amiable, sensible, or even of good character, you did not, nor could not then know; except perhaps you might infer the last from the company you found her in. All you then did or could know of her was her *personal appearance and deportment*; and these, if they impress at all, impress the *heart* and not the head.

[1] Miss Fanny Henning.

Say candidly, were not those heavenly *black eyes* the whole basis of all your earthly *reasoning* on the subject?

After you and I had once been at her residence, did you not go and take me all the way to Lexington and back, for no other purpose but to get to see her again, on our return, in that seeming to take a trip for that express object?

What earthly consideration would you take to find her scouting and despising you, and giving herself up to another? But of this you have no apprehension; and therefore you cannot bring it home to your feelings.

I shall be so anxious about you, that I want you to write me every mail. Your friend

To Joshua Speed, whose fiancée was critically ill.
Springfield, 3 February 1842

Dear Speed: Your letter of the 25th Jany. came to hand to-day. You well know that I do not feel my own sorrows much more keenly than I do yours, when I know of them; and yet I assure you I was not much hurt by what you wrote me of your excessively bad feeling at the time you wrote. Not that I am less capable of sympathizing with you now than ever; not that I am less your friend than ever; but because I hope and believe that your present anxiety and distress about *her*[1] health and *her* life, must and will forever banish those horrid doubts which I know you sometimes felt, as to the truth of your affection for her. If they can be once and forever removed (and I almost feel a presentiment that the Almighty has sent your present affliction expressly for that object), surely nothing can come in their stead to fill their immeasurable measure of misery. The death scenes of those we love are surely painful enough; but these we are prepared to, and expect to see. They happen to all, and all know they must happen. Painful as they are, they are not an unlooked-for sorrow. Should she, as you fear, be destined to an early grave, it is indeed a great consolation to know that she is so well prepared to meet it. Her religion, which you once disliked so much, I will venture you now prize most highly.

But I hope your melancholy bodings as to her early death are not well founded. I even hope that ere this reaches you she will

---

[1] Miss Fanny Henning.

have returned with improved and still improving health; and that you will have met her and forgotten the sorrows of the past in the enjoyment of the present.

I would say more if I could; but it seems I have said enough. It really appears to me that you yourself ought to rejoice and not sorrow at this indubitable evidence of your undying affection for her. Why, Speed, if you did not love her, although you might not wish her death, you would most calmly be resigned to it. Perhaps this point is no longer a question with you, and my pertinacious dwelling upon it is a rude intrusion upon your feelings. If so, you must pardon me. You know the hell I have suffered on that point, and how tender I am upon it. You know I do not mean wrong.

I have been quite clear of hypo[1] since you left, even better than I was along in the fall.

I have seen Sarah but once. She seemed very cheerful and so I said nothing to her about what we spoke of.

Old Uncle Billy Herndon is dead; and it is said this evening that Uncle Ben Ferguson will not live. This I believe is all the news, and enough at that unless it were better.

Write me immediately on the receipt of this. Your friend, as ever

To Joshua Speed, just married.
Springfield, 13 February 1842

Dear Speed: Yours of the 1st inst. came to hand three or four days ago. When this shall reach you, you will have been Fanny's husband several days. You know my desire to befriend you is everlasting – that I will never cease, while I know how to do anything.

But you will always hereafter be on ground that I have never occupied, and consequently, if advice were needed, I might advise wrong.

I do fondly hope, however, that you will never again need any comfort from abroad. But should I be mistaken in this – should excessive pleasure still be accompanied with a painful counterpart at times, still let me urge you, as I have ever done, to remember in the depth and even the agony of despondency, that very shortly

---

[1] Hypochondria, or hypochondriasis, meaning, roughly, a state of depression bordering on the abnormal. It seems to have been a fairly popular affliction in the western United States at this period.

you are to feel well again. I am now fully convinced that you love her as ardently as you are capable of loving. Your ever being happy in her presence, and your intense anxiety about her health, if there were nothing else, would place this beyond all dispute in my mind. I incline to think it probable that your nerves will fail you occasionally for a while; but once you get them fairly graded now, that trouble is over forever.

I think if I were you, in case my mind were not exactly right, I would avoid being *idle*; I would immediately engage in some business, or go to making preparations for it, which would be the same thing.

If you went through the ceremony *calmly*, or even with sufficient composure not to excite alarm in any present, you are safe, beyond question, and in two or three months, to say the most, will be the happiest of men.

I hope with tolerable confidence that this letter is a plaster for a place that is no longer sore. God grant it may be so.

I would desire you to give my particular respects to Fanny, but perhaps you will not wish her to know you have received this, lest she should desire to see it. Make her write me an answer to my last letter to her at any rate. I would set great value upon another letter from her.

Write me whenever you have leisure. Yours forever

To Joshua F. Speed, who has confessed that his marriage has brought him happiness.

Springfield, 25 February 1842

Dear Speed: I received yours of the 12th written the day you went down to William's place, some days since; but delayed answering it till I should receive the promised one of the 16th, which came last night. I opened the latter with intense anxiety and trepidation – so much, that although it turned out better than I expected, I have hardly yet, at the distance of ten hours, become calm.

I tell you, Speed, our *forebodings*, for which you and I are rather peculiar, are all the worst sort of nonsense. I fancied, from the time I received your letter of *Saturday*, that the one of *Wednesday* was never to come; and yet it *did* come, and what is more, it is perfectly clear, both from its *tone* and *handwriting*, that you were much *happier*, or, if you think the term preferable, *less miserable*, when you wrote *it*, than when you wrote the last one before. You had so obviously improved, at the very time I so much feared you would have grown worse. You say that 'something indescribably horrible and alarming still haunts you.' You will not say *that* three months from now, I will venture. When your nerves once get steady now, the whole trouble will be over forever. Nor should you become impatient at their being even very slow in becoming steady. Again, you say you much fear that the Elysium of which you have dreamed so much is never to be realized. Well, if it shall not, I dare swear it will not be the fault of her who is now your wife. I now have no doubt that it is the peculiar misfortune of both you and me to dream dreams of Elysium far exceeding all that anything earthly can realize. Far short of your dreams as you may be, no woman could do more to realize them than that same black-eyed Fanny. If you could but contemplate her through my imagination, it would appear ridiculous to you that anyone should for a moment think of being unhappy with her. My old Father used to have a saying that 'If you make a bad bargain, *hug* it the tighter'; and it occurs to me that if the bargain you have just closed can possibly be called a bad one, it is certainly the most *pleasant one* for applying that maxim to, which my fancy can, by any effort, picture.

I write another letter enclosing this, which you can show her if she desires it. I do this because she would think strangely perhaps should you tell her that you receive no letters from me; or, telling her you do, should refuse to let her see them.

I close this, entertaining the confident hope that every successive letter I shall have from you (which I here pray may not be few, nor far between), may show you possessing a more steady hand and cheerful heart than the last preceding it. As ever, your friend

To Joshua F. Speed, for his wife's eye.

Springfield, 25 February 1842

Dear Speed: Yours of the 16th inst. announcing that Miss Fanny and you 'are no more twain, but one flesh,' reached me this morning. I have no way of telling how much happiness I wish you both; tho' I believe you both can conceive it. I feel somewhat jealous of both of you now; you will be so exclusively concerned for one another that I shall be forgotten entirely. My acquaintance with Miss Fanny (I call her thus, lest you should think I am speaking of your mother), was too short for me to reasonably hope to long be remembered by her; and still, I am sure, I shall not forget her soon. Try if you cannot remind her of that debt she owes me; and be sure you do not interfere to prevent her paying it.

I regret to learn that you have resolved to not return to Illinois. I shall be very lonesome without you. How miserably things seem to be arranged in this world. If we have no friends, we have no pleasure; and if we have them, we are sure to lose them and be doubly pained by the loss. I did hope she and you would make your home here; but I own I have no right to insist. You owe obligations to her, ten thousand times more sacred than any you can owe to others; and, in that light, let them be respected and observed. It is natural that she should desire to remain with her relatives and friends. As to friends, however, *she* could not need them anywhere; she would have them in abundance here.

Give my kind remembrance to Mr Williamson and his family, particularly Miss Elizabeth – also to your mother, brothers, and sisters. Ask little Eliza Davis if she will ride to town with me if I come there again.

And, finally, give Fanny a double reciprocation of all the love she sent me. Write me often, and believe me Yours forever

From a letter to Joshua F. Speed in which Lincoln reveals his own torment.

Springfield, 27 March 1842

Dear Speed: Yours of the 10th inst. was received three or four days since. You know I am sincere when I tell you the pleasure its contents gave me was and is inexpressible. As to your farm matter, I have no sympathy with you. *I* have no farm, nor ever expect to have; and, consequently, have not studied the subject enough to be much interested with it. I can only say that I am glad *you* are satisfied and pleased with it.

But on that other subject, to me of the most intense interest, whether in joy or sorrow, I never had the power to withhold my sympathy from you. It cannot be told how it now thrills me with joy to hear you say you are '*far happier than you ever expected to be.*' That much I know is enough. I know you too well to suppose your expectations were not, at least sometimes, extravagant; and if the reality exceeds them all, I say, enough, dear Lord. I am not going beyond the truth when I tell you that the short space it took me to read your last letter gave me more pleasure than the total sum of all I have enjoyed since that fatal first of Jany. '41.[1] Since then, it seems to me, I should have been entirely happy, but for the never-absent idea that there is *one* still unhappy whom I have contributed to make so. That still kills my soul. I cannot but reproach myself for even wishing to be happy while she is otherwise. She accompanied a large party on the railroad cars to Jacksonville last Monday; and on her return spoke, so that I heard of it, of having enjoyed the trip exceedingly. God be praised for that.

You know with what sleepless vigilance I have watched you, ever since the commencement of your affair; and altho' I am now almost confident it is useless, I cannot forbear once more to say that I think it is even yet possible for your spirits to flag down and leave you miserable. If they should, don't fail to remember that they cannot long remain so. . .

The sweet violet you enclosed came safely to hand, but it was so dry and mashed so flat that it crumbled to dust at the first attempt to handle it. The juice that mashed out of it stained a place on the letter, which I mean to preserve and cherish for the sake of her who procured it to be sent. My renewed good wishes to her, in particular, and generally to all such of your relatives as know me. As ever

From a letter to Joshua F. Speed on the writer's own irresolution.
Springfield, 4 July 1842

Dear Speed: Yours of the 16th June was received only a day or two since. It was not mailed at Louisville till the 25th. You speak of the great time that has elapsed since I wrote you. Let me explain that. Your letter reached here a day or two after I started on the circuit; I was gone five or six weeks, so that I got the letter only a few days before Butler started to your country. I thought it scarcely worth while to write you the news, which he could and would tell you more in detail. On his return he told me you would write me soon; and so I waited for your letter. As to my having been displeased with your advice, surely you know better than that. I know you do; and therefore I will not labor to convince you. True, that subject is painful to me; but it is not your silence,

---

[1] The date on which Lincoln's engagement to Mary Todd was broken.

or the silence of all the world, that can make me forget it. I acknowledge the correctness of your advice too; but before I resolve to do the one thing or the other, I must regain my confidence in my own ability to keep my resolves when they are made. In that ability, you know, I once prided myself as the only, or at least the chief, gem of my character; that gem I lost – how, and when, you too well know. I have not yet regained it; and until I do I cannot trust myself in any matter of much importance. I believe now that, had you understood my case at the time, as well as I understood yours afterwards, by the aid you would have given me I should have sailed through clear; but that does not now afford me sufficient confidence to begin that, or the like of that, again.

You make a kind acknowledgment of your obligations to me for your present happiness. I am much pleased with that acknowledgment; but a thousand times more am I pleased to know that you enjoy a degree of happiness worthy of an acknowledgment. The truth is, I am not sure there was any merit, with me, in the part I took in your difficulty; I was drawn to it as by fate; if I would, I could not have done less than I did. I always was superstitious; and as part of my superstition, I believe God made me one of the instruments of bringing your Fanny and you together, which union, I have no doubt, He had fore-ordained. Whatever he designs, he will do for *me* yet. 'Stand *still* and see the salvation of the Lord' is my text just now. If, as you say, you have told Fanny *all*, I should have no objection to her seeing this letter, but for its reference to our friend here. Let her seeing it depend upon whether she has ever known anything of my affair; and if she has not, do not let her.

I do not think I can come to Kentucky this season. I am so poor and make so little headway in the world that I drop back in a month of idleness as much as I gain in a year's rowing. I should like to visit you again. I should like to see that 'Sis' of yours, that was absent when I was there; tho' I suppose she would run away again, if she were to hear I was coming . . . Ever yours

To Joshua Speed, on an epidemic of dueling fever – and experience of marriage.

Springfield, 5 October 1842

Dear Speed: You have heard of my duel with Shields,[1] and I have

___

[1] James Shields, Illinois State Auditor, whom Lincoln had lampooned in a

now to inform you that the dueling business still rages in this city. Day before yesterday Shields challenged Butler, who accepted, and proposed fighting next morning at sun-rising in Bob Allen's meadow, one hundred yards distance with rifles. To this, Whitesides, Shields' second, said 'No' because of the law. Thus ended duel No. 2. Yesterday, Whitesides chose to consider himself insulted by Dr Merryman, and so sent him a kind of *quasi* challenge inviting him to meet him at the Planter's House in St Louis on the next Friday to settle their difficulty. Merryman made me his friend, and sent W. a note inquiring to know if he meant his note as a challenge, and, if so, that he would, according to the law in such case made and provided, prescribe the terms of the meeting. W. returned for answer that if M. would meet him at the Planter's House as desired, he would challenge him. M. replied in a note that he denied W.'s right to dictate time and place; but that he, M., would waive the question of *time*, and meet him at Louisiana, Missouri. Upon my presenting this note to W. and stating verbally its contents he declined receiving it, saying he had business at St Louis, and it was as near as Louisiana. Merryman then directed me to notify Whitesides that he should publish the correspondence between them with such comments as he thought fit. This I did. Thus it stood at bed time last night. This morning Whitesides, by his friend Shields, is praying for a new trial, on the ground that he was mistaken in Merryman's proposition to meet at Louisiana, Missouri, thinking it was the state of Louisiana. This Merryman hoots at, and is preparing his publication – while the town is in a ferment and a street fight somewhat anticipated.

But I began this letter not for what I have been writing, but to say something on that subject which you know to be of such infinite solicitude to me. The immense suffering you endured from the first days of September till the middle of February you never tried to conceal from me, and I well understood. You have now been the husband of a lovely woman nearly eight months. That you are happier now than you were the day you married her I well know; for without, you would not be living. But I have your word for it too; and the returning elasticity of spirits which is manifested in your letters. But I want to ask a closer question – 'Are you now, in *feeling* as well as *judgment*, glad you are married as you are?' From anybody but me this would be an impudent

communication to the *Sangamo Journal*. Shields had sent a challenge, which Lincoln accepted, but the two men composed their differences on the dueling ground.

question not to be tolerated; but I know you will pardon it in me. Please answer it quickly as I feel impatient to know.

I have sent my love to your Fanny so often that I fear she is getting tired of it; however, I venture to tender it again. Yours forever

To James S. Irwin, a client of Logan & Lincoln, on fees.
Springfield, 2 November 1842

Owing to my absence, yours of the 22nd ult. was not received till this moment.

Judge Logan[1] and myself are willing to attend to any business in the Supreme Court you may send us. As to fees, it is impossible to establish a rule that will apply in all, or even a great many cases. We believe we are never accused of being very unreasonable in this particular; and we would always be easily satisfied, provided we could see the money — but whatever fees we earn at a distance, if not paid *before*, we have noticed we never hear of after the work is done. We therefore are growing a little sensitive on that point. Yours etc.

To Samuel D. Marshall: a lawyer's letter, with a personal announcement.
Springfield, 11 November 1842

Dear Sam: Yours of the 10th Oct. enclosing five dollars was taken from the office in my absence by Judge Logan who neglected to hand it to me till about a week ago, and just an hour before I took a wife. Your other of the 3rd inst. is also received. The Forbes and Hill case, of which you speak, has not been brought up as yet.

I have looked into the Dorman and Lane case, till I believe I understand the facts of it; and I also believe we can reverse it. In the last I may be mistaken, but I think the case at least worth the experiment; and if Dorman will risk the cost, I will do my best for the 'biggest kind of a fee' as you say, if we succeed, and nothing if we fail. I have not had a chance to consult Logan since I read your letters, but if the case comes up, I can have the use of him if I need him.

I would advise you to procure the record and send it up

---

[1] Lincoln entered into a law partnership with Stephen T. Logan in the spring of 1841.

immediately. Attend to the making out of the record yourself, or most likely the clerk will not get it all together right.

Nothing new here, except my marrying,[1] which to me is matter of profound wonder. Yours forever

[1] Lincoln and Mary Todd were married on 4 November 1842.

Chapter 2
Congressman, Husband and Father
1843–52

Abraham Lincoln never lacked political ambition, but the timing of his bid for election to the House of Representatives was dictated by the curious rotation principle which operated among prominent Illinois Whigs, who took it in turns to stand for a single two-year term. Elected in 1846, Lincoln served his two years in Washington from 1847 to 1849. This was not one of the most distinguished phases of his political career, and he made no great enduring impact. The war against Mexico (1846–8) was the dominant issue in Congressional debate, and Lincoln, like most Whigs, especially from the North, opposed it. His 'spot resolutions', demanding to know the spot on American soil where the Mexicans had first shed American blood, attracted some brief notoriety, and attacks from political opponents at home, who condemned as disloyal his opposition to the war.

Lincoln's speech deriding the military record of Democratic presidential candidate Lewis Cass is a good example of his talent for mockery (including self-mockery). The correspondence over the post of Commissioner of the General Land Office suggests the importance of patronage and jobs in the party politics of the day.

The disruption of family life affected both Abraham and Mary Lincoln, and his letters to her show genuine warmth and concern. In sharp contrast, his letters to his stepbrother, John D. Johnston, show a much harsher side to his nature. They also reveal something of his very distant relationship with his father. Warned in 1851 that his father was desperately ill, Lincoln made his not altogether convincing excuses, and attended neither his father's bedside nor his funeral. During the rest of his life, he never made adequate arrangements to mark his father's grave.

This was also the period when the young William Herndon entered Lincoln's life, as law partner, aide and confidant – and as dyed-in-the-wool enemy of Mrs Lincoln. In later years, Herndon was to be the source of many of the most ill-founded and unreliable stories about the early life of the president.

To Richard S. Thomas, a Whig residing in Lincoln's congressional district.

Springfield, 14 February 1843

Friend Richard: ... Now if you should hear anyone say that Lincoln don't want to go to Congress, I wish you as a personal friend of mine would tell him you have reason to believe he is mistaken. The truth is, I would like to go very much. Still, circumstances may happen which may prevent my being a candidate.

If there are any who be my friends in such an enterprise, what I now want is that they shall not throw me away just yet. Yours as ever

From a letter to Joshua F. Speed announcing a political reversal.

Springfield, 24 March 1843

... We had a meeting of the Whigs of the county here on last Monday to appoint delegates to a district convention, and Baker[1] beat me and got the delegation instructed to go for him. The meeting, in spite of my attempt to decline it, appointed me one of the delegates; so that in getting Baker the nomination, I shall be 'fixed' a good deal like a fellow who is made groomsman to the man what has cut him out, and is marrying his own dear 'gal.' About the prospect of your having a namesake at our house, can't say, exactly yet.

From a letter to Joshua F. Speed.

Springfield, 18 May 1843

Dear Speed: Yours of the 9th inst. is duly received, which I do not meet as a 'bore,' but as a most welcome visitor ...

[1] Edward D. Baker. See p. 104n.

In relation to our congress matter here, you were right in supposing I would support the nominee. Neither Baker nor I, however, is the man; but *Hardin*.[1] So far as I can judge from present appearances, we shall have no split or trouble about the matter; all will be harmony. In relation to the 'coming events'[2] about which Butler wrote you, I had not *heard* one word before I got your letter; but I have so much confidence in the judgment of a Butler on such a subject, that I incline to think there may be some reality in it. What *day* does Butler appoint? By the way, how do 'events' of the same sort come on in your family? Are you possessing houses and lands, and oxen and asses, and men-servants and maid-servants, and begetting sons and daughters? We are not keeping house; but boarding at the Globe tavern, which is very well kept now by a widow lady of the name of Beck. Our room (the same Dr Wallace occupied there) and boarding only costs four dollars a week. Ann Todd was married something more than a year since to a fellow by the name of Campbell, and who, Mary says, is pretty much of a 'dunce' though he has a little money and property. They live in Boonville, Missouri; and have not been heard from lately enough to enable me to say anything about her health. I reckon it will scarcely be in our power to visit Kentucky this year. Besides poverty, and the necessity of attending to business, those 'coming events' I suspect would be somewhat in the way. I most heartily wish you and your Fanny would not fail to come. Just let us know the time a week in advance, and we will have a room provided for you at our house, and all be merry together for awhile. Be sure to give my respects to your mother and family. Assure her that if I ever come near her I will not fail to call and see her. Mary joins in sending love to your Fanny and you. Yours as ever

To Williamson Durley, a friend and supporter who lived in the strongly anti-slavery town of Hennepin, Putnam County, Illinois.
Springfield, 3 October 1845

Friend Durley: When I saw you at home, it was agreed that I should write to you and your brother Madison. Until I then saw you, I was not aware of your being what is generally called an

---

[1] John J. Hardin, a popular Whig of Jacksonville, Illinois.
[2] Robert Todd Lincoln was born 1 August 1843.

abolitionist, or, as you call yourself, a Liberty-man; though I well knew there were many such in your county. I was glad to hear you say that you intend to attempt to bring about, at the next election in Putnam, a union of the Whigs proper, and such of the Liberty-men as are Whigs in principle on all questions save only that of slavery. So far as I can perceive, by such union, neither party need yield anything, on *the* point in difference between them. If the Whig abolitioɪists of New York had voted with us last fall, Mr Clay would now be president, Whig principles in the ascendant, and Texas not annexed; whereas by the division, all that either had at stake in the contest was lost. And, indeed, it was extremely probable, beforehand, that such would be the result. As I always understood, the Liberty-men deprecated the annexation of Texas extremely; and, this being so, why they should refuse to so cast their votes as to prevent it, even to me seemed wonderful. What was their process of reasoning, I can only judge from what a single one of them told me. It was this: 'We are not to do *evil* that *good* may come.' This general proposition is doubtless correct; but did it apply? If by your votes you could have prevented the *extension*, etc., of slavery, would it not have been *good* and not *evil* so to have used your votes, even though it involved the casting of them for a slaveholder? By the *fruit* the tree is to be known. An *evil* tree cannot bring forth *good* fruit. If the fruit of electing Mr Clay would have been to prevent the extension of slavery, could the act of electing have been *evil*?

But I will not argue further. I perhaps ought to say that individually I never was much interested in the Texas question. I never could see much good to come of annexation; inasmuch as they were already a free republican people on our own model; on the other hand, I never could very clearly see how the annexation would augment the evil of slavery. It always seemed to me that slaves would be taken there in about equal numbers, with or without annexation. And if more *were* taken because of annexation, still there would be just so many the fewer left, where they were taken from. It is possibly true, to some extent, that with annexation some slaves may be sent to Texas and continued in slavery that otherwise might have been liberated. To whatever extent this may be true, I think annexation an evil. I hold it to be a paramount duty of us in the free states, due to the Union of the states, and perhaps to liberty itself (paradox though it may seem) to let the slavery of the other states alone; while, on the other hand, I hold it to be equally clear that we should never knowingly lend ourselves directly or indirectly to prevent that slavery from dying a natural death – to find new places for it to live in, when it can no longer exist in the old. Of course I am not now considering what would be our duty, in cases of insurrection among the slaves.

To recur to the Texas question, I understand the Liberty-men to have viewed annexation as a much greater evil than I ever did; and I would like to convince you if I could, that they could have prevented it, without violation of principle, if they had chosen.

I intend this letter for you and Madison together; and if you and he or either shall think fit to drop me a line, I shall be pleased. Yours with respect

To Robert Boal, a Whig of Marshall County, Illinois.
Springfield, 7 January 1846

Dear Doctor: Since I saw you last fall, I have often thought of writing you as it was then understood I would, but on reflection I have always found that I had nothing new to tell you. All has happened as I then told you I expected it would – Baker's declining, Hardin's taking the track, and so on.

If Hardin and I stood precisely equal – that is, if *neither* of us had been to Congress, or if we *both* had – it would only accord with what I have always done, for the sake of peace, to give way to him; and I expect I should do it. That I *can* voluntarily postpone my pretensions, when they are no more than equal to those to which they are postponed, you have yourself seen. But to yield to Hardin under present circumstances seems to me as nothing else than yielding to one who would gladly sacrifice me altogether. This I would rather not submit to. That Hardin is talented, energetic, usually generous and magnanimous, I have, before this, affirmed to you, and do not now deny. You know that my only argument is that 'turn about is fair play.' This he, practically at least, denies.

If it would not be taxing you too much, I wish you would write me, telling the aspect of things in your county, or rather your district; and also send the names of some of your Whig neighbors, to whom I might with propriety write. Unless I can get someone to do this, Hardin with his old franking list will have the advantage of me. My reliance for a fair shake (and I want nothing more) in your county is chiefly on you, because of your position and standing, and because I am acquainted with so few others. Let this be strictly confidential, and any letter you may write me shall be the same if you desire. Let me hear from you soon.

Yours truly

To Andrew Johnston, of Quincy, Illinois: a poem.
Springfield, 24 February 1846

Dear Johnston: Feeling a little poetic this evening, I have concluded to redeem my promise this evening by sending you the piece you expressed the wish to have.[1] You find it enclosed. I wish I could think of something else to say; but I believe I cannot. By the way, would you like to see a piece of poetry of my own making? I have a piece that is almost done, but I find a deal of trouble to finish it.

Give my respects to Mr Williams, and have him, together with yourself, to understand that if there is anything I can do in connection with your business in the courts, I shall take pleasure in doing it, upon notice. Yours forever

'MY CHILDHOOD-HOME I SEE AGAIN'

My childhood-home I see again,[2]
  And gladden with the view;
And still as mem'ries crowd my brain,
  There's sadness in it too.

O memory! thou mid-way world
  'Twixt Earth and Paradise,
Where things decayed, and loved ones lost
  In dreamy shadows rise.

And freed from all that's gross or vile,
  Seem hallowed, pure, and bright,
Like scenes in some enchanted isle,
  All bathed in liquid light.

As distant mountains please the eye,
  When twilight chases day –
As bugle-tones, that, passing by,
  In distance die away –

[1] 'Mortality,' by William Knox – beyond question, Lincoln's favorite poem.
[2] From 1816 to 1830 Lincoln had lived in Spencer County, Indiana. See pp. 131, 144.

As leaving some grand waterfall
  We ling'ring, list its roar,
So memory will hallow all
  We've known, but know no more.

Now twenty years have passed away,
  Since here I bid farewell
To woods, and fields, and scenes of play
  And schoolmates loved so well.

Where many were, how few remain
  Of old familiar things!
But seeing these to mind again
  The lost and absent brings.

The friends I left that parting day —
  How changed, as time has sped!
Young childhood grown, strong manhood grey,
  And half of all are dead.

I hear the lone survivors tell
  How nought from death could save,
Till every sound appears a knell,
  And every spot a grave.

I range the fields with pensive tread,
  And pace the hollow rooms;
And feel (companions of the dead)
  I'm living in the tombs.

And here's an object more of dread,
  Than ought the grave contains —
A human-form, with reason fled,
  While wretched life remains.

Poor Matthew! Once of genius bright, —
  A fortune-favored child —
Now locked for aye, in mental night,
  A haggard mad-man wild.

Poor Matthew! I have ne'er forgot
  When first with maddened will,
Yourself you maimed, your father fought,
  And mother strove to kill;

And terror spread, and neighbors ran,
  Your dang'rous strength to bind;
And soon a howling crazy man,
  Your limbs were fast confined.

How then you writhed and shrieked aloud,
  Your bones and sinews bared;
And fiendish on the gaping crowd,
  With burning eyeballs glared.

And begged, and swore, and wept, and prayed,
  With maniac laughter joined —
How fearful are the signs displayed,
  By pangs that kill the mind!

And when at length, tho' drear and long,
  Time soothed your fiercer woes —
How plaintively your mournful song,
  Upon the still night rose.

I've heard it oft, as if I dreamed,
  Far-distant, sweet, and lone;
The funeral dirge it ever seemed
  Of reason dead and gone.

To drink its strains, I've stole away,
  All silently and still,
Ere yet the rising god of day
  Had streaked the Eastern hill.

Air held his breath; the trees all still
  Seemed sorr'wing angels round.
Their swelling tears in dew-drops fell
  Upon the list'ning ground.

But this is past, and nought remains
  That raised you o'er the brute.
Your mad'ning shrieks and soothing strains
  Are like forever mute.

Now fare thee well: more thou the cause
  Than subject now of woe.
All mental pangs, but time's kind laws,
  Hast lost the power to know.

And now away to seek some scene
  Less painful than the last —
With less of horror mingled in
  The present and the past.

The very spot where grew the bread
  That formed my bones, I see.
How strange, old field, on thee to tread,
  And feel I'm part of thee!

A handbill replying to charges of unbelief.

31 July 1846

Fellow-Citizens: A charge having got into circulation in some of the neighborhoods of this District, in substance that I am an open scoffer at Christianity,[1] I have by the advice of some friends concluded to notice the subject in this form. That I am not a member of any Christian Church, is true; but I have never denied the truth of the Scriptures; and I have never spoken with intentional disrespect of religion in general, or of any denomination of Christians in particular. It is true that in early life I was inclined to believe in what I understand is called the 'Doctrine of Necessity' – that is, that the human mind is impelled to action, or held in rest by some power over which the mind itself has no control; and I have sometimes (with one, two, or three, but never publicly) tried to maintain this opinion in argument. The habit of arguing thus, however, I have entirely left off for more than five years. And I add here, I have always understood this same opinion to be held by several of the Christian denominations. The foregoing is the whole truth, briefly stated, in relation to myself, upon this subject.

I do not think I could myself be brought to support a man for office whom I knew to be an open enemy of, and scoffer at, religion. Leaving the higher matter of eternal consequences between him and his Maker, I still do not think any man has the right thus to insult the feelings, and injure the morals, of the community in which he may live. If, then, I was guilty of such conduct, I should blame no man who should condemn me for it; but I do blame those, whoever they may be, who falsely put such a charge in circulation against me.

A. LINCOLN.

From a letter to Joshua F. Speed.

Springfield, 22 October 1846

. . . I should be much pleased to see you here again; but I must, in candor, say I do not perceive how your personal presence would do any good in the business matter.

You, no doubt, assign the suspension of our correspondence to

---

[1] The charge was circulated by Lincoln's Democratic opponent, Peter Cartwright, famed as a Methodist circuit-rider.

the true philosophical cause, though it must be confessed, by both of us, that this is rather a cold reason for allowing a friendship such as ours, to die by degrees. I propose now that, on the receipt of this, you shall be considered in my debt, and under obligation to pay soon, and that neither shall remain long in arrears hereafter. Are you agreed?

Being elected to Congress, though I am very grateful to our friends for having done it, has not pleased me as much as I expected.

We have another boy, born the 10th of March last.[1] He is very much such a child as Bob was at his age – rather of a longer order. Bob is 'short and low,' and, I expect, always will be. He talks very plainly – almost as plainly as anybody. He is quite smart enough. I sometimes fear he is one of the little rare-ripe sort, that are smarter at about five than ever after. He has a great deal of that sort of mischief that is the offspring of much animal spirits. Since I began this letter a messenger came to tell me Bob was lost; but by the time I reached the house, his mother had found him, and had him whipped – and, by now, very likely he is run away again.

Mary has read your letter, and wishes to be remembered to Mrs S. and you, in which I most sincerely join her. As ever Yours

The lone Whig Representative from Illinois to his law partner.[2]
Washington, 8 January 1848

Dear William: Your letter of 27th December was received a day or two ago. I am much obliged to you for the trouble you have taken, and promise to take in my little business there. As to speech-making, by way of getting the hang of the House I made a little speech two or three days ago on a post-office question of no general interest. I find speaking here and elsewhere about the same thing. I was about as badly scared, and no worse, as I am when I speak in court. I expect to make one within a week or two, in which I hope to succeed well enough to wish you to see it.

It is very pleasant to learn from you that there are some who desire that I should be re-elected. I most heartily thank them for their kind partiality; and I can say, as Mr Clay said of the annexation of Texas, that 'personally I would not object' to a re-election, although I thought at the time, and still think, it would be

---

[1] Edward Baker Lincoln, who died 1 February 1850.
[2] Lincoln had formed a partnership with William H. Herndon in December 1844.

quite as well for me to return to the law at the end of a single term. I made the declaration that I would not be a candidate again, more from a wish to deal fairly with others, to keep peace among our friends, and to keep the district from going to the enemy, than for any cause personal to myself; so that, if it should so happen that nobody else wishes to be elected, I could not refuse the people the right of sending me again. But to enter myself as a competitor of others, or to authorize anyone so to enter me, is what my word and honor forbid.

I got some letters intimating a probability of so much difficulty amongst our friends as to lose us the district; but I remember such letters were written to Baker when my own case was under consideration, and I trust there is no more ground for such apprehension now than there was then. Remember I am always glad to receive a letter from you. Most truly your friend

From a letter to Usher F. Linder, an Illinois Whig who had criticized Lincoln for opposing the Mexican War.
Washington, 22 March 1848

... Towards the close of your letter you ask three questions, the first of which is 'Would it not have been just as easy to have elected Genl. Taylor without opposing the war as by opposing it?' I answer, I suppose it would, if we could do *neither* – could be *silent* on the question; but the Locofocos[1] here will not let the Whigs be *silent*. Their very first act in Congress was to present a preamble declaring that war existed by the act of Mexico, and the Whigs were obliged to vote on it – and this policy is followed up by them; so that they are compelled to *speak* and their only option is whether they will, when they do speak, tell the *truth*, or tell a foul, villainous, and bloody falsehood. But, while on this point, I protest against your calling the condemnation of Polk 'opposing the war.' In thus assuming that all must be opposed to the war, even though they vote supplies, who do not endorse Polk, with due deference I say I think you fall into one of the artfully set traps of Locofocoism.

Your next question is 'And suppose we could succeed in proving .: a wicked and unconstitutional war, do we not thereby strip Taylor and Scott of more than half their laurels?' Whether it

---

[1] A slang term applied to the Democratic party by its opponents.

would so strip them is not matter of demonstration, but of *opinion* only; and my opinion is that it would not; but as your opinion seems to be different, let us call in some others as umpire. There are in this H.R.[1] some more than forty members who support Genl. Taylor for the Presidency, every one of whom has voted that the war was 'unnecessarily and unconstitutionally commenced by the President,' every one of whom has spoken to the same effect, who has spoken at all, and not one of whom supposes he thereby strips Genl. [Taylor] of any laurels. More than this: two of these, Col. Haskell and Major Gaines, themselves fought in Mexico; and yet they vote and speak just as the rest of us do, without ever dreaming that they 'strip' themselves of any laurels. There may be others, but Capt. Bishop is the only intelligent Whig who has been to Mexico that I have heard of taking different ground.

Your third question is 'And have we as a party, ever gained anything by falling in company with abolitionists?' Yes. We gained our only national victory by falling in company with them in the election of Genl. Harrison. Not that we fell into abolition doctrines; but that we took up a man whose position induced them to join us in his election. But this question is not so significant as a *question*, as it is as a charge of abolitionism against those who have chosen to speak their minds against the President. As you and I perhaps would again differ as to the justice of his charge, let us once more call in our umpire. There are in this H.R. Whigs from the slave states as follows: one from Louisiana, one from Mississippi, one from Florida, two from Alabama, four from Georgia, five from Tennessee, six from Kentucky, six from North Carolina, six from Virginia, four from Maryland, and one from Delaware, making thirty-seven in all, and all slave-holders, every one of whom votes the commencement of the war 'unnecessary and unconstitutional' and so falls subject to your charge of abolitionism! . . . Very respectfully

To Mary Todd Lincoln, visiting her family in Lexington, Kentucky.

Washington, 16 April 1848

Dear Mary: In this troublesome world we are never quite

---

[1] House of Representatives of US Congress.

satisfied. When you were here, I thought you hindered me some in attending to business; but now, having nothing but business – no variety – it has grown exceedingly tasteless to me. I hate to sit down and direct documents, and I hate to stay in this old room by myself. You know I told you in last Sunday's letter, I was going to make a little speech during the week; but the week has passed away without my getting a chance to do so; and now my interest in the subject has passed away too. Your second and third letters have been received since I wrote before. Dear Eddy thinks father is 'gone tapila.'[1] Has any further discovery been made as to the breaking into your grandmother's house? If I were she, I would not remain there alone. You mention that your uncle John Parker is likely to be at Lexington. Don't forget to present him my very kindest regards.

I went yesterday to hunt the little plaid stockings, as you wished; but found that McKnight has quit business, and Allen had not a single pair of the description you give, and only one plaid pair of any sort that I thought would fit 'Eddy's dear little feet.' I have a notion to make another trial to-morrow morning. If I could get them, I have an excellent chance of sending them. Mr Warrick Tunstall of St Louis is here. He is to leave early this week, and to go by Lexington. He says he knows you, and will call to see you; and he voluntarily asked if I had not some package to send to you.

I wish you to enjoy yourself in every possible way; but is there no danger of wounding the feelings of your good father by being so openly intimate with the Wickcliffe family?

Mrs Broome has not removed yet; but she thinks of doing so to-morrow. All the house – or rather, all with whom you were on decided good terms – send their love to you. The others say nothing.

Very soon after you went away, I got what I think a very pretty set of shirt-bosom studs – modest little ones, jet, set in gold, only costing 50 cents apiece, or $1.50 for the whole.

Suppose you do not prefix the 'Hon.' to the address on your letters to me any more. I like the letters very much, but I would rather they should not have that upon them. It is not necessary, as I suppose you have thought, to have them to come free.

And you are entirely free from headache? That is good – good –

---

[1] Probably a child's attempt to say 'to the capitol.'

considering it is the first spring you have been free from it since we were acquainted. I am afraid you will get so well, and fat, and young, as to be wanting to marry again. Tell Louisa I want her to watch you a little for me. Get weighed, and write me how much you weigh.

I did not get rid of the impression of that foolish dream about dear Bobby till I got your letter written the same day. What did he and Eddy think of the little letters father sent them? Don't let the blessed fellows forget father.

A day or two ago Mr Strong, here in Congress, said to me that Matilda would visit here within two or three weeks. Suppose you write her a letter, and enclose it in one of mine; and if she comes I will deliver it to her, and if she does not, I will send it to her. Most affectionately

To Mary Todd Lincoln.

Washington, 12 June 1848

My dear wife: On my return from Philadelphia, yesterday, where, in my anxiety, I had been led to attend the Whig convention, I found your last letter. I was so tired and sleepy, having ridden all night, that I could not answer it till to-day; and now I have to do so in the H.R. The leading matter in your letter is your wish to return to this side of the mountains. Will you be a *good girl* in all things, if I consent? Then come along, and that as *soon* as possible. Having got the idea in my head, I shall be impatient till I see you. You will not have money enough to bring you; but I presume your uncle will supply you, and I will refund him here. By the way, you do not mention whether you have received the fifty dollars I sent you. I do not much fear but that you got it because the want of it would have induced you to say something in relation to it. If your uncle is already at Lexington, you might induce him to start on earlier than the first of July; he could stay in Kentucky longer on his return, and so make up for lost time. Since I began this letter, the H.R. has passed a resolution for adjourning on the 17th July, which probably will pass the Senate. I hope this letter will not be disagreeable to you; which, together with the circumstances under which I write, I hope will excuse me for not writing a longer one. Come on just as soon as you can. I want to see you, and our dear — *dear* boys very much. Everybody here wants to see our dear Bobby. Affectionately

To William H. Herndon: a letter from a man 'old' at the age of thirty-nine.

Washington, 10 July 1848

Dear William: Your letter covering the newspaper slips was received last night. The subject of that letter is exceedingly painful to me; and I cannot but think there is some mistake in your impression of the motives of the old men. I suppose I am now one of the old men – and I declare on my veracity, which I think is good with you, that nothing could afford me more satisfaction than to learn that you and others of my young friends at home were doing battle in the contest, and endearing themselves to the people, and taking a stand far above any I have ever been able to reach, in their admiration. I cannot conceive that other old men feel differently. Of course I cannot demonstrate what I say; but I was young once, and I am sure I was never ungenerously thrust back. I hardly know what to say. The way for a young man to rise is to improve himself every way he can, never suspecting that anybody wishes to hinder him. Allow me to assure you that suspicion and jealousy never did help any man in any situation. There may sometimes be ungenerous attempts to keep a young man down; and they will succeed too if he allows his mind to be diverted from its true channel to brood over the attempted injury. Cast about, and see if this feeling has not injured every person you have ever known to fall into it.

Now, in what I have said, I am sure you will suspect nothing but sincere friendship. I would save you from a fatal error. You have been a laborious studious young man. You are far better informed on almost all subjects than I have ever been. You cannot fail in any laudable object, unless you allow your mind to be improperly directed. I have some the advantage of you in the world's experience, merely by being older; and it is this that induces me to advise . . . Your friend, as ever

From a speech ridiculing Lewis Cass, of Michigan, Democratic candidate for the Presidency. In the House of Representatives.

27 July 1848

. . . But in my hurry I was very near closing on the subject of military tails before I was done with it. There is one entire article of the sort I have not discussed yet; I mean the military tail you

Democrats are now engaged in dovetailing on to the great Michigander. Yes sir, all his biographers (and they are legion) have him in hand, tying him to a military tail, like so many mischievous boys tying a dog to a bladder of beans. True, the material they have is very limited; but they drive at it, might and main. He *in*vaded Canada without resistance, and he *out*vaded it without pursuit. As he did both under orders, I suppose there was, to him, neither credit or discredit in them; but they are made to constitute a large part of the tail. He was not at Hull's surrender, but he was close by; he was volunteer aid to Gen. Harrison on the day of the Battle of the Thames; and, as you said in 1840, Harrison was picking huckleberries two miles off while the battle was fought, I suppose it is a just conclusion with you to say Cass was aiding Harrison to pick huckleberries. This is about all, except the mooted question of the broken sword. Some authors say he broke it, some say he threw it away, and some others who ought to know, say nothing about it. Perhaps it would be a fair historical compromise to say, if he did not break it he didn't do anything else with it.

By the way, Mr Speaker, did you know I am a military hero? Yes sir; in the days of the Black Hawk war, I fought, bled, and came away. Speaking of Gen. Cass's career reminds me of my own. I was not at Stillman's defeat, but I was about as near it as Cass was to Hull's surrender; and, like him, I saw the place very soon afterwards. It is quite certain I did not break my sword, for I had none to break; but I bent a musket pretty badly on one occasion. If Cass broke his sword, the idea is, he broke it in desperation; I bent the musket by accident. If Gen. Cass went in advance of me in picking huckleberries, I guess I surpassed him in charges upon the wild onions. If he saw any live, fighting Indians, it was more than I did; but I had a good many bloody struggles with the mosquitoes; and, although I never fainted from loss of blood, I can truly say I was often very hungry. Mr Speaker, if I should ever conclude to doff whatever our Democratic friends may suppose there is of black cockade Federalism about me, and thereupon they shall take me up as their candidate for the Presidency, I protest they shall not make fun of me, as they have of Gen. Cass, by attempting to write me into a military hero.

To John D. Johnston, Lincoln's stepbrother.
                                    Washington, 24 December 1848

Dear Johnston: Your request for eighty dollars, I do not think it best to comply with now. At the various times when I have helped you a little, you have said to me 'We can get along very well now' but in a very short time I find you in the same difficulty again. Now this can only happen by some defect in your *conduct*. What that defect is, I think I know. You are not *lazy*, and still you *are* an *idler*. I doubt whether since I saw you, you have done a good whole day's work, in any one day. You do not very much dislike to work; and still you do not work much, merely because it does not seem to you that you could get much for it. This habit of uselessly wasting time is the whole difficulty; and it is vastly important to you, and still more so to your children, that you should break this habit. It is more important to them, because they have longer to live, and can keep out of an idle habit before they are in it, easier than they can get out after they are in.

You are now in need of some ready money; and what I propose is, that you shall go to work 'tooth and nails' for somebody who will give you money for it. Let father and your boys take charge of things at home – prepare for a crop, and make the crop; and you go to work for the best money wages, or in discharge of any debt you owe, that you can get. And to secure you a fair reward for your labor, I now promise you that for every dollar you will, between this and the first of next May, get for your own labor, either in money or in your own indebtedness, I will then give you one other dollar. By this, if you hire yourself at ten dollars a month, from me you will get ten more, making twenty dollars a month for your work. In this I do not mean you shall go off to St Louis, or the lead mines, or the gold mines, in California, but I mean for you to go at it for the best wages you can get close to home in Coles county. Now if you will do this, you will soon be out of debt, and what is better, you will have a habit that will keep you from getting in debt again. But if I should now clear you out, next year you will be just as deep in as ever. You say you would almost give your place in heaven for $70 or $80. Then you value your place in heaven very cheaply for I am sure you can with the offer I make you get the seventy or eighty dollars for four or five months' work. You say if I furnish you the money you will deed me the land, and, if you don't pay the money back, you will deliver possession. Nonsense! If you can't now live *with* the land, how will you then live without it? You have always been kind to me, and I do not now mean to be unkind to you. On the contrary, if you will but follow my advice, you will find it worth more than eight times eighty dollars to you. Affectionately your brother

To William B. Warren and others, Illinois Whigs.
Springfield, 7 April 1849

Gentlemen: In answer to your note concerning the General Land-Office I have to say that if the office can be secured to Illinois by my consent to accept it, and not otherwise, I give that consent. Some months since I gave my word to secure the appointment to that office of Mr Cyrus Edwards, if in my power, in case of a vacancy; and more recently I stipulated with Col. Baker that if Mr Edwards and Col. J. L. D. Morrison could arrange with each other for one of them to withdraw, we would jointly recommend the other. In relation to these pledges, I must not only be chaste but above suspicion. If the office shall be tendered to me, I must be permitted to say 'Give it to Mr Edwards, or, if so agreed by them, to Col. Morrison, and I decline it; if not, I accept.' With this understanding, you are at liberty to procure me the offer of the appointment if you can; and I shall feel complimented by your effort, and still more by its success. It should not be overlooked that Col. Baker's position entitles him to a large share of control in this matter; however, one of your number, Col. Warren, knows that Baker has at all times been ready to recommend me, if I would consent. It must also be understood that if at any time, previous to an appointment being made, I shall learn that Mr Edwards and Col. Morrison have agreed, I shall at once carry out my stipulation with Col. Baker, as above stated. Yours truly

To Joseph Gillespie, a Whig lawyer of Edwardsville, Illinois.
Springfield, 13 July 1849

Dear Gillespie: Mr Edwards[1] is unquestionably offended with me in connection with the matter of the General Land-Office. He wrote a letter against me, which was filed at the Department. The better part of one's life consists of his friendships; and, of these,

---

[1] Cyrus Edwards, of Edwardsville, Illinois.

mine with Mr Edwards was one of the most cherished. I have not been false to it. At a word, I could have had the office any time before the Department was committed to Mr Butterfield – at least Mr Ewing and the President say as much. That word I forebore to speak, partly for other reasons, but chiefly for Mr Edwards's sake. Losing the office that he might gain it, I was always for; but to lose his *friendship* by the effort for him would oppress me very much, were I not sustained by the utmost consciousness of rectitude. I first determined to be an applicant, unconditionally, on the 2nd of June; and I did so then upon being informed by a telegraphic dispatch that the question was narrowed down to Mr B. and myself, and that the Cabinet had postponed the appointment three weeks for my benefit. Not doubting that Mr Edwards was wholly out of the question, I nevertheless would not then have become an applicant had I supposed he would thereby be brought to suspect me of treachery to him. Two or three days afterwards a conversation with Levi Davis convinced me Mr E. was dissatis-fied; but I was then too far in to get out. His own letter, written on the 25th of April, after I had fully informed him of all that had passed up to within a few days of that time, gave assurance I had that entire confidence from him which I felt my uniform and strong friendship for him entitled me to. Among other things it says 'whatever course your judgment may dictate as proper to be pursued, shall never be excepted to by me.' I also had had a letter from Washington, saying Chambers of the Republican had brought a rumor then that Mr E. had declined in my favor, which rumor I judged came from Mr E. himself, as I had not then breathed of his letter to any living creature.

In saying I had never before the 2nd of June determined to be an applicant *unconditionally*, I mean to admit that before then I had said substantially I would take the office rather than it should be lost to the state, or given to one in the state whom the Whigs did not want; but I aver that in every instance in which I spoke of myself, I intended to keep, and now believe I did keep, Mr E. ahead of myself. Mr Edwards's first suspicion was that I had allowed Baker to overreach me, as his friend, in behalf of Don. Morrison. I knew this was a mistake; and the result has proved it. I understand his view now is that if I had gone to open war with Baker I could have ridden him down, and had the thing all my own way. I believe no such thing. With Baker and some strong men from the Military tract, and elsewhere for Morrison; and we and some strong men from the Wabash and elsewhere for Mr E., it was not possible for either to succeed. I *believed* this in March, and I *know* it now. The only thing which gave either any chance was the very thing Baker and I proposed – an adjustment with themselves.

You may wish to know how Butterfield finally beat me. I cannot tell you particulars now, but will when I see you. In the meantime let it be understood I am not greatly dissatisfied. I wish the office had been so bestowed as to encourage our friends in future contests, and I regret exceedingly Mr Edwards's feelings towards me. These two things away, I should have no regrets – at least I think I would not.

Write me soon. Your friend, as ever

To George W. Rives, of Edgar County, Illinois, a disgruntled office-seeker.
Springfield, 15 December 1849

Dear Sir: On my return from Kentucky I found your letter of the 7th of November, and have delayed answering it till now for the reason I now briefly state. From the beginning of our acquaintance I had felt the greatest kindness for you, and had supposed it was reciprocated on your part. Last summer, under circumstances which I mentioned to you, I was painfully constrained to withhold a recommendation which you desired; and shortly afterwards I learned, in such way as to believe it, that you were indulging open abuse of me. Of course my feelings were wounded. On receiving your last letter, the question occurred whether you were attempting to *use* me, at the same time you would *injure* me, or whether you might not have been misrepresented to me. If the former, I ought not to answer you; if the latter I ought, and so I have remained in suspense. I now enclose you a letter which you may use if you think fit. Yours etc.

To Abram Bale, of Petersburg, Illinois.
Springfield, 22 February 1850

Dear Sir: I understand Mr Hickox will go, or send to Petersburg to-morrow, for the purpose of meeting you to settle the difficulty about the wheat. I sincerely hope you will settle it. I think you *can* if you *will*, for I have always found Mr Hickox a fair man in his dealings. If you settle, I will charge nothing for what I have done, and thank you to boot. By settling, you will most likely get your money sooner; and with much less trouble and expense. Yours truly

Notes for a law lecture.

[1 July 1850?]

I am not an accomplished lawyer. I find quite as much material for a lecture in those points wherein I have failed, as in those wherein I have been moderately successful. The leading rule for the lawyer, as for the man of every other calling, is diligence. Leave nothing for to-morrow which can be done to-day. Never let your correspondence fall behind. Whatever piece of business you have in hand, before stopping, do all the labor pertaining to it which can then be done. When you bring a common-law suit, if you have the facts for doing so, write the declaration at once. If a law point be involved, examine the books and note the authority you rely on upon the declaration itself, where you are sure to find it when wanted. The same of defenses and pleas. In business not likely to be litigated — ordinary collection cases, foreclosures, partitions, and the like — make all examinations of titles and note them, and even draft orders and decrees in advance. This course has a triple advantage; it avoids omissions and neglect, saves your labor when once done, performs the labor out of court when you have leisure, rather than in court when you have not. Extemporaneous speaking should be practised and cultivated. It is the lawyer's avenue to the public. However able and faithful he may be in other respects, people are slow to bring him business if he cannot make a speech. And yet there is not a more fatal error to young lawyers than relying too much on speech-making. If anyone, upon his rare powers of speaking, shall claim an exemption from the drudgery of the law, his case is a failure in advance.

Discourage litigation. Persuade your neighbors to compromise whenever you can. Point out to them how the nominal winner is often a real loser — in fees, expenses, and waste of time. As a peacemaker the lawyer has a superior opportunity of being a good man. There will still be business enough.

Never stir up litigation. A worse man can scarcely be found than one who does this. Who can be more nearly a fiend than he who habitually overhauls the register of deeds in search of defects in titles, whereon to stir up strife, and put money in his pocket? A moral tone ought to be infused into the profession which should drive such men out of it.

The matter of fees is important, far beyond the mere question of bread and butter involved. Properly attended to, fuller justice is done to both lawyer and client. An exorbitant fee should never be claimed. As a general rule never take your whole fee in advance, nor any more than a small retainer. When fully paid beforehand, you are more than a common mortal if you can feel the same interest in the case, as if something was still in prospect for you, as well as for your client. And when you lack interest in the case the job will very likely lack skill and diligence in the performance. Settle the amount of fee and take a note in advance. Then you will feel that you are working for something, and you are sure to do your work faithfully and well. Never sell a fee note – at least not before the consideration service is performed. It leads to negligence and dishonesty – negligence by losing interest in the case, and dishonesty in refusing to refund when you have allowed the consideration to fail.

There is a vague popular belief that lawyers are necessarily dishonest. I say vague, because when we consider to what extent confidence and honors are reposed in and conferred upon lawyers by the people, it appears improbable that their impression of dishonesty is very distinct and vivid. Yet the impression is common, almost universal. Let no young man choosing the law for a calling for a moment yield to the popular belief – resolve to be honest at all events; and if in your own judgment you cannot be an honest lawyer, resolve to be honest without being a lawyer. Choose some other occupation rather than one in the choosing of which you do, in advance, consent to be a knave.

To John D. Johnston, stepbrother.

Springfield, 12 January 1851

Dear Brother: On the day before yesterday I received a letter from Harriett, written at Greenup. She says she has just returned from your house; and that Father is very low and will hardly recover. She also says you have written me two letters; and that, although you do not expect me to come now, you wonder that I do not write. I received both your letters, and although I have not answered them, it is not because I have forgotten them or been uninterested about them – but because it appeared to me I could write nothing which could do any good. You already know I desire that neither Father or Mother shall be in want of any comfort either in health or sickness while they live; and I feel sure you have not failed to use my name, if necessary, to procure a doctor, or anything else for Father in his present sickness. My business is such that I could hardly leave home now, if it were not, as it is, that my own wife is sick abed. (It is a case of baby-sickness, and I suppose is not dangerous.) I sincerely hope Father may yet recover his health; but at all events tell him to remember to call upon, and confide in, our great, and good, and merciful Maker, who will not turn away from him in any extremity. He notes the fall of a sparrow, and numbers the hairs of our heads; and He will not forget the dying man, who puts his trust in Him. Say to him that if we could meet now, it is doubtful whether it would not be more painful than pleasant; but that if it be his lot to go now, he will soon have a joyous meeting with many loved ones gone before; and where the rest of us, through the help of God, hope ere long to join them.[1]

Write me again when you receive this. Affectionately

From a letter to John D. Johnston.
Springfield, 4 November 1851.

Dear Brother: When I came into Charleston day before yesterday I learned that you are anxious to sell the land where you live and move to Missouri. I have been thinking of this ever since; and cannot but think such a notion is utterly foolish. What can you do in Missouri better than here? Is the land any richer? Can you there, any more than here, raise corn, and wheat and oats, without work? Will anybody there, any more than here, do your work for you? If you intend to go to work, there is no better place than right where you are; if you do not intend to go to work, you cannot get along anywhere. Squirming and crawling about from place to place can do no good. You have raised no crop this year, and what you really want is to sell the land, get the money and spend it – part with the land you have, and my life upon it, you will never after own a spot big enough to bury you in. Half you will get for the land you spend in moving to Missouri, and the other half you will eat and drink, and wear out, and no foot of

---

[1] Thomas Lincoln died in Coles County, Illinois, on 15 January 1851.

land will be bought. Now I feel it is my duty to have no hand in such a piece of foolery. I feel that it is so even on your own account; and particularly on *Mother*'s account. The eastern forty acres I intend to keep for Mother while she lives – if you *will not cultivate it*; it will rent for enough to support her – at least it will rent for something. Her dower in the other two forties she can let you have, and no thanks to me.

Now do not misunderstand this letter. I do not write it in any unkindness. I write it in order, if possible, to get you to *face* the truth – which truth is, you are destitute because you have *idled* away all your time. Your thousand pretenses for not getting along better are all nonsense – they deceive nobody but yourself. *Go to work* is the only cure for your case . . .

To Charles R. Welles: a letter in behalf of William Florville, Lincoln's Negro barber.

Bloomington, Illinois, 27 September 1852

Dear Sir: I am in a little trouble here. I am trying to get a decree for our 'Billy the Barber' for the conveyance of certain town lots sold to him by Allen, Gridly & Prickett. I made you a party, as administrator of Prickett, but the Clerk omitted to put your name in the writ, and so you are not served. Billy will blame me if I do not get the thing fixed up this time. If, therefore, you will be so kind as to sign the authority below and send it to me by *return mail*, I shall be greatly obliged, and will be careful that you shall not be involved, or your rights invaded by it. Yours as ever

Chapter 3
Kansas-Nebraska and the Return to Active Politics
1854-7

It was the question of slavery and its further extension into the western territories which brought Lincoln back into political life, after an interlude as a busy and successful lawyer in Illinois. The Compromise of 1850 had dealt with many of the issues arising from the acquisition of new territory from Mexico, including California. In 1854, Stephen A. Douglas introduced his Kansas-Nebraska Bill, which, in organizing two new territories, adopted the principle of 'popular sovereignty' – that is, allowing the settlers in a territory to decide for or against the admission of slavery. The price exacted by Southerners for their support was the explicit repeal of the Missouri Compromise of 1820, which had banned slavery from territory north of the Mason-Dixon line. Lincoln's speech of 16 October 1854 set out many of the themes which dominated his thoughts for the remainder of the decade: his hatred of slavery and his horror at the prospect of its unrestricted spread; his stand on the principles of the Declaration of Independence; and his awareness of slavery as a blot on American democracy and America's world reputation.

The Kansas-Nebraska Act produced chaos in Kansas, and provoked the creation of the new Republican party, devoted to the principle of 'free soil' – that is, keeping slavery out of the territories. Lincoln's hopes of election to the Senate were foiled in 1855, and he moved only gradually from his old Whig allegiance into the new party.

In its Dred Scott decision in 1857, the Supreme Court ruled that a slave could never become a citizen, and that Congress had no power to bar slavery from the territories. In his speech of 26 June 1857 on the Dred Scott decision, Lincoln addressed the racial implications of the slavery issue much more explicitly than before. He insisted that the rights set out in the Declaration of Independence applied to everyone, including blacks, but he also accepted the need to separate the races, and advocated overseas colonization of blacks.

Fragment on government.

[1 July 1854?]

Government is a combination of the people of a country to effect certain objects by joint effort. The best framed and best administered governments are necessarily expensive; while by errors in frame and maladministration most of them are more onerous than they need be, and some of them very oppressive. Why, then, should we have government? Why not each individual take to himself the whole fruit of his labor, without having any of it taxed away, in services, corn, or money? Why not take just so much land as he can cultivate with his own hands, without buying it of anyone?

The legitimate object of government is 'to do for the people what needs to be done, but which they cannot, by individual effort, do at all, or do so well, for themselves.' There are many such things – some of them exist independently of the injustice in the world. Making and maintaining roads, bridges, and the like; providing for the helpless young and afflicted; common schools; and disposing of deceased men's property, are instances.

But a far larger class of objects springs from the injustice of men. If one people will make war upon another, it is a necessity with that other to unite and co-operate for defense. Hence the military department. If some men will kill, or beat, or constrain others, or despoil them of property, by force, fraud, or non-compliance with contracts, it is a common object with peaceful and just men to prevent it. Hence the criminal and civil departments.

Fragment on slavery.

[1 July 1854?]

If A. can prove, however conclusively, that he may, of right, enslave B. – why may not B. snatch the same argument, and prove equally that he may enslave A.?

You say A. is white, and B. is black. It is *color*, then; the lighter

having the right to enslave the darker? Take care. By this rule, you
are to be slave to the first man you meet with a fairer skin than
your own.

You do not mean *color* exactly? You mean the whites are
intellectually the superiors of the blacks, and therefore have the
right to enslave them? Take care again. By this rule, you are to be
slave to the first man you meet with an intellect superior to your
own.

But, say you, it is a question of *interest*; and, if you can make it
your *interest*, you have the right to enslave another. Very well.
And if he can make it his interest, he has the right to enslave you.

*To John M. Palmer, a Democrat disturbed by his party's
sponsorship of the Kansas-Nebraska Bill.*
Springfield, 7 September 1854

Dear Sir: You know how anxious I am that this Nebraska
measure shall be rebuked and condemned everywhere. Of course I
hope something from your position; yet I do not expect you to do
anything which may be wrong in your own judgment; nor would I
have you do anything personally injurious to yourself. You are,
and always have been, *honestly* and *sincerely* a democrat; and I
know how painful it must be to an honest sincere man to be urged
by his party to the support of a measure which on his conscience
he believes to be wrong. You have had a severe struggle with
yourself, and you have determined *not* to swallow the *wrong*. Is it
not just to yourself that you should, in a few public speeches, state
your reasons, and thus justify yourself? I wish you would; and yet
I say 'don't do it if you think it will injure you.' You may have given
your word to vote for Major Harris,[1] and if so, of course you will
stick to it. But allow me to suggest that you should avoid speaking
of this; for it probably would induce some of your friends, in like
manner, to cast their votes. You understand. And now let me beg
your pardon for obtruding this letter upon you, to whom I have
ever been opposed in politics. Had your party omitted to make
Nebraska a test of party fidelity, you probably would have been
the Democratic candidate for Congress in the district. You
deserved it, and I believe it would have been given you. In that case
I should have been quite happy that Nebraska was to be rebuked

---

[1] Thomas L. Harris, Democratic candidate for Congress.

at all events. I still should have voted for the Whig candidate; but I should have made no speeches, written no letters; and you would have been elected by at least a thousand majority. Yours truly

From a speech in reply to Senator Stephen A. Douglas of Illinois, sponsor and defender of the Kansas-Nebraska Bill.

Peoria, 16 October 1854

. . . We have before us the chief material enabling us to correctly judge whether the repeal of the Missouri Compromise[1] is right or wrong.

I think, and shall try to show, that it is wrong; wrong in its direct effect, letting slavery into Kansas and Nebraska – and wrong in its prospective principle, allowing it to spread to every other part of the wide world, where men can be found inclined to take it.

This *declared* indifference, but as I must think, covert *real* zeal for the spread of slavery, I cannot but hate. I hate it because of the monstrous injustice of slavery itself. I hate it because it deprives our republican example of its just influence in the world – enables the enemies of free institutions, with plausibility, to taunt us as hypocrites – causes the real friends of freedom to doubt our sincerity, and especially because it forces so many really good men amongst ourselves into an open war with the very fundamental principles of civil liberty – criticizing the Declaration of Independence, and insisting that there is no right principle of action but *self-interest*.

Before proceeding, let me say I think I have no prejudice against the southern people. They are just what we would be in their situation. If slavery did not now exist amongst them, they would not introduce it. If it did now exist amongst us, we should not instantly give it up. This I believe of the masses north and south. Doubtless there are individuals, on both sides, who would not hold slaves under any circumstances; and others who would gladly introduce slavery anew, if it were out of existence. We know that some southern men do free their slaves, go north, and become tip-top abolitionists; while some northern ones go south, and become most cruel slave-masters.

---

[1] The Kansas-Nebraska Act specifically repealed the Missouri Compromise (1820), by which, after the admission of Missouri as a state, slavery was to be prohibited in the remainder of the Louisiana Purchase north of the line of 36° 30′.

When southern people tell us they are no more responsible for the origin of slavery than we, I acknowledge the fact. When it is said that the institution exists, and that it is very difficult to get rid of it in any satisfactory way, I can understand and appreciate the saying. I surely will not blame them for not doing what I should not know how to do myself. If all earthly power were given me, I should not know what to do as to the existing institution. My first impulse would be to free all the slaves and send them to Liberia — to their own native land. But a moment's reflection would convince me that whatever of high hope (as I think there is) there may be in this in the long run, its sudden execution is impossible. If they were all landed there in a day, they would all perish in the next ten days; and there are not surplus shipping and surplus money enough in the world to carry them there in many times ten days. What then? Free them all, and keep them among us as underlings? Is it quite certain that this betters their condition? I think I would not hold one in slavery, at any rate; yet the point is not clear enough for me to denounce people upon. What next? Free them, and make them politically and socially our equals? My own feelings will not admit of this; and if mine would, we well know that those of the great mass of white people will not. Whether this feeling accords with justice and sound judgment is not the sole question, if indeed it is any part of it. A universal feeling, whether well or ill founded, cannot be safely disregarded. We cannot, then, make them equals. It does seem to me that systems of gradual emancipation might be adopted; but for their tardiness in this, I will not undertake to judge our brethren of the south.

When they remind us of their constitutional rights, I acknowledge them, not grudgingly, but fully and fairly; and I would give them any legislation for the reclaiming of their fugitives, which should not, in its stringency, be more likely to carry a free man into slavery than our ordinary criminal laws are to hang an innocent one . . .

Equal justice to the south, it is said, requires us to consent to the extending of slavery to new countries. That is to say, inasmuch as you do not object to my taking my hog to Nebraska, therefore I must not object to you taking your slave. Now I admit this is perfectly logical if there is no difference between hogs and Negroes. But while you thus require me to deny the humanity of the Negro, I wish to ask whether you of the south yourselves have ever been willing to do as much? It is kindly provided that of all those who come into the world only a small percentage are natural tyrants. That percentage is no larger in the slave states than in the free. The great majority, south as well as north, have human sympathies, of which they can no more divest themselves than they can of their sensibility to physical pain. These sympathies in the bosoms of the southern people manifest in many ways their sense of the wrong of slavery, and their consciousness that, after all, there is humanity in the Negro. If they deny this, let me address them a few plain questions. In 1820 you joined the north, almost unanimously, in declaring the African slave-trade piracy, and in annexing to it the punishment of death. Why did you do this? If you did not feel that it was wrong, why did you join in providing that men should be hung for it? The practice was no more than bringing wild Negroes from Africa, to sell to such as would buy them. But you never thought of hanging men for catching and selling wild horses, wild buffaloes, or wild bears . . .

But one great argument in the support of the repeal of the Missouri Compromise is still to come. That argument is 'the sacred right of self-government.' It seems our distinguished Senator has found great difficulty in getting his antagonists, even in the Senate, to meet him fairly on this argument; some poet has said

'Fools rush in where angels fear to tread.'

At the hazard of being thought one of the fools of this quotation, I meet that argument – I rush in, I take that bull by the horns.

I trust I understand and truly estimate the right of self-government. My faith in the proposition that each should do precisely as he pleases with all which is exclusively his own, lies at the foundation of the sense of justice there is in me. I extend the principles to communities of men, as well as to individuals. I so extend it, because it is politically wise, as well as naturally just: politically wise in saving us from broils about matters which do not concern us. Here, or at Washington, I would not trouble myself with the oyster laws of Virginia, or the cranberry laws of Indiana.

The doctrine of self-government is right – absolutely and eternally right – but it has no just application as here attempted. Or perhaps I should rather say that whether it has such just application depends upon whether a Negro is *not* or *is* a man. If he is *not* a man, why in that case he who *is* a man may, as a matter of self-government, do just as he pleases with him. But if the Negro *is* a man, is it not to that extent a total destruction of self-government to say that he too shall not govern *himself*? When the white man governs himself that is self-government; but when he governs himself, and also governs *another* man, that is *more* than self-government – that is despotism. If the Negro is a *man*, why then my ancient faith teaches me that 'all men are created equal'; and that there can be no moral right in connection with one man's making a slave of another.

Judge Douglas frequently, with bitter irony and sarcasm, paraphrases our argument by saying 'The white people of Nebraska are good enough to govern themselves, *but they are not good enough to govern a few miserable Negroes!*'

Well I doubt not that the people of Nebraska are, and will continue to be, as good as the average of people elsewhere. I do not say the contrary. What I do say is, that no man is good enough to govern another man, *without that other's consent*. I say this is the leading principle – the sheet anchor of American republicanism. Our Declaration of Independence says:

'We hold these truths to be self evident: that all men are created equal; that they are endowed by their Creator with certain inalienable rights; that among these are life, liberty, and the pursuit of happiness. That to secure these rights, governments are instituted among men, DERIVING THEIR JUST POWERS FROM THE CONSENT OF THE GOVERNED.'

I have quoted so much at this time merely to show that according to our ancient faith the just powers of governments are derived from the consent of the governed. Now the relation of masters and slaves is, *pro tanto*, a total violation of this principle. The master not only governs the slave without his consent; but he governs him by a set of rules altogether different from those which he prescribes for himself. Allow *all* the governed an equal voice in the government, and that, and that only, is self-government . . .

The Missouri Compromise ought to be restored. For the sake of the Union, it ought to be restored. We ought to elect a House of Representatives which will vote its restoration. If by any means we omit to do this, what follows? Slavery may or may not be established in Nebraska. But whether it be or not, we shall have repudiated – discarded from the councils of the Nation – the *Spirit of Compromise*; for who after this will ever trust in a national compromise? The spirit of mutual concession – that spirit which first gave us the Constitution, and which has thrice saved the Union – we shall have strangled and cast from us forever. And what shall we have in lieu of it? The South flushed with triumph and tempted to excesses; the North, betrayed, as they believe, brooding on wrong and burning for revenge. One side will provoke; the other resent. The one will taunt, the other defy; one aggresses, the other retaliates. Already a few in the North defy all constitutional restraints, resist the execution of the fugitive slave law, and even menace the institution of slavery in the states where it exists.

Already a few in the South claim the constitutional right to take to and hold slaves in the free states – demand the revival of the slave trade; and demand a treaty with Great Britain by which fugitive slaves may be reclaimed from Canada. As yet they are but few on either side. It is a grave question for the lovers of the Union, whether the final destruction of the Missouri Compromise, and with it the spirit of all compromise, will or will not embolden and embitter each of these, and fatally increase the numbers of both.

But restore the compromise, and what then? We thereby restore the national faith, the national confidence, the national feeling of brotherhood. We thereby reinstate the spirit of concession and compromise – that spirit which has never failed us in past perils, and which may be safely trusted for all the future. The South ought to join in doing this. The peace of the nation is as dear to them as to us. In memories of the past and hopes of the future, they share as largely as we. It would be on their part a great act – great in its spirit, and great in its effect. It would be worth to the nation a hundred years' purchase of peace and prosperity. And what of sacrifice would they make? They only surrender to us what they gave us for a consideration long, long ago; what they have not now asked for, struggled or cared for; what has been thrust upon them, not less to their own astonishment than to ours.

But it is said we cannot restore it; that though we elect every member of the lower house, the Senate is still against us. It is quite true, that of the senators who passed the Nebraska bill, a majority of the whole Senate will retain their seats in spite of the elections of this and the next year. But if at these elections, their several constituencies shall clearly express their will against Nebraska, will these senators disregard their will? Will they neither obey, nor make room for those who will?

But even if we fail to technically restore the compromise, it is still a great point to carry a popular vote in favor of the restoration. The moral weight of such a vote cannot be estimated too highly. The authors of Nebraska are not at all satisfied with the destruction of the compromise – an endorsement of this *principle*, they proclaim to be the great object. With them, Nebraska alone is a small matter – to establish a principle, for *future use*, is what they particularly desire.

That future use is to be the planting of slavery wherever in the wide world, local and unorganized opposition cannot prevent it. Now if you wish to give them this endorsement – if you wish to establish this principle – do so. I shall regret it; but it is your right. On the contrary, if you are opposed to the principle – intend to give it no such endorsement – let no wheedling, no sophistry, divert you from throwing a direct vote against it.

Some men, mostly Whigs, who condemn the repeal of the Missouri Compromise, nevertheless hesitate to go for its restoration, lest they be thrown in company with the abolitionist. Will they allow me as an old Whig to tell them good humoredly that I think this is very silly? Stand with anybody that stands *right*. Stand with him while he is right and *part* with him when he goes wrong. Stand *with* the abolitionist in restoring the Missouri Compromise; and stand *against* him when he attempts to repeal the fugitive slave law. In the latter case you stand with the southern disunionist. What of that? you are still right. In both cases you are right. In both cases you oppose the dangerous extremes. In both you stand on middle ground and hold the ship level and steady. In both you are national and nothing less than national. This is good old Whig ground. To desert such ground, because of any company, is to be less than a Whig – less than a man – less than an American . . .

Little by little, but steadily as man's march to the grave, we have been giving up the *old* for the *new* faith. Near eighty years ago we began by declaring that all men are created equal; but now from that beginning we have run down to the other declaration, that for *some* men to enslave *others* is a 'sacred right of self-government.' These principles cannot stand together. They are as opposite as God and mammon; and whoever holds to the one must despise the other. When Pettit, in connection with his support of the Nebraska bill, called the Declaration of Independence 'a self-evident lie' he only did what consistency and candor require all other Nebraska men to do. Of the forty odd Nebraska senators who sat present and heard him, no one rebuked him. Nor am I apprised that any Nebraska newspaper, or any Nebraska orator, in the whole nation, has ever yet rebuked him. If this had been said among Marion's men, southerners though they were, what would have become of the man who said it? If this had been said to the men who captured André,[1] the man who said it would probably have been hung sooner than André was. If it had been said in old Independence Hall, seventy-eight years ago, the very door-keeper would have throttled the man, and thrust him into the street.

Let no one be deceived. The spirit of seventy-six and the spirit of Nebraska are utter antagonisms; and the former is being rapidly displaced by the latter.

Fellow countrymen – Americans south, as well as north, shall we make no effort to arrest this? Already the liberal party throughout the world express the apprehension 'that the one retrograde institution in America is undermining the principles of progress, and fatally violating the noblest political system the world ever saw.' This is not the taunt of enemies, but the warning of friends. Is it quite safe to disregard it – to despise it? Is there no danger to liberty itself in discarding the earliest practice and first precept of our ancient faith? In our greedy chase to make profit of the Negro, let us beware, lest we 'cancel and tear to pieces' even the white man's charter of freedom.

Our republican robe is soiled, and trailed in the dust. Let us repurify it. Let us turn and wash it white, in the spirit if not the blood of the Revolution. Let us turn slavery from its claims of 'moral right,' back upon its existing legal rights, and its arguments of 'necessity.' Let us return it to the position our fathers gave it; and there let it rest in peace. Let us readopt the Declaration of Independence, and with it the practices and policy which harmonize with it. Let north and south – let all Americans – let all lovers of liberty everywhere – join in the great and good work. If we do this, we shall not only have saved the Union; but we shall have so saved it as to make, and to keep it, forever worthy of the saving. We shall have so saved it that the succeeding millions of

---

[1] Major John André, adjutant-general of the British Army in North America during the Revolution, was the go-between between British headquarters and the American traitor, Benedict Arnold. André was captured in civilian clothes and hanged as a spy on 2 October 1780.

free happy people, the world over, shall rise up and call us blessed, to the latest generations . . .

To Joseph Gillespie.

Springfield, 1 December 1854

My dear Sir: I have really got it into my head to try to be United States Senator; and if I could have your support my chances would be reasonably good. But I know, and acknowledge, that you have as just claims to the place as I have; and therefore I do not ask you to yield to me, if you are thinking of becoming a candidate yourself. If, however, you are not, then I should like to be remembered affectionately by you; and also, to have you make a mark for me with the Anti-Nebraska members, down your way. If you know, and have no objection to tell, let me know whether Trumbull intends to make a push. If he does, I suppose the two men in St Clair and one or both in Madison will be for him.

We have the Legislature clearly enough on joint ballot;[1] but the Senate is very close; and Calhoun told me to-day that the Nebraska men will stave off the election if they can. Even if we get into joint vote, we shall have difficulty to unite our forces.

Please write me, and let this be confidential. Your friend as ever

From a letter to William H. Henderson, on being defeated for the Senate.

Springfield, 21 February 1855

. . . The election is over, the session is ended, and I am *not* Senator. I have to content myself with the honor of having been the first choice of a large majority of the fifty-one members who finally made the election. My larger number of friends had to surrender to Trumbull's smaller number, in order to prevent the election of Matteson, which would have been a Douglas victory.[2] I started with 44 votes and T. with 5. It was rather hard for the 44 to have to surrender to the 5 – and a less good-humored man than I, perhaps, would not have consented to it – and it would not have

---

[1] The reader must remember here, and in connection with Lincoln's campaign against Douglas in 1858, that prior to the adoption of the Seventeenth Amendment in 1913 Senators were elected by state legislatures.

[2] Lyman Trumbull was an Anti-Nebraska Democrat; Joel A. Matteson, then Governor of Illinois, a Democrat who supported the Nebraska policy of his party.

been done without my consent. I could not, however, let the whole political result go to ruin on a point merely personal to myself.

Your son kindly and firmly stood by me from first to last; and for which he has my everlasting gratitude. Your friend as ever

To George Robertson, professor of law in Transylvania College at Lexington, Kentucky.

Springfield, 15 August 1855

My dear Sir: The volume you left for me has been received. I am really grateful for the honor of your kind remembrance, as well as for the book.[1] The partial reading I have already given it has afforded me much of both pleasure and instruction. It was new to me that the exact question which led to the Missouri Compromise had arisen before it arose in regard to Missouri; and that you had taken so prominent a part in it. Your short but able and patriotic speech upon that occasion has not been improved upon since by those holding the same views; and, with all the lights you then had, the views you took appear to me as very reasonable.

You are not a friend of slavery in the abstract. In that speech you spoke of '*the peaceful extinction* of *slavery*' and used other expressions indicating your belief that the thing was, at some time, to have an end. Since then we have had thirty-six years of experience; and this experience has demonstrated, I think, that there is no peaceful extinction of slavery in prospect for us. The signal failure of Henry Clay and other good and great men, in 1849, to effect anything in favor of gradual emancipation in Kentucky, together with a thousand other signs, extinguishes that hope utterly. On the question of liberty, as a principle, we are not what we have been. When we were the political slaves of King George, and wanted to be free, we called the maxim that 'all men are created equal' a self-evident truth; but now when we have grown fat, and have lost all dread of being slaves ourselves, we have become so greedy to be *masters* that we call the same maxim 'a self-evident lie.' The fourth of July has not quite dwindled away; it is still a great day – *for burning fire-crackers!!!*

That spirit which desired the peaceful extinction of slavery has itself become extinct, with the *occasion*, and the *men* of the

---

[1] A collection of Robertson's speeches and papers entitled *Scrap Book on Law and Politics, Men and Times.*

Revolution. Under the impulse of that occasion, nearly half the states adopted systems of emancipation at once; and it is a significant fact that not a single state has done the like since. So far as peaceful, voluntary emancipation is concerned, the condition of the Negro slave in America, scarcely less terrible to the contemplation of a free mind, is now as fixed, and hopeless of change for the better, as that of the lost souls of the finally impenitent. The Autocrat of all the Russias will resign his crown and proclaim his subjects free republicans sooner than will our American masters voluntarily give up their slaves.

Our political problem now is 'Can we, as a nation, continue together *permanently* – *forever* – half slave, and half free?' The problem is too mighty for me. May God, in his mercy, superintend the solution. Your much obliged friend, and humble servant

To Joshua F. Speed.

Springfield, 24 August 1855

Dear Speed: You know what a poor correspondent I am. Ever since I received your very agreeable letter of the 22nd of May I have been intending to write you in answer to it. You suggest that in political action now, you and I would differ. I suppose we would; not quite as much, however, as you may think. You know I dislike slavery; and you fully admit the abstract wrong of it. So far there is no cause of difference. But you say that sooner than yield your legal right to the slave – especially at the bidding of those who are not themselves interested – you would see the Union dissolved. I am not aware that *anyone* is bidding you to yield that right; very certainly *I* am not. I leave that matter entirely to yourself. I also acknowledge *your* rights and *my* obligations, under the Constitution, in regard to your slaves. I confess I hate to see the poor creatures hunted down, and caught, and carried back to their stripes, and unrewarded toils; but I bite my lip and keep quiet. In 1841 you and I had together a tedious low-water trip on a steamboat from Louisville to St Louis. You may remember, as I well do, that from Louisville to the mouth of the Ohio there were, on board, ten or a dozen slaves, shackled together with irons. That sight was a continual torment to me;[1] and I see something

---

[1] Compare this verdict with Lincoln's description of the same incident in his letter to Mary Speed, p. 18.

like it every time I touch the Ohio, or any other slave-border. It is hardly fair for you to assume that I have no interest in a thing which has, and continually exercises, the power of making me miserable. You ought rather to appreciate how much the great body of the northern people do crucify their feelings, in order to maintain their loyalty to the Constitution and the Union.

I do oppose the extension of slavery, because my judgment and feelings so prompt me; and I am under no obligation to the contrary. If for this you and I must differ, differ we must. You say if you were President, you would send an army and hang the leaders of the Missouri outrages upon the Kansas elections; still, if Kansas fairly votes herself a slave state, she must be admitted, or the Union must be dissolved. But how if she votes herself a slave state *unfairly* – that is, by the very means for which you say you would hang men? Must she still be admitted, or the Union be dissolved? That will be the phase of the question when it first becomes a practical one. In your assumption that there may be a *fair* decision of the slavery question in Kansas, I plainly see you and I would differ about the Nebraska law. I look upon that enactment not as a *law*, but as *violence* from the beginning. It was conceived in violence, passed in violence, is maintained in violence, and is being executed in violence. I say it was *conceived* in violence, because the destruction of the Missouri Compromise, under the circumstances, was nothing less than violence. It was *passed* in violence, because it could not have passed at all but for the votes of many members, in violent disregard of the known will of their constituents. It is *maintained* in violence because the elections since clearly demand its repeal, and this demand is openly disregarded. *You* say men ought to be hung for the way they are executing that law; and *I* say the way it is being executed is quite as good as any of its antecedents. It is being executed in the precise way which was intended from the first; else why does no Nebraska man express astonishment or condemnation? Poor Reeder is the only public man who has been silly enough to believe that anything like fairness was ever intended; and he has been bravely undeceived.

That Kansas will form a slave constitution, and, with it, will ask to be admitted into the Union, I take to be an already settled question; and so settled by the very means you so pointedly condemn. By every principle of law ever held by any court, north or south, every Negro taken to Kansas is free; yet in utter disregard of this – in the spirit of violence merely – that beautiful legislature gravely passes a law to hang men who shall venture to inform a Negro of his legal rights. This is the substance and real object of the law. If, like Haman, they should hang upon the gallows of their own building, I shall not be among the mourners for their fate.

In my humble sphere I shall advocate the restoration of the Missouri Compromise, so long as Kansas remains a territory; and when, by all these foul means, it seeks to come into the Union as a slave-state, I shall oppose it. I am very loth, in any case, to withhold my assent to the enjoyment of property *acquired*, or *located*, in good faith; but I do not admit that *good faith*, in taking a Negro to Kansas, to be held in slavery, is a *possibility* with any man. Any man who has sense enough to be the controller of his own property has too much sense to misunderstand the outrageous character of this whole Nebraska business. But I digress. In my opposition to the admission of Kansas I shall have some company; but we may be beaten. If we are, I shall not, on that account, attempt to dissolve the Union. On the contrary, if we succeed, there will be enough of us to take care of the Union. I think it probable, however, we shall be beaten. Standing as a unit among yourselves, you can, directly and indirectly, bribe enough of our men to carry the day – as you could on an open proposition to establish monarchy. Get hold of some man in the north, whose position and ability is such that he can make the support of your measure – whatever it may be – a *Democratic party necessity*, and the thing is done. *Apropos* of this, let me tell you an anecdote. Douglas introduced the Nebraska bill in January. In February afterwards, there was a call session of the Illinois legislature. Of the one hundred members composing the two branches of that body, about seventy were Democrats. These latter held a caucus, in which the Nebraska bill was talked of, if not formally discussed. It was thereby discovered that just three, and no more, were in favor of the measure. In a day or two Douglas's orders came on to have resolutions passed approving the bill; and they were passed by large majorities!!! The truth of this is vouched for by a bolting Democratic member. The masses too, Democratic as well as Whig, were even nearer unanimous against it; but as soon as the party necessity of supporting it became apparent, the way the Democracy began to see the *wisdom* and *justice* of it was perfectly astonishing.

You say if Kansas fairly votes herself a free state, as a Christian you will rather rejoice at it. All decent slave-holders *talk* that way; and I do not doubt their candor. But they never *vote* that way. Although in a private letter, or conversation, you will express your preference that Kansas shall be free, you would vote for no man for Congress who would say the same thing publicly. No such man could be elected from any district in any slave-state. You think Stringfellow and Co. ought to be hung; and yet, at the next presidential election, you will vote for the exact type and representative of Stringfellow. The slave-breeders and slave-traders are a small, odious, and detested class among you; and yet in politics they dictate the course of all of you, and are as completely your masters as you are the masters of your own Negroes.

You inquire where I now stand. That is a disputed point. I think I am a Whig; but others say there are no Whigs, and that I am an abolitionist. When I was at Washington I voted for the Wilmot Proviso as good as forty times, and I never heard of anyone attempting to unwhig me for that. I now do no more than oppose the *extension* of slavery.

I am not a Know-Nothing. That is certain. How could I be? How can anyone who abhors the oppression of Negroes be in favor of degrading classes of white people? Our progress in degeneracy appears to me to be pretty rapid. As a nation, we began by declaring that '*all men are created equal.*' We now practically read it 'all men are created equal, *except Negroes.*' When the Know-Nothings get control, it will read 'all men are created equal, except Negroes, *and foreigners, and catholics.*' When it comes to this I should prefer emigrating to some country where they make no pretence of loving liberty — to Russia, for instance, where despotism can be taken pure, and without the base alloy of hypocrisy.

Mary will probably pass a day or two in Louisville in October. My kindest regards to Mrs Speed. On the leading subject of this letter, I have more of her sympathy than I have of yours.

And yet let me say I am Your friend forever

To Isham Reavis, on studying law.
                                        Springfield, 5 November 1855

My dear Sir: I have just reached home, and found your letter of the

23rd ult. I am from home too much of my time for a young man to read law with me advantageously. If you are resolutely determined to make a lawyer of yourself, the thing is more than half done already. It is but a small matter whether you read *with* anybody or not. I did not read with anyone. Get the books, and read and study them till you understand them in their principal features; and that is the main thing. It is of no consequence to be in a large town while you are reading. I read at New Salem, which never had three hundred people living in it. The *books*, and your *capacity* for understanding them, are just the same in all places. Mr Dummer is a very clever man and an excellent lawyer (much better than I, in law-learning); and I have no doubt he will cheerfully tell you what books to read, and also loan you the books.

Always bear in mind that your own resolution to succeed is more important than any other one thing. Very truly Your friend

To George P. Floyd, hotel keeper of Quincy, Illinois.
Springfield, 21 February 1856

Dear Sir: I have just received yours of 16th, with check on Flagg and Savage for twenty-five dollars. You must think I am a high-priced man. You are too liberal with your money.

Fifteen dollars is enough for the job. I send you a receipt for fifteen dollars, and return to you a ten-dollar bill. Yours truly

To Julian M. Sturtevant, president of Illinois College at Jackson-ville, Illinois.
Springfield, 27 September 1856

My dear Sir: Owing to absence yours of the 16th was not received till the day before yesterday. I thank you for your good opinion of me personally, and still more for the deep interest you take in the cause of our common country. It pains me a little that you have deemed it necessary to point out to me how I may be compensated for throwing myself in the breach now. This assumes that I am merely calculating the chances of personal advancement. Let me assure you that I decline to be a candidate for Congress on my clear conviction that my running would *hurt*, and not *help* the cause. I am willing to make any personal sacrifice, but I am not willing to do what in my own judgment is a sacrifice of the cause itself. Very truly Yours

From a speech in Chicago, after Republican defeat in the presidential election of 1856.

10 December 1856

Our government rests in public opinion. Whoever can change public opinion can change the government, practically just so much. Public opinion, on any subject, always has a '*central idea*,' from which all its minor thoughts radiate. That 'central idea' in our political public opinion, at the beginning was, and until recently has continued to be, 'the equality of men.' And although it was always submitted patiently to, whatever of inequality there seemed to be as matter of actual necessity, its constant working has been a steady progress towards the practical equality of all men. The late presidential election was a struggle, by one party, to discard that central idea, and to substitute for it the opposite idea that slavery is right, in the abstract, the workings of which, as a central idea, may be the perpetuity of human slavery, and its extension to all countries and colors. Less than a year ago the Richmond *Enquirer*, an avowed advocate of slavery, regardless of color, in order to favor his views, invented the phrase, 'State equality,' and now the President, in his message, adopts the *Enquirer*'s catch-phrase, telling us the people 'have asserted the constitutional equality of each and all the states of the Union as states.' The President flatters himself that the new central idea is completely inaugurated; and so, indeed, it is, so far as the mere fact of a presidential election can inaugurate it. To us it is left to know that the majority of the people have not yet declared for it, and to hope that they never will.

All of us who did not vote for Mr Buchanan, taken together, are a majority of four hundred thousand. But, in the late contest we were divided between Fremont and Fillmore. Can we not come together, for the future? Let everyone who really believes, and is resolved, that free society is not, *and shall not be*, a failure, and who can conscientiously declare that in the past contest he has done only what he thought best – let every such one have charity to believe that every other one can say as much. Thus let bygones be bygones. Let past differences, as nothing be; and with steady eye on the real issue, let us reinaugurate the good old 'central ideas' of the Republic. We *can* do it. The human heart *is* with us – God is with us. We shall again be able not to declare, that 'all states as states, are equal,' nor yet that 'all citizens as citizens are equal,' but to renew the broader, better declaration, including both these and much more, that 'all *men* are created equal.'

From a speech on the Dred Scott decision in reply to Stephen A. Douglas.

Springfield, 26 June 1857

Fellow-Citizens: I am here to-night, partly by the invitation of some of you, and partly by my own inclination. Two weeks ago Judge Douglas spoke here on the several subjects of Kansas, the Dred Scott decision, and Utah. I listened to the speech at the time, and have read the report of it since. It was intended to controvert opinions which I think just, and to assail (politically, not personally) those men who, in common with me, entertain those opinions. For this reason I wished then, and still wish, to make some answer to it, which I now take the opportunity of doing ...

And now as to the Dred Scott decision.[1] That decision declares two propositions – first, that a Negro cannot sue in the US courts; and secondly, that Congress cannot prohibit slavery in the territories. It was made by a divided court – dividing differently on the different points. Judge Douglas does not discuss the merits of the decision; and, in that respect, I shall follow his example, believing I could no more improve on McLean and Curtis than he could on Taney.

He denounces all who question the correctness of that decision, as offering violent resistance to it. But who resists it? Who has, in spite of the decision, declared Dred Scott free, and resisted the authority of his master over him?

Judicial decisions have two uses – first, to absolutely determine the case decided, and secondly, to indicate to the public how other similar cases will be decided when they arise. For the latter use, they are called 'precedents' and 'authorities.'

We believe, as much as Judge Douglas (perhaps more) in obedience to, and respect for, the judicial department of government. We think its decisions on constitutional questions, when fully settled, should control, not only the particular cases decided, but the general policy of the country, subject to be disturbed only

---

[1] Decided by the Supreme Court of the United States on 6 March 1857. Although all seven majority judges wrote opinions, that of Chief Justice Taney is usually accepted as the opinion of the Court. Justices McLean and Curtis dissented.

by amendments of the Constitution as provided in that instrument itself. More than this would be revolution. But we think the Dred Scott decision is erroneous. We know the court that made it has often overruled its own decisions, and we shall do what we can to have it to overrule this. We offer no *resistance* to it.

Judicial decisions are of greater or less authority as precedents, according to circumstances. That this should be so accords both with common sense and the customary understanding of the legal profession.

If this important decision had been made by the unanimous concurrence of the judges, and without any apparent partisan bias, and in accordance with legal public expectation, and with the steady practice of the departments throughout our history, and had been in no part based on assumed historical facts which are not really true; or, if wanting in some of these, it had been before the court more than once, and had there been affirmed and reaffirmed through a course of years, it then might be, perhaps would be, factious, nay, even revolutionary, to not acquiesce in it as a precedent.

But when, as it is true, we find it wanting in all these claims to the public confidence, it is not resistance, it is not factious, it is not even disrespectful, to treat it as not having yet quite established a settled doctrine for the country . . .

Three years and a half ago, Judge Douglas brought forward his famous Nebraska bill. The country was at once in a blaze. He scorned all opposition, and carried it through Congress. Since then he has seen himself superseded in a presidential nomination, by one indorsing the general doctrine of his measure, but at the same time standing clear of the odium of its untimely agitation, and its gross breach of national faith; and he has seen that successful rival constitutionally elected, not by the strength of friends, but by the division of adversaries, being in a popular minority of nearly four hundred thousand votes. He has seen his chief aids in his own state, Shields and Richardson, politically speaking, successively tried, convicted, and executed, for an offense not their own, but his. And now he sees his own case, standing next on the docket for trial.

There is a natural disgust in the minds of nearly all white people to the idea of an indiscriminate amalgamation of the white and black races; and Judge Douglas evidently is basing his chief hope upon the chances of being able to appropriate the benefit of this disgust to himself. If he can, by much drumming and repeating, fasten the odium of that idea upon his adversaries, he thinks he can struggle through the storm. He therefore clings to this hope, as a drowning man to the last plank. He makes an occasion for lugging it in from the opposition to the Dred Scott decision. He finds the Republicans insisting that the Declaration of Independence includes ALL men, black as well as white; and forthwith he boldly denies that it includes Negroes at all, and proceeds to argue gravely that all who contend it does, do so only because they want to vote, and eat, and sleep, and marry with Negroes! He will have it that they cannot be consistent else. Now I protest against that counterfeit logic which concludes that, because I do not want a black woman for a slave, I must necessarily want her for a wife. I need not have her for either, I can just leave her alone. In some respects, she is certainly not my equal; but in her natural right to eat the bread she earns with her own hands without asking leave of any one else, she is my equal, and the equal of all others.

Chief Justice Taney, in his opinion in the Dred Scott case, admits that the language of the Declaration is broad enough to include the whole human family, but he and Judge Douglas argue that the authors of the instrument did not intend to include Negroes, by the fact that they did not at once actually place them on an equality with the whites. Now this grave argument comes to just nothing at all, by the other fact, that they did not at once, or ever afterwards, actually place all white people on an equality with one or another. And this is the staple argument of both the Chief Justice and the Senator, for doing this obvious violence to the plain unmistakable language of the Declaration. I think the authors of that notable instrument intended to include all men, but they did not intend to declare all men equal in all respects. They did not mean to say all were equal in color, size, intellect, moral developments, or social capacity. They defined with tolerable distinctness in what respects they did consider all men created equal — equal in 'certain inalienable rights, among which are life, liberty and the pursuit of happiness.' This they said, and this meant. They did not mean to assert the obvious untruth, that all were then actually enjoying that equality, nor yet, that they were about to confer it immediately upon them. In fact they had no power to confer such a boon. They meant simply to declare the right, so that the enforcement of it might follow as fast as circumstances should permit. They meant to set up a standard maxim for free society, which should be familiar to all, and revered by all; constantly looked to, constantly labored for, and even though never perfectly attained, constantly approximated, and thereby constantly spreading and deepening its influence, and augmenting the happiness and value of life to all people of all colors everywhere . . .

This very Dred Scott case affords a strong test as to which party most favors amalgamation, the Republicans or the dear Union-saving Democracy. Dred Scott, his wife and two daughters, were all involved in the suit. We desired the court to have held that they were citizens so far at least as to entitle them to a hearing as to whether they were free or not; and then, also, that they were in fact and in law really free. Could we have had our way, the chances of these black girls ever mixing their blood with that of white people would have been diminished at least to the extent that it could not have been without their consent. But Judge Douglas is delighted to have them decided to be slaves, and not human enough to have a hearing, even if they were free, and thus left subject to the forced concubinage of their masters, and liable to become the mothers of mulattos in spite of themselves – the very state of case that produces nine-tenths of all the mulattos – all the mixing of blood in the nation.

Of course, I state this case as an illustration only, not meaning to say or intimate that the master of Dred Scott and his family, or any more than a percentage of masters generally, are inclined to exercise this particular power which they hold over their female slaves.

I have said that the separation of the races is the only perfect preventive of amalgamation. I have no right to say all the members of the Republican party are in favor of this, nor to say that as a party they are in favor of it. There is nothing in their platform directly on the subject. But I can say a very large proportion of its members are for it, and that the chief plank in their platform – opposition to the spread of slavery – is most favorable to that separation.

Such separation, if ever effected at all, must be effected by colonization; and no political party, as such, is now doing anything directly for colonization. Party operations at present only favor or retard colonization incidentally. The enterprise is a difficult one; but 'when there is a will there is a way'; and what colonization needs most is a hearty will. Will springs from the two elements of moral sense and self-interest. Let us be brought to believe it is morally right, and, at the same time, favorable to, or, at least, not against, our interest, to transfer the African to his native clime, and we shall find a way to do it, however great the task may be. The children of Israel, to such numbers as to include four hundred thousand fighting men, went out of Egyptian bondage in a body.

How differently the respective courses of the Democratic and Republican parties incidentally bear on the question of forming a will — a public sentiment — for colonization, is easy to see. The Republicans inculcate, with whatever of ability they can, that the Negro is a man; that his bondage is cruelly wrong, and that the field of his oppression ought not to be enlarged. The Democrats deny his manhood; deny, or dwarf to insignificance, the wrong of his bondage; so far as possible, crush all sympathy for him, and cultivate and excite hatred and disgust against him; compliment themselves as Union-savers for doing so; and call the indefinite outspreading of his bondage 'a sacred right of self-government.'

The plainest print cannot be read through a gold eagle; and it will be ever hard to find many men who will send a slave to Liberia, and pay his passage, while they can send him to a new country, Kansas, for instance, and sell him for fifteen hundred dollars, and the rise.

Chapter 4
The Debates with
Stephen A. Douglas
1858

The Lincoln-Douglas debates have become an American political classic, but they were never designed to be so. In 1858, Stephen A. Douglas, the Democratic champion of the North-west, ran for re-election as a Senator from Illinois. As his Republican opponent, and very much as the underdog against a major national figure, Lincoln challenged Douglas to a series of debates at various locations around the state.

Lincoln's speeches show many of the skills of both the lawyer and the politician, in presentation of a case, and in exposure of the weak points of the opposing case. He hammered away at the moral issues raised by slavery, and the threat which it posed to the preservation of the Union. In his speech at Freeport, and also elsewhere, he forced Douglas to confront the embarrassing clash between the Dred Scott decision which ruled that Congress could not prohibit slavery in the territories, and the doctrine of popular sovereignty, under which Congress delegated that power to others. Douglas took refuge in the argument that, even if permitted to enter a territory, slavery could not in practice survive without local legislation (that is, a slave code) to sustain it. In doing so, he inevitably forfeited much Southern support.

In attempting to counter Douglas's exploitation of the racial prejudices of the electorate, Lincoln asserted his belief in the superiority of the white race, but re-affirmed his belief that blacks were covered by the terms of the Declaration of Independence.

Lincoln may have won the debate (although that verdict is not unanimously accepted), but he did not win the Senate seat. In the nineteenth century, elections to the Senate were decided by state legislatures, and not by direct popular vote, and the Democratic majority in the legislature duly elected Douglas for another term. But the campaign elevated Lincoln into much greater national prominence, and made him at least an outside contender for the Republican presidential nomination in 1860.

To Jediah F. Alexander, editor of the Greenville, Illinois, Advocate.

Springfield, 15 May 1858

My dear Sir: I reached home a week ago and found yours of the 1st inviting me to name a time to meet and address a political meeting in Bond county. It is too early, considering that when I once begin making political speeches I shall have no respite till November. The *labor* of that I might endure, but I really cannot spare the time from my business.

Nearer the time I will try to meet the people of Bond, if they desire.

I will only say now that, as I understand, there remains all the difference there ever was between Judge Douglas and the Republicans – *they* insisting that Congress *shall*, and *he* insisting that Congress *shall not*, keep slavery out of the territories *before and up to the time* they form state constitutions. No Republican has ever contended that *when* a constitution is to be formed, any but the *people* of the territory shall form it. Republicans have never contended that Congress should *dictate* a constitution to any state or territory; but they have contended that the people should be *perfectly* free to form their constitution in their own way – as *perfectly* free from the *presence* of *slavery* amongst them as from every other improper influence.

In voting together in opposition to a constitution being forced upon the people of Kansas, neither Judge Douglas nor the Republicans has conceded anything which was ever in dispute between them. Yours very truly

Speech at Springfield accepting the Republican nomination for the United States Senate in opposition to Stephen A. Douglas, Democrat.

16 June 1858

Mr President and Gentlemen of the Convention: If we could

first know *where* we are, and *whither* we are tending, we could then better judge *what* to do, and *how* to do it.

We are now far into the *fifth* year since a policy was initiated with the *avowed* object, and *confident* promise, of putting an end to slavery agitation.

Under the operation of that policy, that agitation has not only *not ceased*, but has *constantly augmented*.

In *my* opinion, it *will* not cease until a *crisis* shall have been reached, and passed.

'A house divided against itself cannot stand.'

I believe this government cannot endure, permanently half *slave* and half *free*.

I do not expect the Union to be *dissolved* – I do not expect the house to *fall* – but I *do* expect it will cease to be divided.

It will become *all* one thing, or *all* the other.

Either the *opponents* of slavery will arrest the further spread of it, and place it where the public mind shall rest in the belief that it is in course of ultimate extinction; or its *advocates* will push it forward till it shall become alike lawful in *all* the states, *old* as well as *new* – *north* as well as *south*.

Have we no *tendency* to the latter condition?

Let anyone who doubts, carefully contemplate that now almost complete legal combination – piece of *machinery* so to speak – compounded of the Nebraska doctrine and the Dred Scott decision. Let him consider not only *what work* the machinery is adapted to do, and *how well* adapted; but also, let him study the *history* of its construction, and trace, if he can, or rather *fail*, if he can, to trace the evidences of design, and concert of action, among its chief bosses from the beginning.

But, so far, *Congress* only had acted; and an *indorsement* by the people, *real* or apparent, was indispensable to *save* the point already gained, and give chance for more.

The new year of 1854 found slavery excluded from more than half the states by state constitutions, and from most of the national territory by congressional prohibition.

Four days later commenced the struggle which ended in repealing that congressional prohibition.

This opened all the national territory to slavery; and was the first point gained.

This necessity had not been overlooked; but had been provided for, as well as might be, in the notable argument of '*squatter* sovereignty,' otherwise called 'sacred right of self-government,' which latter phrase, though expressive of the only rightful basis of any government, was so perverted in this attempted use of it as to amount to just this: That if any *one* man choose to enslave *another*, no *third* man shall be allowed to object.

That argument was incorporated into the Nebraska bill itself, in the language which follows: '*It being the true intent and meaning of this act not to legislate slavery into any Territory or state, nor exclude it therefrom; but to leave the people thereof perfectly free to form and regulate their domestic institutions in their own way, subject only to the Constitution of the United States.*'

Then opened the roar of loose declamation in favor of 'Squatter Sovereignty,' and 'Sacred right of self-government.'

'But,' said opposition members, 'let us be more *specific* – let us *amend* the bill so as to expressly declare that the people of the territory may exclude slavery.' 'Not we,' said the friends of the measure; and down they voted the amendment.

While the Nebraska bill was passing through Congress, a *law case*, involving the question of a Negro's freedom, by reason of his owner having voluntarily taken him first into a free state and then a territory covered by the congressional prohibition, and held him as a slave, for a long time in each, was passing through the US Circuit Court for the District of Missouri; and both Nebraska bill and lawsuit were brought to a decision in the same month of May 1854. The Negro's name was 'Dred Scott,' which name now designates the decision finally made in the case.

Before the *then* next presidential election, the law case came *to*, and was argued *in* the Supreme Court of the United States; but the *decision* of it was deferred until *after* the election. Still, *before* the election, Senator Trumbull, on the floor of the Senate, requests the leading advocate of the Nebraska bill to state *his opinion* whether the people of a territory can constitutionally exclude slavery from their limits; and the latter answers, 'That is a question for the Supreme Court.'

The election came. Mr Buchanan was elected, and the *indorsement*, such as it was, secured. That was the *second* point gained. The indorsement, however, fell short of a clear popular majority by nearly four hundred thousand votes, and so, perhaps, was not overwhelmingly reliable and satisfactory.

The *outgoing* President, in his last annual message, as impressively as possible *echoed back* upon the people the *weight* and *authority* of the indorsement.

The Supreme Court met again; *did not* announce their decision, but ordered a re-argument.

The presidential inauguration came, and still no decision of the court; but the *incoming* President, in his inaugural address, fervently exhorted the people to abide by the forthcoming decision, *whatever it might be.*

Then, in a few days, came the decision.

The reputed author of the Nebraska bill finds an early occasion to make a speech at this capitol indorsing the Dred Scott decision, and vehemently denouncing all opposition to it.

The new President, too, seizes the early occasion of the Silliman letter to *indorse* and strongly *construe* that decision, and to express his *astonishment* that any different view had ever been entertained.

At length a squabble springs up between the President and the author of the Nebraska bill, on the *mere* question of *fact*, whether the Lecompton Constitution was or was not, in any just sense, made by the people of Kansas; and in that squabble the latter declares that all he wants is a fair vote for the people, and that he *cares* not whether slavery be voted *down* or voted *up*. I do not understand his declaration that he cares not whether slavery be voted down or voted up, to be intended by him other than as an *apt definition* of the *policy* he would impress upon the public mind – the *principle* for which he declares he has suffered much, and is ready to suffer to the end.

And well may he cling to that principle. If he has any parental feeling, well may he cling to it. That principle is the only *shred* left of his original Nebraska doctrine. Under the Dred Scott decision 'squatter sovereignty' squatted out of existence, tumbled down like temporary scaffolding – like the mold at the foundry served through one blast and fell back into loose sand – helped to carry an election, and then was kicked to the winds. His late *joint* struggle with the Republicans, against the Lecompton Constitution, involves nothing of the original Nebraska doctrine. That struggle was made on a point, the right of a people to make their own constitution, upon which he and the Republicans have never differed.

The several points of the Dred Scott decision, in connection with Senator Douglas's 'care not' policy, constitute the piece of machinery, in its *present* state of advancement. This was the third point gained.

The *working* points of that machinery are:

First, that no Negro slave, imported as such from Africa, and no descendant of such slave can ever be a *citizen* of any state, in the sense of that term as used in the Constitution of the United States.

This point is made in order to deprive the Negro, in every possible event, of the benefit of this provision of the United States Constitution, which declares that —

'The citizens of each state shall be entitled to all privileges and immunities of citizens in the several states.'

Secondly, that 'subject to the Constitution of the United States,' neither *Congress* nor a *territorial legislature* can exclude slavery from any United States territory.

This point is made in order that individual men may *fill up* the territories with slaves, without danger of losing them as property, and thus to enhance the chances of *permanency* to the institution through all the future.

Thirdly, that whether the holding a Negro in actual slavery in a free state makes him free, as against the holder, the United States courts will not decide, but will leave to be decided by the courts of any slave state the Negro may be forced into by the master.

This point is made, not to be pressed *immediately*; but, if acquiesced in for a while, and apparently *indorsed* by the people at an election, *then* to sustain the logical conclusion that what Dred Scott's master might lawfully do with Dred Scott, in the free state of Illinois, every other master may lawfully do with any other *one*, or one *thousand* slaves, in Illinois, or in any other free state.

Auxiliary to all this, and working hand in hand with it, the Nebraska doctrine, or what is left of it, is to *educate* and *mold* public opinion, at least *northern* public opinion, to not *care* whether slavery is voted *down* or voted *up*.

This shows exactly where we now *are* and *partially* also, whither we are tending.

It will throw additional light on the latter to go back and run the mind over the string of historical facts already stated. Several things will *now* appear less *dark* and *mysterious* than they did *when* then were transpiring. The people were to be left 'perfectly free' 'subject only to the Constitution.' What the *Constitution* had to do with it, outsiders could not *then* see. Plainly enough *now*, it was an exactly fitted *niche*, for the Dred Scott decision to afterwards come in, and declare the *perfect freedom* of the people, to be just no freedom at all.

Why was the amendment, expressly declaring the right of the people to exclude slavery, voted down? Plainly enough *now*, the adoption of it would have spoiled the niche for the Dred Scott decision.

Why was the court decision held up? Why, even a Senator's individual opinion withheld, till *after* the presidential election? Plainly enough *now*, the speaking out *then* would have damaged the '*perfectly free*' argument upon which the election was to be carried.

Why the *outgoing* President's felicitation on the indorsement? Why the delay of a re-argument? Why the incoming President's *advance* exhortation in favor of the decision?

These things *look* like the cautious *patting* and *petting* a spirited horse, preparatory to mounting him, when it is dreaded that he may give the rider a fall.

And why the hasty after-indorsements of the decision by the President and others?

We cannot absolutely *know* that all these exact adaptations are the result of preconcert. But when we see a lot of framed timbers, different portions of which we know have been gotten out at different times and places and by different workmen – Stephen, Franklin, Roger, and James,[1] for instance – and when we see these timbers joined together, and see they exactly make the frame of a house or a mill, all the tenons and mortices exactly fitting, and all the lengths and proportions of the different pieces exactly adapted to their respective places, and not a piece too many or too few – not omitting even scaffolding – or, if a single piece be lacking, we can see the place in the frame fitted and prepared to yet bring such piece in – in *such* a case, we find it impossible to not *believe* that Stephen and Franklin and Roger and James all understood one another from the beginning, and all worked upon a common *plan* or *draft* drawn up before the first lick was struck.

It should not be overlooked that, by the Nebraska bill, the people of a *state* as well as *territory*, were to be left '*perfectly free*' '*subject only to the Constitution.*'

[1] Stephen A. Douglas, sponsor of the Kansas-Nebraska Bill; Franklin Pierce, President, 1853–7; Roger B. Taney, Chief Justice of the United States; and James Buchanan, President, 1857–61.

Why mention a *state*? They were legislating for *territories*, and not *for* or *about* states. Certainly the people of a state *are* and *ought to be* subject to the Constitution of the United States; but why is mention of this *lugged* into this merely *territorial* law? Why are the people of a *territory* and the people of a *state* therein *lumped* together, and their relation to the Constitution therein treated as being *precisely* the same?

While the opinion of *the court*, by Chief Justice Taney, in the Dred Scott case, and the separate opinions of all the concurring judges, expressly declare that the Constitution of the United States neither permits Congress nor a territorial legislature to exclude slavery from any United States territory, they all *omit* to declare whether or not the same Constitution permits a *state*, or the people of a state, to exclude it.

Possibly this was a mere *omission*; but who can be *quite* sure, if McLean or Curtis had sought to get into the opinion a declaration of unlimited power in the people of a *state* to exclude slavery from their limits, just as Chase and Macy sought to get such declaration, in behalf of the people of a territory, into the Nebraska bill—I ask, who can be quite *sure* that it would not have been voted down, in the one case, as it had been in the other.

The nearest approach to the point of declaring the power of a state over slavery is made by Judge Nelson. He approaches it more than once, using the precise idea, and *almost* the language too, of the Nebraska Act. On one occasion his exact language is, 'except in cases where the power is restrained by the Constitution of the United States, the law of the state is supreme over the subject of slavery within its jurisdiction.'

In what *cases* the power of the *states is* so restrained by the US Constitution is left an *open* question, precisely as the same question, as to the restraint on the power of the *territories* was left open in the Nebraska Act. Put *that* and *that* together, and we have another nice little niche, which we may, ere long, see filled with another Supreme Court decision, declaring that the Constitution of the United States does not permit a *state* to exclude slavery from its limits.

And this may especially be expected if the doctrine of 'care not whether slavery be voted *down* or voted *up*,' shall gain upon the public mind sufficiently to give promise that such a decision can be maintained when made.

Such a decision is all that slavery now lacks of being alike lawful in all the states.

Welcome or unwelcome, such decision *is* probably coming, and will soon be upon us, unless the power of the present political dynasty shall be met and overthrown.

We shall *lie down* pleasantly dreaming that the people of *Missouri* are on the verge of making their state *free*; and we shall *awake* to the *reality*, instead, that the *Supreme* Court has made *Illinois* a *slave* state.

To meet and overthrow the power of that dynasty is the work now before all those who would prevent that consummation.

That is *what* we have to do.

But *how* can we best do it?

There are those who denounce us *openly* to their *own* friends, and yet whisper *us softly*, that *Senator Douglas* is the *aptest* instrument there is, with which to effect that object. *They* do *not* tell us, nor has *he* told us, that he *wishes* any such object to be effected. They wish us to *infer* all, from the facts, that he now has a little quarrel with the present head of the dynasty; and that he has regularly voted with us, on a single point, upon which he and we have never differed.

They remind us that *he* is a very *great man*, and that the largest of *us* are very small ones. Let this be granted. But 'a *living dog* is better than a *dead lion*.' Judge Douglas, if not a *dead* lion *for this work*, is at least a *caged* and *toothless* one. How can he oppose the advances of slavery? He don't *care* anything about it. His avowed *mission is impressing* the 'public heart' to *care* nothing about it.

A leading Douglas Democratic newspaper thinks Douglas's superior talent will be needed to resist the revival of the African slave trade.

Does Douglas believe an effort to revive that trade is approaching? He has not said so. Does he *really* think so? But if it is, how can he resist it? For years he has labored to prove it a *sacred right* of white men to take Negro slaves into the new territories. Can he possibly show that it is *less* a sacred right to *buy* them where they can be bought cheapest? And unquestionably they can be bought *cheaper in Africa* than in *Virginia*.

He has done all in his power to reduce the whole question of slavery to one of a mere *right of property*; and as such, how can *he* oppose the foreign slave trade – how can he refuse that trade in that 'property' shall be 'perfectly free' – unless he does it as a *protection* to the home production? And as the home *producers* will probably not *ask* the protection, he will be wholly without a ground of opposition.

Senator Douglas holds, we know, that a man may rightfully be *wiser to-day* than he was *yesterday* – that he may rightfully *change* when he finds himself wrong.

But, can we for that reason, run ahead, and *infer* that he *will* make any particular change, of which he, himself, has given no intimation? Can we *safely* base *our* action upon any such *vague* inference?

Now, as ever, I wish to not *misrepresent* Judge Douglas's *position*, question his *motives*, or do aught that can be personally offensive to him.

Whenever, *if ever*, he and we can come together on *principle* so that *our great cause* may have assistance from *his great ability*, I hope to have interposed no adventitious obstacle.

But clearly he is not *now* with us – he does not *pretend* to be – he does not *promise* to *ever* be.

Our cause, then, must be intrusted to, and conducted by its own undoubted friends – those whose hands are free, whose hearts are in the work – who *do care* for the result.

Two years ago the Republicans of the nation mustered over thirteen hundred thousand strong.

We did this under the single impulse of resistance to a common danger, with every external circumstance against us.

Of *strange, discordant,* and even *hostile* elements, we gathered from the four winds, and *formed* and fought the battle through, under the constant hot fire of a disciplined, proud, and pampered enemy.

Did we brave all *then*, to *falter* now? – *now* – when that same enemy is *wavering,* dissevered and belligerent?

The result is not doubtful. We shall not fail – if we stand firm, we shall not fail.

Wise councils may *accelerate* or *mistakes delay* it, but, sooner or later, the victory is *sure* to come.

To John L. Scripps, editor of the Chicago Daily Democratic Press.

Springfield, 23 June 1858

My dear Sir: Your kind note of yesterday is duly received. I am much flattered by the estimate you place on my late speech; and yet I am much mortified that any part of it should be construed so differently from anything intended by me. The language, 'place it where the public mind shall rest in the belief that it is in course of ultimate extinction,' I used deliberately, not dreaming then, nor believing now, that it asserts, or intimates, any power or purpose to interfere with slavery in the states where it exists. But, to not cavil about language, I declare that whether the clause used by me will bear such construction or not, I never so intended it. I have declared a thousand times, and now repeat that, in my opinion, neither the general government, nor any other power outside of the slave states, can constitutionally or rightfully interfere with slaves or slavery where it already exists. I believe that whenever the effort to spread slavery into the new territories, by whatever means, and into the free states themselves, by Supreme Court decisions, shall be fairly headed off, the institution will then be in course of ultimate extinction; and by the language used I meant only this.

I do not intend this for publication; but still you may show it to anyone you think fit. I think I shall, as you suggest, take some early occasion to publicly repeat the declaration I have already so often made as before stated. Yours very truly

From a speech at Chicago in which Lincoln opened his campaign.
10 July 1858

My Fellow-Citizens: On yesterday evening, upon the occasion of the reception given to Senator Douglas, I was furnished with a seat very convenient for hearing him, and was otherwise very courteously treated by him and his friends, and for which I thank him and them. During the course of his remarks my name was mentioned in such a way as I suppose renders it at least not improper that I should make some sort of reply to him. I shall not attempt to follow him in the precise order in which he addressed the assembled multitude upon that occasion, though I shall perhaps do so in the main . . .

Judge Douglas made two points upon my recent speech at Springfield. He says they are to be the issues of this campaign. The first one of these points he bases upon the language in a speech which I delivered at Springfield, which I believe I can quote correctly from memory. I said there that 'we are now far into the fifth year since a policy was instituted for the avowed object and with the confident promise of putting an end to slavery agitation;

under the operation of that policy, that agitation had not only not ceased, but has constantly augmented. I believe it will not cease until a crisis shall have been reached and passed. A house divided against itself cannot stand. I believe this government cannot endure permanently half slave and half free. I do not expect the Union to be dissolved' – I am quoting from my speech – 'I do not expect the house to fall, but I do expect it will cease to be divided. It will become all one thing or the other. Either the opponents of slavery will arrest the spread of it, and place it where the public mind shall rest in the belief that it is in the course of ultimate extinction, or its advocates will push it forward until it shall become alike lawful in all the states, north as well as south.'

. . . In this paragraph which I have quoted in your hearing, and to which I ask the attention of all, Judge Douglas thinks he discovers great political heresy. I want your attention particularly to what he has inferred from it. He says I am in favor of making all the states of this Union uniform in all their internal regulations; that in all their domestic concerns I am in favor of making them entirely uniform. He draws this inference from the language I have quoted to you. He says that I am in favor of making war by the North upon the South for the extinction of slavery; that I am also in favor of inviting (as he expresses it) the South to a war upon the North, for the purpose of nationalizing slavery. Now, it is singular enough, if you will carefully read that passage over, that I did not say that I was in favor of anything in it. I only said what I expected would take place. I made a prediction only – it may have been a foolish one perhaps. I did not even say that I desired that slavery should be put in course of ultimate extinction. I do say so now, however, so there need be no longer any difficulty about that . . .

Gentlemen, Judge Douglas informed you that this speech of mine was probably carefully prepared. I admit that it was. I am not master of language; I have not a fine education; I am not capable of entering into a disquisition upon dialectics, as I believe you call it; but I do not believe the language I employed bears any such construction as Judge Douglas put upon it. But I don't care about a quibble in regard to words. I know what I meant, and I will not leave this crowd in doubt, if I can explain it to them, what I really meant in the use of that paragraph.

I am not, in the first place, unaware that this government has endured eighty-two years, half slave and half free. I know that. I am tolerably well acquainted with the history of the country, and I know that it has endured eighty-two years, half slave and half free. I *believe* – and that is what I meant to allude to there – I *believe* it has endured because, during all that time, until the introduction of the Nebraska bill, the public mind did rest, all the time, in the belief that slavery was in course of ultimate extinction. That was what gave us the rest that we had through that period of eighty-two years; at least, so I believe. I have always hated slavery, I think as much as any abolitionist. I have been an Old Line Whig. I have always hated it, but I have always been quiet about it until this new era of the introduction of the Nebraska bill began. I always believed that everybody was against it, and that it was in course of ultimate extinction. [Pointing to Mr Browning, who stood near by.] Browning thought so; the great mass of the nation have rested in the belief that slavery was in course of ultimate extinction. They had reason so to believe.

The adoption of the Constitution and its attendant history led the people to believe so; and that such was the belief of the framers of the Constitution itself. Why did those old men, about the time of the adoption of the Constitution, decree that slavery should not go into the new territory, where it had not already gone? Why declare that within twenty years the African slave trade, by which slaves are supplied, might be cut off by Congress? Why were all these acts? I might enumerate more of these acts – but enough. What were they but a clear indication that the framers of the Constitution intended and expected the ultimate extinction of that institution. And now, when I say, as I said in my speech that Judge Douglas has quoted from, when I say that I think the opponents of slavery will resist the farther spread of it, and place it where the public mind shall rest with the belief that it is in course of ultimate extinction, I only mean to say that they will place it where the founders of this government originally placed it.

I have said a hundred times, and I have now no inclination to take it back, that I believe there is no right, and ought to be no inclination in the people of the free states to enter into the slave states, and interfere with the question of slavery at all. I have said that always. Judge Douglas has heard me say it – if not quite a hundred times, at least as good as a hundred times; and when it is said that I am in favor of interfering with slavery where it exists, I know it is unwarranted by anything I have ever *intended*, and, as I believe, by anything I have ever *said*. If, by any means, I have ever used language which could fairly be so construed (as, however, I believe I never have), I now correct it.

So much then for the inference that Judge Douglas draws, that I am in favor of setting the sections at war with one another. I know that I never meant any such thing, and I believe that no fair mind can infer any such thing from anything I have ever said.

Now in relation to his inference that I am in favor of a general consolidation of all the local institutions of the various states. I will attend to that for a little while, and try to inquire, if I can, how on earth it could be that any man could draw such an inference from anything I said. I have said, very many times, in Judge Douglas's hearing, that no man believed more than I in the principle of self-government; that it lies at the bottom of all my ideas of just government, from beginning to end. I have denied that his use of that term applies properly. But for the thing itself, I deny that any man has ever gone ahead of me in his devotion to the principle, whatever he may have done in efficiency in advocating it. I think that I have said it in your hearing — that I believe each individual is naturally entitled to do as he pleases with himself and the fruit of his labors, so far as it in no wise interferes with any other man's rights — that each community, as a state, has a right to do exactly as it pleases with all the concerns within that state that interfere with the rights of no other state, and that the general government, upon principle, has no right to interfere with anything other than that general class of things that does concern the whole. I have said that at all times. I have said, as illustrations, that I do not believe in the right of Illinois to interfere with the cranberry laws of Indiana, the oyster laws of Virginia, or the liquor laws of Maine. I have said these things over and over again, and I repeat them here as my sentiments.

How is it, then, that Judge Douglas infers, because I hope to see slavery put where the public mind shall rest in the belief that it is in the course of ultimate extinction, that I am in favor of Illinois going over and interfering with the cranberry laws of Indiana? What can authorize him to draw any such inference? I suppose there might be one thing that at least enabled *him* to draw such an inference that would not be true with me or with many others, that is, because he looks upon all this matter of slavery as an exceedingly little thing — this matter of keeping one-sixth of the population of the whole nation in a state of oppression and tyranny unequaled in the world. He looks upon it as being an exceedingly little thing – only equal to the question of the cranberry laws of Indiana – as something having no moral question in it – as something on a par with the question of whether a man shall pasture his land with cattle, or plant it with tobacco – so little and so small a thing, that he concludes, if I could desire that anything should be done to bring about the ultimate extinction of that little thing, I must be in favor of bringing about an amalgamation of all the other little things in the Union. Now, it so happens – and there, I presume, is the foundation of this mistake – that the Judge thinks thus; and it so happens that there is a vast portion of the American people that do *not* look upon that matter as being this very little thing. They look upon it as a vast moral evil; they can prove it is such by the writings of those who gave us the blessings of liberty which we enjoy, and that they so looked upon it, and not as an evil merely confining itself to the states where it is situated; and while we agree that, by the Constitution we assented to, in the states where it exists we have no right to interfere with it because it is in the Constitution and we are by both duty and inclination to stick by that Constitution in all its letter and spirit from beginning to end.

So much then as to my disposition – my wish – to have all the state legislatures blotted out, and to have one general consolidated government, and a uniformity of domestic regulations in all the states, by which I suppose it is meant if we raise corn here, we must make sugar cane grow here too, and we must make those which grow north grow in the south. All this I suppose he understands I am in favor of doing. Now, so much for all this nonsense – for I must call it so. The Judge can have no issue with me on a question of establishing uniformity in the domestic regulations of the states . . .

Now, it happens that we meet together once every year, some time about the 4th of July, for some reason or other. These 4th of July gatherings I suppose have their uses. If you will indulge me, I will state what I suppose to be some of them.

We are now a mighty nation, we are thirty – or about thirty – millions of people, and we own and inhabit about one-fifteenth part of the dry land of the whole earth. We run our memory back over the pages of history for about eighty-two years and we discover that we were then a very small people in point of numbers, vastly inferior to what we are now, with a vastly less extent of country – with vastly less of everything we deem desirable among men – we look upon the change as exceedingly advantageous to us and to our posterity, and we fix upon something that happened away back as in some way or other being connected with this rise of prosperity. We find a race of men living in that day whom we claim as our fathers and grandfathers; they were iron men, they fought for the principle that they were contending for; and we understood that by what they then did it has followed that the degree of prosperity that we now enjoy has come to us. We hold this annual celebration to remind ourselves of all the good done in this process of time, of how it was done and who did it, and how we are historically connected with it; and we go from these meetings in better humor with ourselves – we feel more attached the one to the other, and more firmly bound to the country we inhabit. In every way we are better men in the age, and race, and country in which we live for these celebrations. But after we have done all this we have not yet reached the whole. There is something else connected with it. We have besides these men – descended by blood from our ancestors – among us perhaps half our people who are not descendants at all of these men, they are men who have come from Europe – German, Irish, French, and Scandinavian – men that have come from Europe themselves, or whose ancestors have come hither and settled here, finding themselves our equals in all things. If they look back through this history to trace their connection with those days by blood, they find they have none, they cannot carry themselves back into that glorious epoch and make themselves feel that they are part of us, but when they look through that old Declaration of Independence they find that those old men say that 'We hold these truths to be self-evident, that all men are created equal,' and then they feel that that moral sentiment taught in that day evidences their relation to those men, that it is the father of all moral principle in them, and that they have a right to claim it as though they were blood of the blood, and flesh of the flesh of the men who wrote that Declaration, and so they are. That is the electric cord in that Declaration that links the hearts of patriotic and liberty-loving men together, that will link those patriotic hearts as long as the love of freedom exists in the minds of men throughout the world.

Now, sirs, for the purpose of squaring things with this idea of 'don't care if slavery is voted up or voted down,' for sustaining the Dred Scott decision, for holding that the Declaration of Independence did not mean anything at all, we have Judge

Douglas giving his exposition of what the Declaration of Independence means, and we have him saying that the people of America are equal to the people of England. According to his construction, you Germans are not connected with it. Now I ask you in all soberness, if all these things, if indulged in, if ratified, if confirmed and endorsed, if taught to our children, and repeated to them, do not tend to rub out the sentiment of liberty in the country, and to transform this government into a government of some other form. Those arguments that are made, that the inferior race are to be treated with as much allowance as they are capable of enjoying; that as much is to be done for them as their condition will allow. What are these arguments? They are the arguments that kings have made for enslaving the people in all ages of the world. You will find that all the arguments in favor of kingcraft were of this class; they always bestrode the necks of the people, not that they wanted to do it, but because the people were better off for being ridden. That is their argument, and this argument of the Judge is the same old serpent that says you work and I eat, you toil and I will enjoy the fruits of it. Turn it whatever way you will — whether it come from the mouth of a king, an excuse for enslaving the people of his country, or from the mouth of men of one race as a reason for enslaving the men of another race, it is all the same old serpent, and I hold if that course of argumentation that is made for the purpose of convincing the public mind that we should not care about this, should be granted, it does not stop with the Negro. I should like to know if taking this old Declaration of Independence, which declares that all men are equal upon principle, and making exceptions to it, where will it stop? If one man says it does not mean a Negro, why not another say it does not mean some other man? If that declaration is not the truth, let us get the statute book in which we find it and tear it out! Who is so bold as to do it! If it is not true let us tear it out! Let us stick to it then, let us stand firmly by it then.

It may be argued that there are certain conditions that make necessities and impose them upon us, and to the extent that a necessity is imposed upon a man he must submit to it. I think that was the condition in which we found ourselves when we established this government. We had slavery among us, we could not get our constitution unless we permitted them to remain in slavery, we could not secure the good we did secure if we grasped for more, and having by necessity submitted to that much, it does not destroy the principle that is the charter of our liberties. Let that charter stand as our standard . . .

From a speech at Springfield.

17 July 1858

. . . After Senator Douglas left Washington, as his movements were made known by the public prints, he tarried a considerable time in the city of New York; and it was heralded that, like another Napoleon, he was lying by, and framing the plan of his campaign. It was telegraphed to Washington City, and published in the *Union*, that he was framing his plan for the purpose of going to Illinois to pounce upon and annihilate the treasonable and disunion speech which Lincoln had made here on the 16th of June. Now, I do suppose that the Judge really spent some time in New York maturing the plan of the campaign, as his friends heralded for him. I have been able, by noting his movements since his arrival in Illinois, to discover evidences confirmatory of that allegation. I think I have been able to see what are the material points of that plan. I will, for a little while, ask your attention to some of them. What I shall point out, though not showing the whole plan, are, nevertheless, the main points, as I suppose . . .

When he was preparing his plan of campaign, Napoleon-like, in New York, as appears by two speeches I have heard him deliver since his arrival in Illinois, he gave special attention to a speech of mine, delivered here on the 16th of June last. He says that he carefully read that speech. He told us that at Chicago a week ago last night, and he repeated it at Bloomington last night. Doubtless he repeated it again to-day, though I did not hear him. In the two first places – Chicago and Bloomington – I heard him; to-day I did not. He said he had carefully examined that speech; *when*, he did not say; but there is no reasonable doubt it was when he was in New York preparing his plan of campaign. I am glad he did read it carefully. He says it was evidently prepared with great care. I freely admit it was prepared with care. I claim not to be more free from errors than others – perhaps scarcely so much; but I was very careful not to put anything in that speech as a matter of fact, or make any inferences which did not appear to me to be true, and fully warrantable. If I had made any mistake I was willing to be corrected; if I had drawn any inference in regard to Judge Douglas, or anyone else, which was not warranted, I was fully prepared to modify it as soon as discovered. I planted myself upon the truth, and the truth only, so far as I knew it, or could be brought to know it.

Having made that speech with the most kindly feeling towards Judge Douglas, as manifested therein, I was gratified when I found that he had carefully examined it and had detected no error of fact, nor any inference against him, nor any misrepresentations, of which he thought fit to complain. In neither of the two speeches I have mentioned, did he make any such complaint. I will thank anyone who will inform me that he, in his speech to-day, pointed out anything I had stated, respecting him, as being erroneous. I presume there is no such thing. I have reason to be gratified that the care and caution used in that speech left it so that he, most of all others interested in discovering error, has not been able to point out one thing against him which he could say was wrong. He seizes upon the doctrines he supposes to be included in that speech, and declares that upon them will turn the issues of this campaign. He then quotes, or attempts to quote, from my speech. I will not say that he wilfully misquotes, but he does fail to quote accurately. His attempt at quoting is from a passage which I believe I can quote accurately from memory. I shall make the quotation now, with some comments upon it, as I have already said, in order that the Judge shall be left entirely without excuse for misrepresenting me. I do so now, as I hope, for the last time. I do this in great caution, in order that if he repeats his mis-representation, it shall be plain to all that he does so wilfully. If, after all, he still persists, I shall be compelled to reconstruct the course I have marked out for myself, and draw upon such humble resources as I have, for a new course, better suited to the real exigencies of the case. I set out in this campaign, with the intention of conducting it strictly as a gentleman, in substance at least, if not in the outside polish. The latter I shall never be, but that which constitutes the inside of a gentleman I hope I understand, and am not less inclined to practice than others. It was my purpose and expectation that this canvass would be conducted upon principle, and with fairness on both sides; and it shall not be my fault, if this purpose and expectation shall be given up.

He charges, in substance, that I invite a war of sections; that I propose all the local institutions of the different states shall become consolidated and uniform. What is there in the language of that speech which expresses such purpose, or bears such construction? I have again and again said that I would not enter into any of the states to disturb the institution of slavery. Judge Douglas said, at Bloomington, that I used language most able and ingenious for concealing what I really meant; and that while I had protested against entering into the slave states, I nevertheless did mean to go on the banks of Ohio and throw missiles into Kentucky to disturb them in their domestic institutions.

I said, in that speech, and I meant no more, that the institution of slavery ought to be placed in the very attitude where the framers of this government placed it, and left it. I do not understand that the framers of our Constitution left the people of the free states in the attitude of firing bombs or shells into the slave states. I was not using that passage for the purpose for which he infers I did use it. I said: 'We are now far advanced into the fifth year since a policy was created for the avowed object and with the confident promise of putting an end to slavery agitation. Under the operation of that policy that agitation has not only not ceased, but has constantly augmented. In my opinion it will not cease till a crisis shall have been reached and passed. "A house divided against itself cannot stand." I believe that this government cannot endure permanently half slave and half free. It will become all one thing or all the other. Either the opponents of slavery will arrest the further spread of it, and place it where the public mind shall rest in the belief that it is in the course of ultimate extinction, or its advocates will push it forward till it shall become alike lawful in all the states, old as well as new, north as well as south.'

Now you all see, from that quotation, I did not express my *wish* on anything. In that passage I indicated no wish or purpose of my own; I simply expressed my *expectation*. Cannot the Judge perceive the distinction between a *purpose* and an *expectation*? I have often expressed an expectation to die, but I have never expressed a *wish* to die. I said at Chicago, and now repeat, that I am quite aware this government has endured, half slave and half free, for eighty-two years. I understand that little bit of history. I expressed the opinion I did, because I perceived – or thought I perceived – a new set of causes introduced. I did say, at Chicago, in my speech there, that I do wish to see the spread of slavery arrested and to see it placed where the public mind shall rest in the belief that it is in course of ultimate extinction. I said that because I supposed, when the public mind shall rest in that belief, we shall have peace on the slavery question. I have believed – and now believe – the public mind did rest on that belief up to the introduction of the Nebraska bill.

Although I have ever been opposed to slavery, so far I rested in the hope and belief that it was in course of ultimate extinction. For that reason, it had been a minor question with me. I might have been mistaken; but I had believed, and now believe, that the whole public mind, that is the mind of the great majority, had rested in that belief up to the repeal of the Missouri Compromise. But upon that event, I became convinced that either I had been resting in a delusion, or the institution was being placed on a new basis — a basis for making it perpetual, national, and universal. Subsequent events have greatly confirmed me in that belief. I believe that bill to be the beginning of a conspiracy for that purpose. So believing, I have since then considered that question a paramount one. So believing, I have thought the public mind will never rest till the power of Congress to restrict the spread of it shall again be acknowledged and exercised on the one hand, or on the other, all resistance be entirely crushed out. I have expressed that opinion, and I entertain it to-night. It is denied that there is any tendency to the nationalization of slavery in these states . . .

Now, as to the Dred Scott decision; for upon that he makes his last point at me. He boldly takes ground in favor of that decision.

This is one-half the onslaught, and one-third of the entire plan of the campaign. I am opposed to that decision in a certain sense, but not in the sense which he puts on it. I say that in so far as it decided in favor of Dred Scott's master and against Dred Scott and his family, I do not propose to disturb or resist the decision.

I never have proposed to do any such thing. I think that in respect for judicial authority, my humble history would not suffer in a comparison with that of Judge Douglas. He would have the citizen conform his vote to that decision; the member of Congress, his; the President, his use of the veto power. He would make it a rule of political action for the people and all the departments of the government. I would not. By resisting it as a political rule, I disturb no right of property, create no disorder, excite no mobs . . .

Now, I wish to know what the Judge can charge upon me, with respect to decisions of the Supreme Court which does not lie in all its length, breadth, and proportions at his own door. The plain truth is simply this: Judge Douglas is *for* Supreme Court decisions when he likes them and against them when he does not like them. He is for the Dred Scott decision because it tends to nationalize slavery — because it is part of the original combination for that object. It so happens, singularly enough, that I never stood opposed to a decision of the Supreme Court till this. On the contrary, I have no recollection that he was ever particularly in favor of one till this. He never was in favor of any, nor opposed to any, till the present one, which helps to nationalize slavery.

Free men of Sangamon – free men of Illinois – free men everywhere – judge ye between him and me, upon this issue.

He says this Dred Scott case is a very small matter at most – that it has no practical effect; that at best, or rather, I suppose, at worst, it is but an abstraction. I submit that the proposition that the thing which determines whether a man is free or a slave, is rather *concrete* than *abstract*. I think you would conclude that it was, if your liberty depended upon it, and so would Judge Douglas if his liberty depended upon it. But suppose it was on the question of spreading slavery over the new territories that he considers it as being merely an abstract matter, and one of no importance. How has the planting of slavery in new countries always been effected? It has now been decided that slavery cannot be kept out of our new territories by any legal means. In what does our new territories now differ in this respect, from the old colonies when slavery was first planted within them? It was planted as Mr Clay once declared, and as history proves true, by individual men in spite of the wishes of the people; the mother government refusing to prohibit it, and withholding from the people of the colonies the authority to prohibit it for themselves. Mr Clay says this was one of the great and just causes of complaint against Great Britain by the colonies, and the best apology we can now make for having the institution amongst us. In that precise condition our Nebraska politicians have at last succeeded in placing our own new territories; the government will not prohibit slavery within them, nor allow the people to prohibit it . . .

One more thing. Last night Judge Douglas tormented himself with horrors about my disposition to make Negroes perfectly equal with white men in social and political relations. He did not stop to show that I have said any such thing, or that it legitimately follows from anything I have said, but he rushes on with his assertions. I adhere to the Declaration of Independence. If Judge Douglas and his friends are not willing to stand by it, let them come up and amend it. Let them make it read that all men are created equal except Negroes. Let us have it decided, whether the Declaration of Independence, in this blessed year of 1858, shall be thus amended. In his construction of the Declaration last year he said it only meant that Americans in America were equal to Englishmen in England. Then, when I pointed out to him that by that rule he excludes the Germans, the Irish, the Portuguese, and all the other people who have come amongst us since the Revolution, he reconstructs his construction. In his last speech he tells us it meant Europeans.

I press him a little further, and ask if it meant to include the Russians in Asia? or does he mean to exclude that vast population from the principles of our Declaration of Independence? I expect ere long he will introduce another amendment to his definition. He is not at all particular. He is satisfied with anything which does not endanger the nationalizing of Negro slavery. It may draw white men down, but it must not lift Negroes up. Who shall say, 'I am the superior, and you are the inferior'?

My declarations upon this subject of Negro slavery may be misrepresented, but cannot be misunderstood. I have said that I do not understand the Declaration to mean that all men were created equal in all respects. They are not our equal in color: but I suppose that it does mean to declare that all men are equal in some respects; they are equal in their right to 'life, liberty, and the pursuit of happiness.' Certainly the Negro is not our equal in color – perhaps not in many other respects; still, in the right to put into his mouth the bread that his own hands have earned, he is the equal of every other man, white or black. In pointing out that more has been given you, you cannot be justified in taking away the little which has been given him. All I ask for the Negro is that if you do not like him, let him alone. If God gave him but little, that little let him enjoy.

When our government was established, we had the institution of slavery among us. We were in a certain sense compelled to tolerate its existence. It was a sort of necessity. We had gone through our struggle and secured our own independence. The framers of the Constitution found the institution of slavery amongst their other institutions at the time. They found that by an effort to eradicate it, they might lose much of what they had already gained. They were obliged to bow to the necessity. They gave power to Congress to abolish the slave trade at the end of twenty years. They also prohibited it in the territories where it did not exist. They did what they could and yielded to the necessity for the rest. I also yield to all which follows from that necessity. What I would most desire would be the separation of the white and black races.

One more point on this Springfield speech which Judge Douglas says he has read so carefully. I expressed my belief in the existence of a conspiracy to perpetuate and nationalize slavery. I did not profess to know it, nor do I now. I showed the part Judge Douglas had played in the string of facts constituting, to my mind, the proof of that conspiracy. I showed the parts played by others.

I charged that the people had been deceived into carrying the last presidential election, by the impression that the people of the territories might exclude slavery if they chose, when it was known in advance by the conspirators that the Court was to decide that neither Congress nor the people could so exclude slavery. These charges are more distinctly made than anything else in the speech.

Judge Douglas has carefully read and re-read that speech. He has not, so far as I know, contradicted those charges. In the two speeches which I heard he certainly did not. On his own tacit admission I renew that charge. I charge him with having been a party to that conspiracy and to that deception for the sole purpose of nationalizing slavery.

Letter to Stephen A. Douglas.

Chicago, 24 July 1858

My Dear Sir: Will it be agreeable to you to make an arrangement for you and myself to divide time, and address the same audiences during the present canvass? Mr Judd,[1] who will hand you this, is authorized to receive your answer; and, if agreeable to you, to enter into the terms of such arrangement. Your Obt. Servt.

Letter to Stephen A. Douglas.

Springfield, 31 July 1858

Dear Sir: Yours of yesterday, naming places, times, and terms for joint discussions between us, was received this morning. Although, by the terms, as you propose, you take *four* openings and closes to my *three*, I accede, and thus close the arrangement. I direct this to you at Hillsboro; and shall try to have both your letter and this appear in the *Journal* and *Register* of Monday morning. Your Obt. Servt.

---

[1] Norman B. Judd, chairman of the Republican State Central Committee.

From Lincoln's reply to Douglas in the first joint debate.
                    Ottawa, Illinois, 21 August 1858

. . . I will say here, while upon this subject, that I have no purpose directly or indirectly to interfere with the institution of slavery in the states where it exists. I believe I have no lawful right to do so, and I have no inclination to do so. I have no purpose to introduce political and social equality between the white and the black races. There is a physical difference between the two, which in my judgment will probably forever forbid their living together upon the footing of perfect equality, and inasmuch as it becomes a necessity that there must be a difference, I, as well as Judge Douglas, am in favor of the race to which I belong, having the superior position. I have never said anything to the contrary, but I hold that notwithstanding all this, there is no reason in the world why the Negro is not entitled to all the natural rights enumerated in the Declaration of Independence, the right to life, liberty, and the pursuit of happiness. I hold that he is as much entitled to these as the white man. I agree with Judge Douglas he is not my equal in many respects — certainly not in color, perhaps not in moral or intellectual endowment. But in the right to eat the bread, without leave of anybody else, which his own hand earns, *he is my equal and the equal of Judge Douglas, and the equal of every living man*.

Now I pass on to consider one or two more of these little follies. The Judge is woefully at fault about his early friend Lincoln being a 'grocery keeper.' I don't know as it would be a great sin if I had been, but he is mistaken. Lincoln never kept a grocery[1] anywhere in the world. It is true that Lincoln did work the latter part of one winter in a small still house, up at the head of a hollow. And so I think my friend, the Judge, is equally at fault when he charges me at the time when I was in Congress of having opposed our soldiers who were fighting in the Mexican War. The Judge did not make his charge very distinctly but I can tell you what he can prove by referring to the record. You remember I was an old Whig, and whenever the Democratic party tried to get me to vote that the war had been righteously begun by the President, I would not do it. But whenever they asked for any money, or land warrants, or anything to pay the soldiers there, during all that time, I gave the same votes that Judge Douglas did. You can think as you please as to whether that was consistent. Such is the truth, and the Judge

---

[1] A now obsolete term for a tavern or dram shop.

has the right to make all he can out of it. But when he, by a general charge, conveys the idea that I withheld supplies from the soldiers who were fighting in the Mexican War, or did anything else to hinder the soldiers, he is, to say the least, grossly and altogether mistaken, as a consultation of the records will prove to him.

As I have not used up so much of my time as I had supposed, I will dwell a little longer upon one or two of these minor topics upon which the Judge has spoken. He has read from my speech in Springfield, in which I say that 'a house divided against itself cannot stand.' Does the Judge say it *can* stand? I don't know whether he does or not. The Judge does not seem to be attending to me just now, but I would like to know if it is his opinion that a house divided against itself *can stand*. If he does, then there is a question of veracity, not between him and me, but between the Judge and an authority of a somewhat higher character.

Now, my friends, I ask your attention to this matter for the purpose of saying something seriously. I know that the Judge may readily enough agree with me that the maxim which was put forth by the Saviour is true, but he may allege that I misapply it; and the Judge has a right to urge that, in my application, I do misapply it, and then I have a right to show that I do *not* misapply it. When he undertakes to say that because I think this nation, so far as the question of slavery is concerned, will all become one thing or all the other, I am in favor of bringing about a dead uniformity in the various states, in all their institutions, he argues erroneously. The great variety of the local institutions in the states, springing from differences in the soil, differences in the face of the country, and in the climate, are bonds of union. They do not make 'a house divided against itself,' but they make a house united. If they produce in one section of the country what is called for by the wants of another section, and this other section can supply the wants of the first, they are not matters of discord but bonds of union, true bonds of union. But can this question of slavery be considered as among *these* varieties in the institutions of the country? I leave it to you to say whether, in the history of our government, this institution of slavery has not always failed to be a bond of union, and, on the contrary, been an apple of discord and an element of division in the house. I ask you to consider whether, so long as the moral constitution of men's minds shall continue to be the same, after this generation and assemblage shall sink into the grave, and another race shall arise, with the same moral and intellectual development we have — whether, if that institution is standing in the same irritating position in which it now is, it will not continue an element of division? If so, then I have a right to say that in regard to this question, the Union is a house divided against itself, and when the Judge reminds me that I have often said to him that the institution of slavery has existed for eighty years in some states, and yet it does not exist in some others, I agree to the fact, and I account for it by looking at the position in which our fathers originally placed it — restricting it from the new territories where it had not gone, and legislating to cut off its source by the abrogation of the slave trade, thus putting the seal of legislation *against its spread*. The public mind *did* rest in the belief that it was in the course of ultimate extinction. But lately, I think — and in this I charge nothing on the Judge's motives — lately, I think that he, and those acting with him, have placed that institution on a new basis, which looks to the *perpetuity and nationalization of slavery*. And while it is placed upon this new basis, I say, and I have said, that I believe we shall not have peace upon the question until the opponents of slavery arrest the further spread of it, and place it where the public mind shall rest in the belief that it is in the course of ultimate extinction; or, on the other hand, that its advocates will push it forward until it shall become alike lawful in all the states, old as well as new, north as well as south. Now, I believe if we could arrest the spread, and place it where Washington, and Jefferson, and Madison placed it, it *would be* in the course of ultimate extinction, and the public mind *would*, as for eighty years past, believe that it was in the course of ultimate extinction. The crisis would be past and the institution might be let alone for a hundred years, if it should live so long, in the states where it exists, yet it would be going out of existence in the way best for both the black and the white races.

A VOICE: Then do you repudiate Popular Sovereignty?

MR LINCOLN: Well, then, let us talk about Popular Sovereignty! What is Popular Sovereignty? Is it the right of the people to have slavery or not have it, as they see fit, in the territories? I will state — and I have an able man to watch me — my understanding is that Popular Sovereignty, as now applied to the question of slavery, does allow the people of a territory to have slavery if they want to, but does not allow them *not* to have it if they *do not* want it. I do not mean that if this vast concourse of people were in a territory of the United States, any one of them would be obliged to have a slave if he did not want one; but I do say that, as I understand the Dred Scott decision, if any one man wants slaves, all the rest have no way of keeping that one man from holding them.

When I made my speech at Springfield, of which the Judge complains, and from which he quotes, I really was not thinking of the things which he ascribes to me at all. I had no thought in the world that I was doing anything to bring about a war between the free and slave states. I had no thought in the world that I was doing anything to bring about a political and social equality of the black and white races. It never occurred to me that I was doing anything or favoring anything to reduce to a dead uniformity all the local institutions of the various states. But I must say, in all fairness to him, if he thinks I am doing something which leads to these bad results, it is none the better that I did not mean it. It is just as fatal to the country, if I have any influence in producing it, whether I intend it or not. But can it be true, that placing this institution upon the original basis – the basis upon which our fathers placed it – can have any tendency to set the northern and the southern states at war with one another, or that it can have any tendency to make the people of Vermont raise sugar-cane, because they raise it in Louisiana, or that it can compel the people of Illinois to cut pine logs on the Grand Prairie, where they will not grow, because they cut pine logs in Maine, where they do grow? The Judge says this is a new principle started in regard to this question. Does the Judge claim that he is working on the plan of the founders of government? I think he says in some of his speeches – indeed I have one here now – that he saw evidence of a policy to allow slavery to be south of a certain line, while north of it it should be excluded, and he saw an indisposition on the part of the country to stand upon that policy, and therefore he set about studying the subject upon *original principles*, and upon *original principles* he got up the Nebraska bill! I am fighting it upon these 'original principles' – fighting it in the Jeffersonian, Washingtonian, and Madisonian fashion.

Now, my friends, I wish you to attend for a little while to one or two other things in that Springfield speech. My main object was to show, so far as my humble ability was capable of showing to the people of this country, what I believed was the truth – that there was a *tendency*, if not a conspiracy among those who have engineered this slavery question for the last four or five years, to make slavery perpetual and universal in this nation . . .

. . . I want to ask your attention to a portion of the Nebraska bill, which Judge Douglas has quoted: 'It being the true intent and meaning of this act, not to legislate slavery into any territory or state, nor to exclude it therefrom, but to leave the people thereof perfectly free to form and regulate their domestic institutions in their own way, subject only to the Constitution of the United States.' Thereupon Judge Douglas and others began to argue in favor of 'Popular Sovereignty' – the right of the people to have slaves if they wanted them, and to exclude slavery if they did not want them. 'But,' said, in substance, a Senator from Ohio (Mr Chase, I believe), 'we more than suspect that you do not mean to allow the people to exclude slavery if they wish to, and if you do mean it, accept an amendment which I propose expressly authorizing the people to exclude slavery.' I believe I have the amendment here before me, which was offered, and under which the people of the territory, through their proper representatives, might if they saw fit, prohibit the existence of slavery therein. And now I state it as a *fact*, to be taken back if there is any mistake about it, that Judge Douglas and those acting with him, *voted that amendment down*. I now think that those men who voted it down, had a *real reason* for doing so. They know what that reason was. It looks to us, since we have seen the Dred Scott decision pronounced holding that 'under the Constitution' the people cannot exclude slavery – I say it looks to outsiders, poor, simple, 'amiable, intelligent gentlemen,' as though the niche was left as a place to put that Dred Scott decision in – a niche which would have been spoiled by adopting the amendment. And now, I say again, if *this* was not the reason, it will avail the Judge much more to calmly and good-humoredly point out to these people what that *other* reason was for voting the amendment down, than, swelling himself up, to vociferate that he may be provoked to call somebody a liar.

Again, there is in that same quotation from the Nebraska bill this clause: 'It being the true intent and meaning of this bill not to legislate slavery into any territory or *state*.' I have always been puzzled to know what business the word 'state' had in that connection. Judge Douglas knows. *He put it there*. He knows what he put it there for. We outsiders cannot say what he put it there for. The law they were passing was not about states, and was not making provisions for states. What was it placed there for? After seeing the Dred Scott decision, which holds that the people cannot exclude slavery from a *territory*, if another Dred Scott decision shall come, holding that they cannot exclude it from a *state*, we shall discover that when the word was originally put there, it was in view of something which was to come in due time, we shall see that it was the *other half* of something. I now say again, if there is any different reason for putting it there, Judge Douglas, in a good-humored way, without calling anybody a liar, *can tell what the reason was* . . .

. . . One more word and I am done. Henry Clay, my beau ideal of a statesman, the man for whom I fought all my humble life — Henry Clay once said of a class of men who would repress all tendencies to liberty and ultimate emancipation, that they must, if they would do this, go back to the era of our independence, and muzzle the cannon which thunders its annual joyous return; they must blow out the moral lights around us; they must penetrate the human soul, and eradicate there the love of liberty; and then and not till then, could they perpetuate slavery in this country! To my thinking, Judge Douglas is, by his example and vast influence, doing that very thing in this community, when he says that the Negro has nothing in the Declaration of Independence. Henry Clay plainly understood the contrary. Judge Douglas is going back to the era of our Revolution, and to the extent of his ability, muzzling the cannon which thunders its annual joyous return. When he invites any people willing to have slavery, to establish it, he is blowing out the moral lights around us. When he says he 'cares not whether slavery is voted down or voted up' — that it is a sacred right of self government — he is in my judgment penetrating the human soul and eradicating the light of reason and the love of liberty in this American people. And now I will only say that when, by all these means and appliances, Judge Douglas shall succeed in bringing public sentiment to an exact accordance with his own views — when these vast assemblages shall echo back all these sentiments — when they shall come to repeat his views and to avow his principles, and to say all that he says on these mighty questions — then it needs only the formality of the second Dred Scott decision, which he endorses in advance, to make slavery alike lawful in all the states — old as well as new, north as well as south . . .

From Lincoln's opening speech in the second joint debate.
                              Freeport, Illinois, 27 August 1858

Now, my friends, it will be perceived upon an examination of these questions and answers, that so far I have only answered that I was not *pledged* to this, that, or the other. The Judge has not framed his interrogatories to ask me anything more than this, and I have answered in strict accordance with the interrogatories, and have answered truly that I am not *pledged* at all upon any of the points to which I have answered. But I am not disposed to hang upon the exact form of his interrogatory. I am rather disposed to take up at least some of these questions, and state what I really think upon them.

As to the first one, in regard to the Fugitive Slave law, I have never hesitated to say, and I do not now hesitate to say, that I think, under the Constitution of the United States, the people of the southern states are entitled to a congressional Fugitive Slave law. Having said that, I have had nothing to say in regard to the existing Fugitive Slave law further than that I think it should have been framed so as to be free from some of the objections that pertain to it, without lessening its efficiency. And inasmuch as we are not now in an agitation in regard to an alteration or modification of that law, I would not be the man to introduce it as a new subject of agitation upon the general question of slavery.

In regard to the other question of whether I am pledged to the admission of any more slave states into the Union, I state to you very frankly that I would be exceedingly sorry ever to be put in a position of having to pass upon that question. I should be exceedingly glad to know that there would never be another slave state admitted into the Union; but I must add, that if slavery shall be kept out of the territories during the territorial existence of any one given territory, and then the people shall, having a fair chance and a clear field, when they come to adopt the constitution, do such an extraordinary thing as to adopt a slave constitution, uninfluenced by the actual presence of the institution among them, I see no alternative, if we own the country, but to admit them into the Union.

The third interrogatory is answered by the answer to the second, it being, as I conceive, the same as the second.

The fourth one is in regard to the abolition of slavery in the District of Columbia. In relation to that, I have my mind very distinctly made up. I should be exceedingly glad to see slavery abolished in the District of Columbia. I believe that Congress possesses the constitutional power to abolish it. Yet as a member of Congress, I should not with my present views, be in favor, of *endeavoring* to abolish slavery in the District of Columbia, unless it would be upon these conditions. *First*, that the abolition should be gradual. *Second*, that it should be on a vote of the majority of qualified voters in the District, and *third*, that compensation should be made to unwilling owners. With these three conditions, I confess I would be exceedingly glad to see Congress abolish slavery in the District of Columbia, and, in the language of Henry Clay, 'sweep from our Capital that foul blot upon our nation.'

In regard to the fifth interrogatory, I must say here, that as to the question of the abolition of the slave trade between the different states, I can truly answer, as I have, that I am pledged to nothing about it. It is a subject to which I have not given that mature consideration that would make me feel authorized to state a position so as to hold myself entirely bound by it. In other words, that question has never been prominently enough before me to induce me to investigate whether we really have the constitutional power to do it. I could investigate it if I had sufficient time to bring myself to a conclusion upon that subject, but I have not done so, and I say so frankly to you here, and to Judge Douglas. I must say, however, that if I should be of opinion that Congress does possess the constitutional power to abolish the slave trade among the different states, I should still not be in favor of the exercise of that power unless upon some conservative principle as I conceive it, akin to what I have said in relation to the abolition of slavery in the District of Columbia.

My answer as to whether I desire that slavery should be prohibited in all the territories of the United States is full and explicit within itself, and cannot be made clearer by any comments of mine. So I suppose in regard to the question whether I am opposed to the acquisition of any more territory unless slavery is first prohibited therein, my answer is such that I could add nothing by way of illustration, or making myself better understood, than the answer which I have placed in writing.

Now in all this, the Judge has me and he has me on the record. I suppose he had flattered himself that I was really entertaining one set of opinions for one place and another set for another place — that I was afraid to say at one place what I uttered at another.

What I am saying here I suppose I say to a vast audience as strongly tending to abolitionism as any audience in the state of Illinois, and I believe I am saying that which, if it would be offensive to any persons and render them enemies to myself, would be offensive to persons in this audience.

I now proceed to propound to the Judge the interrogatories, so far as I have framed them. I will bring forward a new instalment when I get them ready. I will bring them forward now, only reaching to number four.

This first one is —

Question 1. If the people of Kansas shall, by means entirely unobjectionable in all other respects, adopt a state constitution, and ask admission into the Union under it, *before* they have the requisite number of inhabitants according to the English bill — some ninety-three thousand — will you vote to admit them?

Question 2. Can the people of a United States territory, in any lawful way, against the wish of any citizen of the United States, exclude slavery from its limits prior to the formation of a state constitution?

Question 3. If the Supreme Court of the United States shall decide that states cannot exclude slavery from their limits, are you in favor of acquiescing in, adopting, and following such decision as a rule of political action?

Question 4. Are you in favor of acquiring additional territory, in disregard of how such acquisition may affect the nation on the slavery question? . . .

From Lincoln's reply in the third joint debate.
                    Jonesboro, Illinois, 15 September 1858

At Freeport I answered several interrogatories that had been propounded to me by Judge Douglas at the Ottawa meeting. The Judge has yet not seen fit to find any fault with the position that I took in regard to those seven interrogatories, which were certainly broad enough, in all conscience, to cover the entire ground. In my answers, which have been printed, and all have had the opportunity of seeing, I take the ground that those who elect me must expect that I will do nothing which is not in accordance with those answers. I have some right to assert that Judge Douglas has no fault to find with them. But he chooses to still try to thrust me upon different ground without paying any attention to my answers, the obtaining of which from me cost him so much trouble and concern. At the same time, I propounded four interrogatories to him, claiming it as a right that he should answer as many interrogatories for me as I did for him, and I would reserve myself for a future instalment when I got them ready. The Judge in answering me upon that occasion put in what I suppose he intends as answers to all four of my interrogatories. The first one of these interrogatories I have before me, and it is in these words:

'Question 1. If the people of Kansas shall, by means entirely unobjectionable in all other respects, adopt a state constitution, and ask admission into the Union under it, *before* they have the requisite number of inhabitants according to the English bill – some ninety-three thousand – will you vote to admit them?'

As I read the Judge's answer in the newspaper, and as I remember it as pronounced at the time, he does not give any answer which is equivalent to yes or no – I will or I won't. He answers at very considerable length, rather quarreling with me for asking the question, and insisting that Judge Trumbull had done something that I ought to say something about; and finally getting out such statements as induce me to infer that he means to be understood he will, in that supposed case, vote for the admission of Kansas. I only bring this forward now for the purpose of saying that if he chooses to put a different construction upon his answer he may do it. But if he does not, I shall from this time forward assume that he will vote for the admission of Kansas in disregard of the English bill. He has the right to remove any misunderstanding I may have. I only mention it now that I may hereafter assume this to be the true construction of his answer, if he does not now choose to correct me.

The second interrogatory that I propounded to him was this:

'Question 2. Can the people of a United States territory, in any lawful way, against the wish of any citizen of the United States, exclude slavery from its limits prior to the formation of a state constitution?'

To this Judge Douglas answered that they can lawfully exclude slavery from the territory prior to the formation of a constitution. He goes on to tell us how it can be done. As I understand him, he holds that it can be done by the territorial legislature refusing to make any enactments for the protection of slavery in the territory, and especially by adopting unfriendly legislation to it. For the sake of clearness I state it again: that they can exclude slavery from the territory, 1st, by withholding what he assumes to be an indispensable assistance to it in the way of legislation; and 2nd, by unfriendly legislation. If I rightly understand him, I wish to ask your attention for a while to his position.

In the first place, the Supreme Court of the United States has decided that any congressional prohibition of slavery in the territories is unconstitutional – that they have reached this proposition as a conclusion from their former proposition that the Constitution of the United States expressly recognizes property in slaves, and from that other constitutional provision that no person shall be deprived of property without due process of law. Hence they reach the conclusion that as the Constitution of the United States expressly recognizes property in slaves, and prohibits any person from being deprived of property without due process of law, to pass an act of Congress by which a man who owned a slave on one side of a line would be deprived of him if he took him on the other side, is depriving him of that property without due process of law. That I understand to be the decision of the Supreme Court. I understand also that Judge Douglas adheres most firmly to that decision; and the difficulty is, how is it possible for any power to exclude slavery from the territory unless in violation of that decision? That is the difficulty . . .

I hold that the proposition that slavery cannot enter a new country without police regulations is historically false. It is not true at all. I hold that the history of this country shows that the institution of slavery was originally planted upon this continent *without* these 'police regulations' which the Judge now thinks necessary for the actual establishment of it. Not only so, but is there not another fact – how came this Dred Scott decision to be made? It was made upon the case of a Negro being taken and actually held in slavery in Minnesota Territory, claiming his freedom because the act of Congress prohibited his being so held there. *Will the Judge pretend that Dred Scott was not held there without police regulations?* There is at least one matter of record as to his having been held in slavery in the territory, not only without police regulations, but in the teeth of congressional legislation supposed to be valid at the time. This shows that there is vigor enough in slavery to plant itself in a new country even against unfriendly legislation. It takes not only law but the *enforcement* of law to keep it out. That is the history of this country upon the subject.

I wish to ask one other question. It being understood that the Constitution of the United States guarantees property in slaves in the territories, if there is any infringement of the right of that property, would not the United States courts, organized for the government of the territory, apply such remedy as might be necessary in that case? It is a maxim held by the courts, that there is no wrong without its remedy; and the courts have a remedy for whatever is acknowledged and treated as a wrong.

Again: I will ask you, my friends, if you were elected members of the legislature, what would be the first thing you would have to do before entering upon your duties? *Swear to support the Constitution of the United States.* Suppose you believe, as Judge Douglas does, that the Constitution of the United States guarantees to your neighbor the right to hold slaves in that territory – that they are his property – how can you clear your oaths unless you give him such legislation as is necessary to enable him to enjoy that property? What do you understand by supporting the Constitution of a state or of the United States? Is it not to give such constitutional helps to the rights established by that Constitution as may be practically needed? Can you, if you swear to support the Constitution, and believe that the Constitution establishes a right, clear your oath, without giving it support? Do you support the Constitution if, knowing or believing there is a right established under it which needs specific legislation, you withhold that legislation? Do you not violate and disregard your oath? I can conceive of nothing plainer in the world. There can be nothing in the words 'support the Constitution,' if you may run counter to it by refusing support to any right established under the Constitution. And what I say here will hold with still more force against the Judge's doctrine of 'unfriendly legislation.' How could you, having sworn to support the Constitution, and believing it guaranteed the right to hold slaves in the territories, assist in legislation *intended to defeat that right*? That would be violating your own view of the Constitution. Not only so, but if you were to do so, how long would it take the courts to hold your votes unconstitutional and void? Not a moment.

Lastly I would ask – is not Congress itself under obligation to give legislative support to any right that is established under the United States Constitution? I repeat the question – is not Congress itself bound to give legislative support to any right that is established in the United States Constitution? A member of

Congress swears to support the Constitution of the United States, and if he sees a right established by that Constitution which needs specific legislative protection, can he clear his oath without giving that protection? Let me ask you why many of us who are opposed to slavery upon principle give our acquiescence to a fugitive slave law? Why do we hold ourselves under obligations to pass such a law, and abide by it when it is passed? Because the Constitution makes provision that the owners of slaves shall have the right to reclaim them. It gives the right to reclaim slaves, and that right is, as Judge Douglas says, a barren right, unless there is legislation that will enforce it.

The mere declaration 'No person held to service or labor in one state under the laws thereof, escaping into another, shall in consequence of any law or regulation therein be discharged from such service or labor, but shall be delivered up on claim of the party to whom such service or labor may be due' is powerless without specific legislation to enforce it. Now on what ground would a member of Congress who is opposed to slavery in the abstract vote for a fugitive law, as I would deem it my duty to do? Because there is a constitutional right which needs legislation to enforce it. And although it is distasteful to me, I have sworn to support the Constitution, and having so sworn I cannot conceive that I do support it if I withheld from that right any necessary legislation to make it practical. And if that is true in regard to a fugitive slave law, is the right to have fugitive slaves reclaimed any better fixed in the Constitution than the right to hold slaves in the territories? For this decision is a just exposition of the Constitution as Judge Douglas thinks. Is the one right any better than the other? Is there any man who while a member of Congress would give support to the one any more than the other? If I wished to refuse to give legislative support to slave property in the territories, if a member of Congress, I could not do it holding the view that the Constitution establishes that right. If I did it at all, it would be because I deny that this decision properly construes the Constitution. But if I acknowledge with Judge Douglas that this decision properly construes the Constitution, I cannot conceive that I would be less than a perjured man if I should refuse in Congress to give such protection to that property as in its nature it needed . . .

From Lincoln's opening speech in the fourth joint debate.
                    Charleston, Illinois, 18 September 1858

While I was at the hotel to-day an elderly gentleman called upon me to know whether I was really in favor of producing a perfect equality between the Negroes and white people. While I had not proposed to myself on this occasion to say much on that subject, yet as the question was asked me I thought I would occupy perhaps five minutes in saying something in regard to it. I will say then that I am not, nor ever have been in favor of bringing about in any way the social and political equality of the white and black races – that I am not nor ever have been in favor of making voters or jurors of Negroes, nor of qualifying them to hold office, nor to intermarry with white people; and I will say in addition to this that there is a physical difference between the white and black races which I believe will forever forbid the two races living together on terms of social and political equality. And inasmuch as they cannot so live, while they do remain together there must be the position of superior and inferior, and I as much as any other man am in favor of having the superior position assigned to the white race. I say upon this occasion I do not perceive that because the white man is to have the superior position the Negro should be denied everything. I do not understand that because I do not want a Negro woman for a slave I must necessarily want her for a wife. My understanding is that I can just let her alone. I am now in my fiftieth year, and I certainly never have had a black woman for either a slave or a wife. So it seems to me quite possible for us to get along without making either slaves or wives of Negroes. I will add to this that I have never seen to my knowledge a man, woman, or child who was in favor of producing a perfect equality, social and political, between Negroes and white men. I recollect of but one distinguished instance that I ever heard of so frequently as to be entirely satisfied of its correctness – and that is the case of Judge Douglas's old friend Col. Richard M. Johnson.[1] I will also add to the remarks I have made (for I am not going to enter at large upon this subject), that I have never had the least apprehension that I or my friends would marry Negroes if there was no law to keep them

---

[1] Democratic Representative and Senator from Kentucky, Vice-President of the United States, 1837–41. According to T. P. Abernethy in the *Dictionary of American Biography*, Johnson 'never married, but had two daughters by Julia Chinn, a mulatto who came to him in the distribution of his father's estate.'

from it, but as Judge Douglas and his friends seem to be in great apprehension that they might, if there were no law to keep them from it, I give him the most solemn pledge that I will to the very last stand by the law of this state, which forbids the marrying of white people with Negroes. I will add one further word, which is this, that I do not understand there is any place where an alteration of the social and political relations of the Negro and the white man can be made except in the state legislature – not in the Congress of the United States – and as I do not really apprehend the approach of any such thing myself, and as Judge Douglas seems to be in constant horror that some such danger is rapidly approaching, I propose as the best means to prevent it that the Judge be kept at home and placed in the state legislature to fight the measure. I do not propose dwelling longer at this time on this subject . . .

From Lincoln's reply in the fifth joint debate.
                    Galesburg, Illinois, 7 October 1858

The Judge has alluded to the Declaration of Independence, and insisted that Negroes are not included in that Declaration; and that it is a slander upon the framers of that instrument to suppose that Negroes were meant therein; and he asks you: Is it possible to believe that Mr Jefferson, who penned the immortal paper, could have supposed himself applying the language of that instrument to the Negro race, and yet held a portion of that race in slavery? Would he not at once have freed them? I only have to remark upon this part of the Judge's speech (and that, too, very briefly, for I shall not detain myself, or you, upon that point for any great length of time), that I believe the entire records of the world, from the date of the Declaration of Independence up to within three years ago, may be searched in vain for one single affirmation, from one single man, that the Negro was not included in the Declaration of Independence. I think I may defy Judge Douglas to show that he ever said so, that Washington ever said so, that any President ever said so, that any member of Congress ever said so, or that any living man upon the whole earth ever said so, until the necessities of the present policy of the Democratic party, in regard to slavery, had to invent that affirmation. And I will remind Judge Douglas and this audience, that while Mr Jefferson was the owner of slaves, as undoubtedly he was, in speaking upon this very subject, he used the strong language that 'he trembled for his country when he remembered that God was just'; and I will offer the highest premium in my power to Judge Douglas if he will show that he, in all his life, ever uttered a sentiment at all akin to that of Jefferson . . .

The Judge has also detained us a while in regard to the distinction between his party and our party. His he assumes to be a national party – ours, a sectional one. He does this in asking the question whether this country has any interest in the maintenance of the Republican party? He assumes that our party is altogether sectional – that the party to which he adheres is national; and the argument is, that no party can be a rightful party – can be based upon rightful principles – unless it can announce its principles everywhere. I presume that Judge Douglas could not go into Russia and announce the doctrine of our national democracy; he could not denounce the doctrine of kings, and emperors, and monarchies, in Russia; and it may be true of this country, that in some places we may not be able to proclaim a doctrine as clearly true as the truth of democracy, because there is a section so directly opposed to it that they will not tolerate us in doing so. Is it the true test of the soundness of a doctrine, that in some places people won't let you proclaim it? Is that the way to test the truth of any doctrine? Why, I understood that at one time the people of Chicago would not let Judge Douglas preach a certain favorite doctrine of his. I commend to his consideration the question, whether he takes that as a test of the unsoundness of what he wanted to preach.

There is another thing to which I wish to ask attention for a little while on this occasion. What has always been the evidence brought forward to prove that the Republican party is a sectional party? The main one was that in the southern portion of the Union the people did not let the Republicans proclaim their doctrine amongst them. That has been the main evidence brought forward – that they had no supporters, or substantially none, in the slave states. The South have not taken hold of our principles as we announce them; nor does Judge Douglas now grapple with those principles. We have a Republican State platform, laid down in Springfield in June last, stating our position all the way through the questions before the country. We are now far advanced in this canvass. Judge Douglas and I have made perhaps forty speeches apiece, and we have now for the fifth time met face to face in debate, and up to this day I have not found either Judge Douglas or any friend of his taking hold of the Republican platform or laying his finger upon anything in it that is wrong. I ask you all to recollect that.

Judge Douglas turns away from the platform of principles to the fact that he can find people somewhere who will not allow us to announce those principles. If he had great confidence that our principles were wrong, he would take hold of them and demonstrate them to be wrong. But he does not do so. The only evidence he has of their being wrong is in the fact that there are people who won't allow us to preach them. I ask again, is that the way to test the soundness of a doctrine? . . .

The Judge tells, in proceeding, that he is opposed to making any odious distinctions between free and slave states. I am altogether unaware that the Republicans are in favor of making any odious distinctions between the free and slave states. But there still is a difference, I think, between Judge Douglas and the Republicans in this. I suppose that the real difference between Judge Douglas and his friends, and the Republicans on the contrary, is that the Judge is not in favor of making any difference between slavery and liberty — that he is in favor of eradicating, of pressing out of view, the questions of preference in this country for free over slave institutions; and consequently every sentiment he utters discards the idea that there is any wrong in slavery. Everything that emanates from him or his coadjutors in their course of policy carefully excludes the thought that there is anything wrong in slavery. If you will take the Judge's speeches, and select the short and pointed sentences expressed by him — as his declaration that he 'don't care whether slavery is voted up or down' — you will see at once that this is perfectly logical, if you do not admit that slavery is wrong. If you do admit that it is wrong, Judge Douglas cannot logically say that he don't care whether a wrong is voted up or voted down. Judge Douglas declares that if any community want slavery they have a right to it. He can say that logically, if he says that there is no wrong in slavery; but if you admit that there is a wrong in it, he cannot logically say that anybody has a right to do wrong. He insists that, upon the score of equality, the owners of slaves and owners of property — of horses and every other sort of property — should be alike and hold them alike in a new territory. That is perfectly logical, if the two species of property are alike and are equally founded in right. But if you admit that one of them is wrong, you cannot institute any equality between right and wrong. And from this difference of sentiment – the belief on the part of one that the institution is wrong, and a policy springing from that belief which looks to the arrest of the enlargement of that wrong; and this other sentiment, that it is no wrong, and a policy sprung from that sentiment which will tolerate no idea of preventing that wrong from growing larger, and looks to there never being an end of it through all the existence of things – arises the real difference between Judge Douglas and his friends, on the one hand, and the Republicans on the other. Now, I confess myself as belonging to that class in the country who contemplate slavery as a moral, social, and political evil, having due regard for its actual existence amongst us and the difficulties of getting rid of it in any satisfactory way, and to all the constitutional obligations which have been thrown about it; but, nevertheless, desire a policy that looks to the prevention of it as a wrong, and looks hopefully to the time when as a wrong it may come to an end . . .

From Lincoln's opening speech in the sixth joint debate.
                    Quincy, Illinois, 13 October 1858

We have in this nation this element of domestic slavery. It is a matter of absolute certainty that it is a disturbing element. It is the opinion of all the great men who have expressed an opinion upon it, that it is a dangerous element. We keep up a controversy in regard to it. That controversy necessarily springs from difference of opinion, and if we can learn exactly – can reduce to the lowest elements – what that difference of opinion is, we perhaps shall be better prepared for discussing the different systems of policy that we would propose in regard to that disturbing element. I suggest that the difference of opinion, reduced to its lowest terms, is no other than the difference between the men who think slavery a wrong and those who do not think it wrong. The Republican party think it wrong – we think it is a moral, a social, and a political wrong. We think it is a wrong not confining itself merely to the persons or the states where it exists, but that it is a wrong in its tendency, to say the least, that extends itself to the existence of the whole nation. Because we think it wrong, we propose a course of policy that shall deal with it as a wrong. We deal with it as with any other wrong, in so far as we can prevent its growing any larger and so deal with it that in the run of time there may be some promise of an end to it. We have a due regard to the actual presence of it amongst us and the difficulties of getting rid of it in any satisfactory way, and all the constitutional obligations thrown about it. I suppose that in reference both to its actual existence in the nation, and to our constitutional obligations, we have no right at all to disturb it in the states where it exists, and we profess that we have no more inclination to disturb it than we have the right to do it. We go further than that; we don't propose to disturb it where, in one instance, we think the Constitution would permit us. We think the Constitution would permit us to disturb it in the District of Columbia. Still we do not propose to do that, unless it should be in terms which I don't suppose the nation is very likely soon to agree to — the terms of making the emancipation gradual and compensating the unwilling owners. Where we suppose we have the constitutional right, we restrain ourselves in deference to the actual existence of the institution and the difficulties thrown about it. We also oppose it as an evil so far as it seeks to spread itself. We insist on the policy that shall restrict it to its present limits. We don't suppose that in doing this we violate anything due to the actual presence of the institution, or anything due to the constitutional guarantees thrown around it. . .

I will say now that there is a sentiment in the country contrary to me — a sentiment which holds that slavery is not wrong, and therefore it goes for policy that does not propose dealing with it as a wrong. That policy is the Democratic policy, and that sentiment is the Democratic sentiment. If there be a doubt in the mind of any one of this vast audience that this is really the central idea of the Democratic party, in relation to this subject, I ask him to bear with me while I state a few things tending, as I think, to prove that proposition. In the first place, the leading man — I think I may do my friend Judge Douglas the honor of calling him such — advocating the present Democratic policy, never himself says it is wrong. He has the high distinction, so far as I know, of never having said slavery is either right or wrong. Almost everybody else says one or the other, but the Judge never does. If there be a man in the Democratic party who thinks it is wrong, and yet clings to that party, I suggest to him in the first place that his leader don't talk as he does, for he never says that it is wrong. In the second place, I suggest to him that if he will examine the policy proposed to be

carried forward, he will find that he carefully excludes the idea
that there is anything wrong in slavery. Perhaps that Democrat
who says he is as much opposed to slavery as I am, will tell me that
I am wrong about this. I wish him to examine his own course in
regard to this matter a moment, and then see if his opinion will not
be changed a little. You say it is wrong; but don't you constantly
object to anybody else saying so? Do you not constantly argue
that this is not the right place to oppose it? You say it must not be
opposed in the free states, because it is there; it must not be
opposed in politics, because that will make a fuss; it must not be
opposed in the pulpit, because it is not religion. Then where is the
place to oppose it? There is no suitable place to oppose it. There is
no place in the country to oppose this evil overspreading the
continent, which you say yourself is coming. Frank Blair and
Gratz Brown tried to get up a system of gradual emancipation in
Missouri, had an election in August and got beat, and you, Mr
Democrat, threw up your hat, and halloed 'Hurrah for
Democracy.' So I say again that in regard to the arguments that
are made, when Judge Douglas says he 'don't care whether slavery
is voted up or voted down,' whether he means that as an
individual expression of sentiment, or only as a sort of statement
of his views on national policy, it is alike true to say that he can
thus argue logically if he don't see anything wrong in it; but he
cannot say so logically if he admits that slavery is wrong. He
cannot say that he would as soon see a wrong voted up as voted
down. When Judge Douglas says that whoever, or whatever community, wants slaves, they have a right to have them, he is
perfectly logical if there is nothing wrong in the institution; but if
you admit that it is wrong, he cannot logically say that anybody
has a right to do wrong. When he says that slave property and
horse and hog property are alike to be allowed to go into the
territories, upon the principles of equality, he is reasoning truly, if
there is no difference between them as property; but if the one is
property, held rightfully, and the other is wrong, then there is no
equality between the right and wrong; so that, turn it in any way
you can, in all the arguments sustaining the Democratic policy,
and in that policy itself, there is a careful, studied exclusion of the
idea that there is anything wrong in slavery. Let us understand
this. I am not, just here, trying to prove that we are right and they
are wrong. I have been stating where we and they stand, and
trying to show what is the real difference between us; and I now

say that whenever we can get the question distinctly stated – can get all these men who believe that slavery is in some of these respects wrong, to stand and act with us in treating it as a wrong –then, and not till then, I think we will in some way come to an end of this slavery agitation.

From Lincoln's reply in the seventh and last joint debate.
                    Alton, Illinois, 15 October 1858

I have stated upon former occasions, and I may as well state again, what I understand to be the real issue in this controversy between Judge Douglas and myself. On the point of my wanting to make war between the free and the slave states, there has been no issue between us. So, too, when he assumes that I am in favor of introducing a perfect social and political equality between the white and black races. These are false issues, upon which Judge Douglas has tried to force the controversy. There is no foundation in truth for the charge that I maintain either of these propositions. The real issue in this controversy – the one pressing upon every mind – is the sentiment on the part of one class that looks upon the institution of slavery *as a wrong*, and of another class that *does not* look upon it as a wrong. The sentiment that contemplates the institution of slavery in this country as a wrong is the sentiment of the Republican party. It is the sentiment around which all their actions – all their arguments circle – from which all their propositions radiate. They look upon it as being a moral, social, and political wrong; and while they contemplate it as such, they nevertheless have due regard for its actual existence among us, and the difficulties of getting rid of it in any satisfactory way and to all the constitutional obligations thrown about it. Yet having a due regard for these, they desire a policy in regard to it that looks to its not creating any more danger. They insist that it should as far as may be, *be treated* as a wrong, and one of the methods of treating it as a wrong is to *make provision that it shall grow no larger*. They also desire a policy that looks to a peaceful end of slavery at some time, as being wrong. . .

On the other hand, I have said there is a sentiment which treats it as *not* being wrong. That is the Democratic sentiment of this day. I do not mean to say that every man who stands within that range positively asserts that it is right. That class will include all who positively assert that it is right, and all who like Judge

Douglas treat it as indifferent and do not say it is either right or wrong. These two classes of men fall within the general class of those who do not look upon it as wrong. And if there be among you anybody who supposes that he as a Democrat can consider himself 'as much opposed to slavery as anybody,' I would like to reason with him. You never treat it as a wrong. What other thing that you consider as a wrong, do you deal with as you deal with that? Perhaps you *say* it is wrong, *but your leader never does; and you quarrel with anybody who says it is wrong*. Although you pretend to say so yourself you can find no fit place to deal with it as a wrong. You must not say anything about it in the free states, *because it is not here*. You must not say anything about it in the slave states, *because it is there*. You must not say anything about it in the pulpit, because that is religion and has nothing to do with it. You must not say anything about it in politics, *because that will disturb the security of 'my place.'* There is no place to talk about it as being a wrong, although you say yourself it *is* a wrong. . .

That is the real issue. That is the issue that will continue in this country when these poor tongues of Judge Douglas and myself shall be silent. It is the eternal struggle between these two principles—right and wrong—throughout the world. They are the two principles that have stood face to face from the beginning of time; and will ever continue to struggle. The one is the common right of humanity and the other the divine right of kings. It is the same principle in whatever shape it develops itself. It is the same spirit that says: 'You work and toil and earn bread, and I'll eat it.' No matter in what shape it comes, whether from the mouth of a king who seeks to bestride the people of his own nation and live by the fruit of their labor, or from one race of men as an apology for enslaving another race, it is the same tyrannical principle. I was glad to express my gratitude at Quincy, and I re-express it here to Judge Douglas — *that he looks to no end of the institution of slavery*. That will help the people to see where the struggle really is. It will hereafter place with us all men who really do wish the wrong may have an end. And whenever we can get rid of the fog which obscures the real question — when we can get Judge Douglas and his friends to avow a policy looking to its perpetuation — we can get out from among them that class of men and bring them to the side of those who treat it as a wrong. Then there will soon be an end of it, and that end will be its 'ultimate extinction.' Whenever the issue can be distinctly made, and all extraneous matter thrown out so that men can fairly see the real difference between the parties, this controversy will soon be settled, and it will be done peaceably too. There will be no war, no violence. It will be placed again where the wisest and best men of the world placed it. Brooks of South Carolina once declared that when this Constitution was framed, its framers did not look to the institution existing until this day. When he said this, I think he stated a fact that is fully borne out by the history of the times. But he also said they were better and wiser men than the men of these days; yet the men of these days had experience which they had not, and by the invention of the cotton gin it became a necessity in this country that slavery should be perpetual. I now say that willingly or unwillingly, purposely or without purpose, Judge Douglas has been the most prominent instrument in changing the position of the institution of slavery which the fathers of the government expected to come to an end ere this – *and putting it upon Brooks's cotton gin basis* – placing it where he openly confesses he has no desire there shall ever be an end of it . . .

From Lincoln's last speech in the senatorial campaign.
Springfield, 30 October 1858

My friends, to-day closes the discussions of this canvass. The planting and the culture are over; and there remains but the preparation and the harvest.

I stand here surrounded by friends – some *political, all personal* friends, I trust. May I be indulged, in this closing scene, to say a few words of myself. I have borne a laborious, and, in some respects to myself, a painful part in the contest. Through all, I have neither assailed, nor wrestled with any part of the Constitution. The legal right of the Southern people to reclaim their fugitives I have constantly admitted. The legal right of Congress to interfere with their institution in the states I have constantly denied. In resisting the spread of slavery to new territory, and with that, what appears to me to be a tendency to subvert the first principle of free government itself, my whole effort has consisted. To the best of my judgment I have labored *for*, and not *against* the Union. As I have not felt, so I have not expressed any harsh sentiment towards our southern brethren. I have constantly declared, as I really believed, the only difference between them and us is the difference of circumstances.

I have meant to assail the motives of no party, or individual; and if I have, in any instance (of which I am not conscious) departed from my purpose, I regret it.

I have said that in some respects the contest has been painful to me. Myself, and those with whom I act, have been constantly accused of a purpose to destroy the Union; and bespattered with every imaginable odious epithet; and some who were friends, as it were but yesterday, have made themselves most active in this. I have cultivated patience, and made no attempt at a retort.

Ambition has been ascribed to me. God knows how sincerely I prayed from the first that this field of ambition might not be opened. I claim no insensibility to political honors; but to-day could the Missouri restriction be restored, and the whole slavery question replaced on the old ground of 'toleration' by *necessity* where it exists, with unyielding hostility to the spread of it, on principle, I would, in consideration, gladly agree, that Judge Douglas should never be *out*, and I never *in*, an office, so long as we both or either, live.

Letter to Henry Asbury.

Springfield, 19 November 1858

My dear Sir: Yours of the 13th was received some days ago. The fight must go on. The cause of civil liberty must not be surrendered at the end of *one*, or even one *hundred* defeats. Douglas had the ingenuity to be supported in the late contest both as the best means to *break down*, and to *uphold* the slave interest. No ingenuity can keep those antagonistic elements in harmony long. Another explosion will soon come. Yours truly

Chapter 5
The Making of the
First Republican President
1859–61

Having done remarkably well in its first presidential contest in 1856, the Republican party had high hopes of success in 1860. Equally, many Southerners dreaded the prospect of victory for the candidate of a purely Northern sectional party, dedicated to preventing the further extension of slavery.

Lincoln's speeches in 1859 and 1860 reinforced his growing reputation, none more so than the Cooper Institute speech in New York in February 1860. His brief essays in autobiography, prepared for campaign purposes, are notable both for what they say and what they omit. At the Republican Convention in Chicago, Lincoln had the advantage of being on home ground, and, as more prominent candidates faltered or canceled each other out, he emerged as the 'available man' – the first choice of comparatively few, but the second choice of many. He faced three other candidates, for the Democratic party had split North and South, and a Constitutional Union party was organized in defense of the Union. Lincoln observed the nineteenth-century convention that presidential candidates did not campaign on their own behalf. He won the election with barely 40 per cent of the popular vote (all of it gathered in the North), but with a comfortable majority in the electoral college.

At this time, there was a four-month gap between the election and the inauguration of a new president. In that period, seven states of the deep South seceded from the Union, and set up a new Southern Confederacy. As Lincoln made his way to Washington for his inauguration, the Union seemed to be crumbling around him, and the prospect of civil war loomed, although it was by no means certain at this stage.

For all his desire to avoid war, Lincoln ruled out any compromise on two basic principles: the preservation of the Union and the prevention of any further extension of slavery. No new president has ever faced a crisis of such proportions on taking office.

From a letter to Theodore Canisius, editor of the Illinois Staats-Anzeiger.

Springfield, 17 May 1859

Dear Sir: Your note asking, in behalf of yourself and other German citizens, whether I am for or against the constitutional provision in regard to naturalized citizens, lately adopted by Massachusetts; and whether I am for or against a fusion of the Republicans and other opposition elements, for the canvass of 1860, is received.

Massachusetts is a sovereign and independent state; and it is no privilege of mine to scold her for what she does. Still, if from what she *has done*, an inference is sought to be drawn as to what I *would do*, I may, without impropriety, speak out. I say then, that, as I understand the Massachusetts provision, I am against its adoption in Illinois, or in any other place , where I have a right to oppose it. Understanding the spirit of our institutions to aim at the *elevation* of men, I am opposed to whatever tends to *degrade* them. I have some little notoriety for commiserating the oppressed condition of the Negro; and I should be strangely inconsistent if I could favor any project for curtailing the existing rights of *white men*, even though born in different lands, and speaking different languages from myself . . .

From an address before the Wisconsin State Agricultural Society.
Milwaukee, 30 September 1859

The world is agreed that *labor* is the source from which human wants are mainly supplied. There is no dispute upon this point. From this point, however, men immediately diverge. Much disputation is maintained as to the best way of applying and controlling the labor element. By some it is assumed that labor is available only in connection with capital – that nobody labors, unless somebody else, owning capital, somehow, by the use of that capital, induces him to do it. Having assumed this, they proceed to consider whether it is best that capital shall *hire* laborers, and thus induce them to work by their own consent; or *buy* them, and drive them to it without their consent. Having proceeded so far they naturally conclude that all laborers are necessarily either *hired* laborers, or *slaves*. They further assume that whoever is once a *hired* laborer, is fatally fixed in that condition for life; and thence again that his condition is as bad as, or worse than, that of a slave. This is the '*mud-sill*' theory.

But another class of reasoners hold the opinion that there is no *such* relation between capital and labor, as assumed; and that there is no such thing as a freeman being fatally fixed for life, in the condition of a hired laborer, that both these assumptions are false, and all inferences from them groundless. They hold that labor is prior to, and independent of, capital; that, in fact, capital is the fruit of labor, and could never have existed if labor had not *first* existed – that labor can exist without capital, but that capital could never have existed without labor. Hence they hold that labor is the superior – greatly the superior – of capital.

They do not deny that there is, and probably always will be, *a* relation between labor and capital. The error, as they hold, is in assuming that the *whole* labor of the world exists within that relation. A few men own capital; and that few avoid labor themselves, and with their capital hire, or buy, another few to labor for them. A large majority belong to neither class – neither work for others, nor have others working for them. Even in all our slave states, except South Carolina, a majority of the whole people of all colors, are neither slaves nor masters. In these free states, a large majority are neither *hirers* nor *hired*. Men, with their families – wives, sons, and daughters – work for themselves, on their farms, in their houses, and in their shops, taking the whole product to themselves, and asking no favors of capital on the one hand, nor of hirelings or slaves on the other. It is not forgotten that a considerable number of persons mingle their own labor with capital; that is, labor with their own hands, and also buy slaves or hire freemen to labor for them; but this is only a *mixed*, and not a *distinct* class. No principle stated is disturbed by the existence of this mixed class. Again, as has already been said, the opponents of the 'mud-sill' theory insist that there is not, of necessity, any such thing as the free hired laborer being fixed to that condition for life. There is demonstration for saying this. Many independent men, in this assembly, doubtless a few years ago were hired laborers. And their case is almost if not quite the general rule.

The prudent, penniless beginner in the world labors for wages awhile, saves a surplus with which to buy tools or land for himself; then labors on his own account another while, and at length hires another new beginner to help him. This, say its advocates, is *free* labor – the just and generous, and prosperous system, which opens the way for all – gives hope to all, and energy, and progress, and improvement of condition to all. If any continue through life in the condition of the hired laborer, it is not the fault of the system but because of either a dependent nature which prefers it, or improvidence, folly, or singular misfortune. I have said this much about the elements of labor generally, as introductory to the consideration of a new phase which that element is in process of assuming. The old general rule was that *educated* people did not perform manual labor. They managed to eat their bread, leaving the toil of producing it to the uneducated. This was not an insupportable evil to the working bees, so long as the class of drones remained very small. But *now*, especially in these free states, nearly all are educated – quite too nearly all, to leave the labor of the uneducated, in any wise adequate to the support of the whole. It follows from this, that henceforth educated people must labor. Otherwise, education itself would become a positive and intolerable evil. No country can sustain, in idleness, more than a small percentage of its numbers. The great majority must labor at something productive. From these premises the problem springs, 'How can *labor* and *education* be the most satisfactorily combined?'

By the 'mud-sill' theory it is assumed that labor and education are incompatible; and any practical combination of them impossible. According to that theory, a blind horse upon a treadmill is a perfect illustration of what a laborer should be – all the better for being blind, that he could not read out of place, or kick understandingly. According to that theory, the education of laborers is not only useless, but pernicious, and dangerous. In fact, it is, in some sort, deemed a misfortune that laborers should have heads at all. Those same heads are regarded as explosive materials, only to be safely kept in damp places, as far as possible from that peculiar sort of fire which ignites them. A Yankee who could invent a strong-*handed* man without a head would receive the everlasting gratitude of the 'mud-sill' advocates.

But Free Labor says 'no!' Free Labor argues that, as the Author of man makes every individual with one head and one pair of hands, it was probably intended that heads and hands should co-operate as friends; and that that particular head should direct and control that particular pair of hands. As each man has one mouth to be fed, and one pair of hands to furnish food, it was probably intended that that particular pair of hands should feed that particular mouth – that each head is the natural guardian, director, and protector of the hands and mouth inseparably connected with it; and that being so, every head should be cultivated, and improved, by whatever will add to its capacity for performing its charge. In one word, Free Labor insists on universal education.

I have so far stated the opposite theories of 'Mud-Sill' and 'Free Labor' without declaring any preference of my own between them. On an occasion like this I ought not to declare any. I suppose, however, I shall not be mistaken in assuming as a fact that the people of Wisconsin prefer free labor, with its natural companion, education . . .

Letter to Jesse W. Fell, Bloomington, Illinois, with an autobiography.

Springfield, 20 December 1859

My dear Sir: Herewith is a little sketch, as you requested. There is not much of it, for the reason, I suppose, that there is not much of me.

If anything be made out of it, I wish it to be modest, and not to go beyond the material. If it were thought necessary to incorporate anything from any of my speeches, I suppose there would be no objection. Of course it must not appear to have been written by myself. Yours very truly

I was born 12th February 1809, in Hardin County, Kentucky. My parents were both born in Virginia, of undistinguished families – second families, perhaps I should say. My mother, who died in my tenth year, was of a family of the name of Hanks, some of whom now reside in Adams, and others in Macon counties, Illinois. My paternal grandfather, Abraham Lincoln, emigrated from Rockingham County, Virginia, to Kentucky, about 1781 or 1782, where, a year or two later, he was killed by Indians, not in battle, but by stealth when he was laboring to open a farm in the forest. His ancestors, who were Quakers, went to Virginia from Berks County, Pennsylvania. An effort to identify them with the New England family of the same name ended in nothing more definite than a similarity of Christian names in both families, such as Enoch, Levi, Mordecai, Solomon, Abraham, and the like.

My father, at the death of his father, was but six years of age; and he grew up, literally without education. He removed from Kentucky to what is now Spencer County, Indiana, in my eighth year. We reached our new home about the time the state came into the Union. It was a wild region, with many bears and other wild animals still in the woods. There I grew up. There were some schools, so called; but no qualification was ever required of a teacher, beyond 'readin, writin, and cipherin,' to the Rule of Three. If a straggler supposed to understand Latin happened to sojourn in the neighborhood, he was looked upon as a wizard. There was absolutely nothing to excite ambition for education. Of course when I came of age I did not know much. Still, somehow, I could read, write, and cipher to the Rule of Three; but that was all. I have not been to school since. The little advance I now have upon this store of education, I have picked up from time to time under the pressure of necessity.

I was raised to farm work, which I continued till I was twenty-two. At twenty-one I came to Illinois, and passed the first year in Illinois – Macon County. Then I got to New Salem (at that time in Sangamon, now in Menard County), where I remained a year as a sort of clerk in a store. Then came the Black-Hawk War; and I was elected a Captain of Volunteers – a success which gave me more pleasure than any I have had since. I went the campaign, was elated [sic], ran for the legislature the same year (1832), and was beaten – the only time I have been beaten by the people. The next, and three succeeding biennial elections, I was elected to the legislature. I was not a candidate afterwards. During the legislative period I had studied law, and removed to Springfield to practice it. In 1846 I was once elected to the lower House of Congress. Was not a candidate for re-election. From 1849 to 1854, both inclusive, practiced law more assiduously than ever before. Always a Whig in politics, and generally on the Whig electoral tickets, making active canvasses. I was losing interest in politics, when the repeal of the Missouri Compromise aroused me again. What I have done since then is pretty well known.

If any personal description of me is thought desirable, it may be said I am, in height, six feet four inches, nearly; lean in flesh, weighing, on an average, one hundred and eighty pounds; dark complexion, with coarse black hair, and gray eyes – no other marks or brands recollected. Yours very truly

From an address at Cooper Institute.
                    New York City, 27 February 1860

. . . If any man at this day sincerely believes that a proper division of local from federal authority, or any part of the Constitution, forbids the federal government to control as to slavery in the federal territories, he is right to say so, and to enforce his position by all truthful evidence and fair argument which he can. But he has no right to mislead others, who have less access to history, and less leisure to study it, into the false belief that 'our fathers, who framed the government under which we live,' were of the same opinion – thus substituting falsehood and deception for truthful evidence and fair argument. If any man at this day sincerely believes 'our fathers who framed the government under which we live,' used and applied principles, in other cases, which ought to have led them to understand that a proper division of local from federal authority or some part of the Constitution, forbids the federal government to control as to slavery in the federal territories, he is right to say so. But he should, at the same time, brave the responsibility of declaring that, in his opinion, he understands their principles better than they did themselves; and especially should he not shirk that responsibility by asserting that they 'understood the question just as well, and even better, than we do now.'

But enough! *Let all who believe that 'our fathers, who framed the government under which we live, understood this question just as well, and even better, than we do now,' speak as they spoke, and act as they acted upon it. This is all Republicans ask – all Republicans desire – in relation to slavery. As those fathers marked it, so let it be again marked, as an evil not to be extended, but to be tolerated and protected only because of and so far as its actual presence among us makes that toleration and protection a necessity. Let all the guarantees those fathers gave it, be, not grudgingly, but fully and fairly maintained.* For this Republicans contend, and with this, so far as I know or believe, they will be content.

And now, if they would listen — as I suppose they will not — I would address a few words to the southern people.

I would say to them: You consider yourselves a reasonable and just people; and I consider that in the general qualities of reason and justice you are not inferior to any other people. Still, when you speak of us Republicans, you do so only to denounce us as reptiles, or, at the best, as no better than outlaws. You will grant a hearing to pirates or murderers, but nothing like it to 'Black Republicans.' In all your contentions with one another, each of you deems an unconditional condemnation of 'Black Republicanism' as the first thing to be attended to. Indeed, such condemnation of us seems to be an indispensable prerequisite — license, so to speak — among you to be admitted or permitted to speak at all. Now, can you, or not, be prevailed upon to pause and to consider whether this is quite just to us, or even to yourselves? Bring forward your charges and specifications, and then be patient long enough to hear us deny or justify.

You say we are sectional. We deny it. That makes an issue; and the burden of proof is upon you. You produce your proof; and what is it? Why, that our party has no existence in your section — gets no votes in your section. The fact is substantially true; but does it prove the issue? If it does, then in case we should, without change of principle, begin to get votes in your section, we should thereby cease to be sectional. You cannot escape this conclusion; and yet, are you willing to abide by it? If you are, you will probably soon find that we have ceased to be sectional, for we shall get votes in your section this very year. You will then begin to discover, as the truth plainly is, that your proof does not touch the issue. The fact that we get no votes in your section is a fact of your making, and not of ours. And if there be fault in that fact, that fault is primarily yours, and remains so until you show that we repel you by some wrong principle or practice. If we do repel you by any wrong principle or practice, the fault is ours; but this brings you to where you ought to have started — to a discussion of the right or wrong of our principle. If our principle, put in practice, would wrong your section for the benefit of ours, or for any other object, then our principle, and we with it, are sectional, and are justly opposed and denounced as such. Meet us, then, on the question of whether our principle, put in practice, would wrong your section; and so meet us as if it were possible that something may be said on our side. Do you accept the challenge?

No! Then you really believe that the principle which 'our fathers who framed the government under which we live' thought so clearly right as to adopt it, and indorse it again and again, upon their official oaths, is in fact so clearly wrong as to demand your condemnation without a moment's consideration.

Some of you delight to flaunt in our faces the warning against sectional parties given by Washington in his Farewell Address. Less than eight years before Washington gave that warning, he had, as President of the United States, approved and signed an Act of Congress, enforcing the prohibition of slavery in the Northwestern Territory, which act embodied the policy of the government upon that subject up to and at that very moment he penned that warning; and about one year after he penned it, he wrote Lafayette that he considered that prohibition a wise measure, expressing in the same connection his hope that we should at some time have a confederacy of free states.

Bearing this in mind, and seeing that sectionalism has since arisen upon this same subject, is that warning a weapon in your hands aginst us, or in our hands against you? Could Washington himself speak, would he cast the blame of that sectionalism upon us, who sustain his policy, or upon you who repudiate it? We respect that warning of Washington, and we commend it to you, together with his example pointing to the right application of it.

But you say you are conservative – eminently conservative – while we are revolutionary, destructive, or something of the sort. What is conservatism? Is it not adherence to the old and tried, against the new and untried? We stick to, contend for, the identical old policy on the point in controversy which was adopted by 'our fathers who framed the government under which we live'; while you with one accord reject, and scout, and spit upon that old policy, and insist upon substituting something new. True, you disagree among yourselves as to what that substitute shall be. You are divided on new propositions and plans, but you are unanimous in rejecting and denouncing the old policy of the fathers. Some of you are for reviving the foreign slave trade; some for a congressional slave-code for the territories; some for Congress forbidding the territories to prohibit slavery within their limits; some for maintaining slavery in the territories through the judiciary; some for the 'gur-reat pur-rinciple' that 'if one man would enslave another, no third man should object,' fantastically called 'Popular Sovereignty'; but never a man among you in favor of federal prohibition of slavery in federal territories, according to the practice of 'our fathers who framed the government under which we live.' Not one of all your various plans can show a precedent or an advocate in the century within which our government originated. Consider, then, whether your claim of conservatism for yourselves, and your charge of destructiveness against us, are based on the most clear and stable foundations.

Again, you say we have made the slavery question more prominent than it formerly was. We deny it. We admit that it is more prominent, but we deny that we made it so. It was not we, but you, who discarded the old policy of the fathers. We resisted, and still resist, your innovation; and thence comes the greater prominence of the question. Would you have that question reduced to its former proportions? Go back to that old policy. What has been will be again, under the same conditions. If you would have the peace of the old times, readopt the precepts and policy of the old times.

You charge that we stir up insurrections among your slaves. We deny it; and what is your proof? Harper's Ferry! John Brown! John Brown was no Republican; and you have failed to implicate a single Republican in his Harper's Ferry enterprise.[1] If any member of our party is guilty in that matter, you know it or you do not know it. If you do know it, you are inexcusable for not designating the man and proving the fact. If you do not know it, you are inexcusable for asserting it, and especially for persisting in the assertion after you have tried and failed to make the proof. You need not be told that persisting in a charge which one does not know to be true, is simply malicious slander.

Some of you admit that no Republican designedly aided or encouraged the Harper's Ferry affair; but still insist that our doctrines and declarations necessarily lead to such results. We do not believe it. We know we hold to no doctrine, and make no declaration, which were not held to and made by 'our fathers who framed the government under which we live.' You never dealt fairly by us in relation to this affair. When it occurred, some important state elections were near at hand, and you were in evident glee with the belief that, by charging the blame upon us

[1] Brown's fanatical raid on the United States armory and arsenal at Harper's Ferry, Virginia (now West Virginia), on 16–18 October 1859, which he hoped would start a slave insurrection. Convicted of treason to the State of Virginia and conspiracy, Brown was hanged on 2 December 1859.

you could get an advantage of us in those elections. The elections came, and your expectations were not quite fulfilled. Every Republican man knew that, as to himself at least, your charge was a slander, and he was not much inclined by it to cast his vote in your favor. Republican doctrines and declarations are accompanied with a continual protest against any interference whatever with your slaves, or with you about your slaves. Surely, this does not encourage them to revolt. True, we do, in common with 'our fathers, who framed the government under which we live,' declare our belief that slavery is wrong; but the slaves do not hear us declare even this. For anything we say or do, the slaves would scarcely know there is a Republican party. I believe they would not, in fact, generally know it but for your misrepresentation of us, in their hearing. In your political contests among yourselves, each faction charges the other with sympathy with Black Republicanism; and then, to give point to the charge, defines Black Republicanism to simply be insurrection, blood and thunder among the slaves.

Slave insurrections are no more common now than they were before the Republican party was organized. What induced the Southampton insurrection, twenty-eight years ago, in which at least three times as many lives were lost as at Harper's Ferry? You can scarcely stretch your very elastic fancy to the conclusion that Southampton was 'got up by Black Republicanism.' In the present state of things in the United States, I do not think a general, or even a very extensive slave insurrection, is possible. The indispensable concert of action cannot be attained. The slaves have no means of rapid communication; nor can incendiary freemen, black or white, supply it. The explosive materials are everywhere in parcels; but there neither are, nor can be supplied, the indispensable connecting trains.

Much is said by southern people about the affection of slaves for their masters and mistresses; and a part of it, at least, is true. A plot for an uprising could scarcely be devised and communicated to twenty individuals before some one of them, to save the life of a favorite master or mistress, would divulge it. This is the rule; and the slave revolution in Haiti was not an exception to it, but a case occurring under peculiar circumstances. The gunpowder plot of British history, though not connected with slaves, was more in point. In that case, only about twenty were admitted to the secret; and yet one of them, in his anxiety to save a friend, betrayed the plot to that friend, and, by consequence, averted the calamity. Occasional poisonings from the kitchen, and open or stealthy assassinations in the field, and local revolts extending to a score or so, will continue to occur as the natural results of slavery; but no general insurrection of slaves, as I think, can happen in this country for a long time. Whoever much fears, or much hopes for such an event, will be alike disappointed.

In the language of Mr Jefferson, uttered many years ago, 'It is still in our power to direct the process of emancipation, and deportation, peaceably, and in such slow degrees, as that the evil will wear off insensibly; and their places be, *pari passu*, filled up by free white laborers. If, on the contrary, it is left to force itself on, human nature must shudder at the prospect held up.'

Mr Jefferson did not mean to say, nor do I, that the power of emancipation is in the federal government. He spoke of Virginia; and, as to the power of emancipation, I speak of the slaveholding states only. The federal government, however, as we insist, has the power of restraining the extension of the institution – the power to insure that a slave insurrection shall never occur on any American soil which is now free from slavery.

John Brown's effort was peculiar. It was not a slave insurrection. It was an attempt by white men to get up a revolt among slaves, in which the slaves refused to participate. In fact, it was so absurd that the slaves, with all their ignorance, saw plainly enough it could not succeed. That affair, in its philosophy, corresponds with the many attempts, related in history, at the assassination of kings and emperors. An enthusiast broods over the oppression of a people till he fancies himself commissioned by Heaven to liberate them. He ventures the attempt, which ends in little else than his own execution. Orsini's attempt on Louis Napoleon, and John Brown's attempt at Harper's Ferry were, in their philosophy, precisely the same. The eagerness to cast blame on old England in the one case, and on New England in the other, does not disprove the sameness of the two things.

And how much would it avail you, if you could, by the use of John Brown, Helper's book,[1] and the like, break up the Republican organization? Human action can be modified to some extent, but human nature cannot be changed. There is a judgment and a feeling

---

[1] *The Impending Crisis of the South*, by Hinton Rowan Helper (1857), was an anti-slavery argument, based on economics, by a North Carolinian. The book, and especially its endorsement by many prominent Republicans, infuriated the South.

against slavery in this nation, which cast at least a million and a half of votes. You cannot destroy that judgment and feeling – that sentiment – by breaking up the political organization which rallies around it. You can scarcely scatter and disperse an army which has been formed into order in the face of your heaviest fire; but if you could, how much would you gain by forcing the sentiment which created it out of the peaceful channel of the ballot-box, into some other channel? What would that other channel probably be? Would the number of John Browns be lessened or enlarged by the operation?

But you will break up the Union rather than submit to a denial of your constitutional rights.

That has a somewhat reckless sound; but it would be palliated, if not fully justified, were we proposing, by the mere force of numbers, to deprive you of some right, plainly written down in the Constitution. But we are proposing no such thing.

When you make these declarations, you have a specific and well-understood allusion to an assumed constitutional right of yours, to take slaves into the federal territories, and to hold them there as property. But no such right is specifically written in the Constitution. That instrument is literally silent about any such right. We, on the contrary, deny that such a right has any existence in the Constitution, even by implication.

Your purpose, then, plainly stated, is, that you will destroy the government, unless you be allowed to construe and enforce the Constitution as you please, on all points in dispute between you and us. You will rule or ruin in all events.

This, plainly stated, is your language. Perhaps you will say the Supreme Court has decided the disputed constitutional question in your favor. Not quite so. But waiving the lawyer's distinction between dictum and decision, the Court have decided the question for you in a sort of way. The Court have substantially said, it is your constitutional right to take slaves into the federal territories, and to hold them there as property. When I say the decision was made in a sort of way, I mean it was made in a divided court, by a bare majority of the Judges, and they not quite agreeing with one another in the reasons for making it; that it is so made as that its avowed supporters disagree with one another about its meaning, and that it was mainly based upon a mistaken statement of fact – the statement in the opinion that 'the right of property in a slave is distinctly and expressly affirmed in the Constitution.'

An inspection of the Constitution will show that the right of property in a slave is not '*distinctly* and *expressly* affirmed' in it. Bear in mind, the Judges do not pledge their judicial opinion that such right is *impliedly* affirmed in the Constitution; but they pledge their veracity that it is '*distinctly* and *expressly*' affirmed there – 'distinctly,' that is, not mingled with anything else – 'expressly,' that is, in words meaning just that, without the aid of any inference, and susceptible of no other meaning.

If they had only pledged their judicial opinion that such right is affirmed in the instrument by implication, it would be open to others to show that neither the word 'slave' nor 'slavery' is to be found in the Constitution, nor the word 'property' even, in any connection with language alluding to the things slave, or slavery, and that wherever in that instrument the slave is alluded to, he is called a 'person'; and wherever his master's legal right in relation to him is alluded to, it is spoken of as 'service or labor which may be due' – as a debt payable in service or labor. Also, it would be open to show, by contemporaneous history, that this mode of alluding to slaves and slavery, instead of speaking of them, was employed on purpose to exclude from the Constitution the idea that there could be property in man.

To show all this is easy and certain.

When this obvious mistake of the Judges shall be brought to their notice, is it not reasonable to expect that they will withdraw the mistaken statement, and reconsider the conclusion based upon it?

And then it is to be remembered that 'our fathers, who framed the government under which we live' – the men who made the Constitution – decided this same constitutional question in our favor, long ago – decided it without division among themselves, when making the decision; without division among themselves about the meaning of it after it was made, and, so far as any evidence is left, without basing it upon any mistaken statement of facts.

Under all these circumstances, do you really feel yourselves justified to break up this government, unless such a court decision as yours is, shall be at once submitted to as a conclusive and final rule of political action? But you will not abide the election of a Republican President! In that supposed event, you say, you will destroy the Union; and then, you say, the great crime of having destroyed it will be upon us! That is cool. A highwayman holds a pistol to my ear, and mutters through his teeth, 'Stand and deliver, or I shall kill you, and then you will be a murderer!'

To be sure, what the robber demanded of me – my money – was my own; and I had a clear right to keep it; but it was no more my own than my vote is my own; and the threat of death to me, to extort my money, and the threat of destruction to the Union, to extort my vote, can scarcely be distinguished in principle.

A few words now to Republicans. *It is exceedingly desirable that all parts of this great Confederacy shall be at peace, and in harmony, one with another. Let us Republicans do our part to have it so. Even though much provoked, let us do nothing through passion and ill temper. Even though the southern people will not so much as listen to us, let us calmly consider their demands, and yield to them, if, in our deliberate view of our duty, we possibly can.* Judging by all they say and do, and by the subject and nature of their controversy with us, let us determine, if we can, what will satisfy them.

Will they be satisfied if the territories be unconditionally surrendered to them? We know they will not. In all their present complaints against us, the territories are scarcely mentioned. Invasions and insurrections are the rage now. Will it satisfy them, if, in the future, we have nothing to do with invasions and insurrections? We know it will not. We so know, because we know we never had anything to do with invasions and insurrections; and yet this total abstaining does not exempt us from the charge and the denunciation.

The question recurs, what will satisfy them? Simply this: We must not only let them alone, but we must, somehow, convince them that we do let them alone. This, we know by experience, is no easy task. We have been so trying to convince them from the very beginning of our organization, but with no success. In all our platforms and speeches we have constantly protested our purpose to let them alone; but this has had no tendency to convince them. Alike unavailing to convince them, is the fact that they have never detected a man of us in any attempt to disturb them.

These natural, and apparently adequate means all failing, what will convince them? This, and this only: cease to call slavery *wrong*, and join them in calling it *right*. And this must be done thoroughly – done in *acts* as well as in *words*. Silence will not be tolerated – we must place ourselves avowedly with them. Senator Douglas's new sedition law must be enacted and enforced, suppressing all declarations that slavery is wrong, whether made in politics, in presses, in pulpits, or in private. We must arrest and return their fugitive slaves with greedy pleasure. We must pull down our free state constitutions. The whole atmosphere must be disinfected from all taint of opposition to slavery, before they will cease to believe that all their troubles proceed from us.

I am quite aware they do not state their case precisely in this way. Most of them would probably say to us: 'Let us alone, *do* nothing to us, and *say* what you please about slavery.' But we do let them alone – have never disturbed them – so that, after all, it is what we say, which dissatisfies them. They will continue to accuse us of doing, until we cease saying.

I am also aware they have not, as yet, in terms, demanded the overthrow of our free-state constitutions. Yet those constitutions declare the wrong of slavery, with more solemn emphasis, than do all other sayings against it; and when all these other sayings shall have been silenced, the overthrow of these constitutions will be demanded, and nothing be left to resist the demand. It is nothing to the contrary, that they do not demand the whole of this just now. Demanding what they do, and for the reason they do, they can voluntarily stop nowhere short of this consummation. Holding, as they do, that slavery is morally right, and socially elevating, they cannot cease to demand a full recognition of it, as a legal right, and a social blessing.

Nor can we justifiably withhold this, on any ground save our conviction that slavery is wrong. If slavery is right, all words, acts, laws, and constitutions against it, are themselves wrong, and should be silenced and swept away. If it is right, we cannot justly object to its nationality – its universality; if it is wrong, they cannot justly insist upon its extension – its enlargement. All they ask, we could readily grant, if we thought slavery right; all we ask, they could as readily grant, if they thought it wrong. Their thinking it right, and our thinking it wrong, is the precise fact upon which depends the whole controversy. Thinking it right, as they do, they are not to blame for desiring its full recognition, as being right; but, thinking it wrong, as we do, can we yield to them? Can we cast our votes with their view, and against our own? In view of our moral, social, and political responsibilities, can we do this?

Wrong as we think slavery is, we can yet afford to let it alone where it is, because that much is due to the necessity arising from its actual presence in the nation; but can we, while our votes will prevent it, allow it to spread into the national territories, and to overrun us here in these free states? If our sense of duty forbids this, then let us stand by our duty, fearlessly and effectively. Let us be diverted by none of those sophistical contrivances wherewith we are so industriously plied and belabored – contrivances such as groping for some middle ground between the right and the wrong, vain as the search for a man who should be neither a living man nor a dead man – such as a policy of 'don't care' on a question about which all true men do care – such as Union appeals beseeching true Union men to yield to Disunionists, reversing the divine rule, and calling, not the sinners, but the righteous to repentance – such as invocations to Washington, imploring men to unsay what Washington said, and undo what Washington did.

Neither let us be slandered from our duty by false accusations against us, nor frightened from it by menaces of destruction to the government nor of dungeons to ourselves. LET US HAVE FAITH THAT RIGHT MAKES MIGHT, AND IN THAT FAITH, LET US, TO THE END, DARE TO DO OUR DUTY AS WE UNDERSTAND IT.

Letter to Samuel Galloway, Ohio Republican leader.
                                        Chicago, 24 March 1860

My dear Sir: I am here attending a trial in court. Before leaving home I received your kind letter of the 15th. Of course I am gratified to know I have friends in Ohio who are disposed to give me the highest evidence of their friendship and confidence. Mr Parrott of the legislature, had written me to the same effect. If I have any chance, it consists mainly in the fact that the *whole* opposition would vote for me if nominated. (I don't mean to include the pro-slavery opposition of the South, of course.) My name is new in the field; and I suppose I am not the *first* choice of a very great many. Our policy, then, is to give no offense to others – leave them in a mood to come to us, if they shall be compelled to give up their first love. This too is dealing justly with all, and leaving us in a mood to support heartily whoever shall be nominated. I believe I have once before told you that I especially wish to do no ungenerous thing towards Governor Chase,[1] because he gave us his sympathy in 1858, when scarcely any other distinguished man did. Whatever you may do for me, consistently with these suggestions, will be appreciated, and gratefully remembered.

Please write me again. Yours very truly

[1] Salmon P. Chase, whom Lincoln would appoint Secretary of the Treasury in 1861.

Letter to George Ashmun, President of the Republican National Convention, accepting the presidential nomination.

Springfield, 23 May 1860

Sir: I accept the nomination tendered me by the convention over which you presided, and of which I am formally apprised in the letter of yourself and others, acting as a committee of the convention, for that purpose.

The declaration of principles and sentiments, which accompanies your letter, meets my approval; and it shall be my care not to violate, or disregard it, in any part.

Imploring the assistance of Divine Providence, and with due regard to the views and feelings of all who were represented in the convention; to the rights of all the states, and territories, and people of the nation; to the inviolability of the Constitution, and the perpetual union, harmony, and prosperity of all, I am most happy to co-operate for the practical success of the principles declared by the convention. Your obliged friend, and fellow-citizen

An autobiography in the third person, written for John L. Scripps of the Chicago *Press and Tribune.*

Springfield, June 1860

Abraham Lincoln was born 12th Feb. 1809, then in Hardin, now in the more recently formed county of Larue, Kentucky. His father, Thomas, and grandfather, Abraham, were born in Rockingham County, Virginia, whither their ancestors had come from Berks County, Pennsylvania. His lineage has been traced no farther back than this. The family were originally Quakers, though in later times they have fallen away from the peculiar habits of that people. The grandfather Abraham had four brothers – Isaac, Jacob, John, and Thomas. So far as known, the descendants of Jacob and John are still in Virginia. Isaac went to a place near where Virginia, North Carolina, and Tennessee, join; and his descendants are in that region. Thomas came to Kentucky, and after many years, died there, whence his descendants went to Missouri. Abraham, grandfather of the subject of this sketch, came to Kentucky, and was killed by Indians about the year 1784. He left a widow, three sons, and two daughters. The eldest son, Mordecai, remained in Kentucky till late in life, when he removed to Hancock County, Illinois, where soon after he died, and where several of his descendants still reside. The second son, Josiah, removed at an early day to a place on Blue River, now within Harrison [Hancock] County, Indiana; but no recent information of him, or his family, has been obtained. The eldest sister, Mary, married Ralph Crume and some of her descendants are now known to be in Breckenridge County, Kentucky. The second sister, Nancy, married William Brumfield, and her family are not known to have left Kentucky, but there is no recent information from them. Thomas, the youngest son, and father of the present subject, by the early death of his father, and very narrow circumstances of his mother, even in childhood was a wandering laboring boy, and grew up literally without education. He never did more in the way of writing than to bunglingly sign his own name. Before he was grown, he passed one year as a hired hand with his Uncle Isaac on Watauga, a branch of the Holsteen [Holston] River. Getting back into Kentucky, and having reached his twenty-eighth year, he married Nancy Hanks — mother of the present subject — in the year 1806. She also was born in Virginia; and relatives of hers of the name of Hanks, and of other names, now reside in Coles, in Macon, and in Adams counties, Illinois, and also in Iowa. The present subject has no brother or sister of the whole or half blood. He had a sister, older than himself, who was grown and married, but died many years ago, leaving no child. Also a brother, younger than himself, who died in infancy. Before leaving Kentucky he and his sister were sent for short periods to A.B.C. schools, the first kept by Zachariah Riney, and the second by Caleb Hazel.

At this time his father resided on Knob Creek, on the road from Bardstown, Kentucky, to Nashville, Tennessee, at a point three or three and a half miles south or south-west of Atherton's ferry on the Rolling Fork. From this place he removed to what is now Spencer County, Indiana, in the autumn of 1816, A.[1] then being in his eighth year. This removal was partly on account of slavery; but chiefly on account of the difficulty in land titles in Kentucky. He settled in an unbroken forest; and the clearing away of surplus wood was the great task ahead. A. though very young was large of his age, and had an axe put into his hands at once; and from that till within his twenty-third year, he was almost constantly

---

[1] Throughout this sketch 'A.' stands for the writer.

handling that most useful instrument – less, of course, in plowing and harvesting seasons. At this place A. took an early start as a hunter, which was never much improved afterwards. (A few days before the completion of his eighth year, in the absence of his father, a flock of wild turkeys approached the new log cabin, and A. with a rifle gun, standing inside, shot through a crack, and killed one of them. He has never since pulled a trigger on any larger game.) In the autumn of 1818 his mother died; and a year afterwards his father married Mrs Sally Johnston, at Elizabethtown, Kentucky – a widow, with three children of her first marriage. She proved a good and kind mother to A. and is still living in Coles County, Illinois. There were no children of this second marriage. His father's residence continued at the same place in Indiana till 1830. While here A. went to A.B.C. schools by littles, kept successively by Andrew Crawford, — Sweeney, and Azel W. Dorsey. He does not remember any other. The family of Mr Dorsey now reside in Schuyler County, Illinois. A. now thinks that the aggregate of all his schooling did not amount to one year. He was never in a college or academy as a student; and never inside of a college or academy building till since he had a law license. What he has in the way of education, he has picked up. After he was twenty-three, and had separated from his father, he studied English grammar, imperfectly of course, but so as to speak and write as well as he now does. He studied and nearly mastered the six books of Euclid, since he was a member of Congress. He regrets his want of education, and does what he can to supply the want. In his tenth year he was kicked by a horse, and apparently killed for a time. When he was nineteen, still residing in Indiana, he made his first trip upon a flat-boat to New Orleans. He was a hired hand merely; and he and a son of the owner, without other assistance, made the trip. The nature of part of the cargo-load, as it was called, made it necessary for them to linger and trade along the Sugar coast – and one night they were attacked by seven Negroes with intent to kill and rob them. They were hurt some in the *mêlée*, but succeeded in driving the Negroes from the boat, and then 'cut cable,' 'weighed anchor,' and left.

March 1st 1830: A. having just completed his twenty-first year, his father and family, with the families of the two daughters and sons-in-law of his stepmother, left the old homestead in Indiana, and came to Illinois. Their mode of conveyance was wagons drawn by ox-teams, or [sic] A. drove one of the teams. They reached the county of Macon, and stopped there some time within the same month of March. His father and family settled a new place on the north side of the Sangamon River, at the junction of the timber-land and prairie, about ten miles westerly from Decatur. Here they built a log cabin, into which they removed, and made sufficient of rails to fence ten acres of ground, fenced and broke the ground, and raised a crop of sown corn upon it the same year. These are, or are supposed to be, the rails about which so much is being said just now, though they are far from being the first, or only rails ever made by A.

The sons-in-law were temporarily settled at other places in the county. In the autumn all hands were greatly afflicted with ague and fever, to which they had not been used, and by which they were greatly discouraged – so much so that they determined on leaving the county. They remained, however, through the succeeding winter, which was the winter of the very celebrated 'deep snow' of Illinois. During that winter, A., together with his stepmother's son, John D. Johnston, and John Hanks, yet residing in Macon County, hired themselves to one Denton Offutt, to take a flat-boat from Beardstown, Illinois, to New Orleans; and for that purpose, were to join him – Offutt – at Springfield, Illinois, so soon as the snow should go off. When it did go off, which was about the 1st of March 1831 – the county was so flooded as to make traveling by land impracticable; to obviate which difficulty they purchased a large canoe and came down the Sangamon River in it. This is the time and the manner of A.'s first entrance into Sangamon County. They found Offutt at Springfield, but learned from him that he had failed in getting a boat at Beardstown. This led to their hiring themselves to him at $12 per month, each; and getting the timber out of the trees and building a boat at old Sangamon Town on the Sangamon River, seven miles north-west of Springfield, which boat they took to New Orleans, substantially upon the old contract. It was in connection with this boat that occurred the ludicrous incident of sewing up the hogs' eyes. Offutt bought thirty odd large, fat, live hogs, but found difficulty in driving them from where [he] purchased them to the boat, and thereupon conceived the whim that he could sew up their eyes and drive them where he pleased. No sooner thought of than decided, he put his hands, including A. at the job, which they completed – all but the driving. In their blind condition they could not be driven out of the lot or field they were in. This expedient failing, they were tied and hauled on carts to the boat. It was near the Sangamon River, within what is now Menard County.

During this boat enterprise acquaintance with Offutt, who was previously an entire stranger, he conceived a liking for A. and believing he could turn him to account, he contracted with him to act as clerk for him, on his return from New Orleans, in charge of a store and mill at New Salem, then in Sangamon, now in Menard County. Hanks had not gone to New Orleans, but having a family, and being likely to be detained from home longer than at first expected, had turned back from St Louis. He is the same John Hanks who now engineers the 'rail enterprise' at Decatur; and is a first cousin to A.'s mother. A.'s father, with his own family and others mentioned, had, in pursuance of their intention, removed from Macon to Coles County. John D. Johnston, the stepmother's son, went to them; and A. stopped indefinitely, and, for the first time, as it were, by himself at New Salem, before mentioned. This was in July 1831. Here he rapidly made acquaintances and friends. In less than a year Offutt's business was failing – had almost failed – when the Black-Hawk War of 1832 broke out. A. joined a volunteer company, and to his own surprise, was elected captain of it. He says he has not since had any success in life which gave him so much satisfaction. He went the campaign, served near three months, met the ordinary hardships of such an expedition, but was in no battle. He now owns in Iowa the land upon which his own warrants for this service were located. Returning from the campaign, and encouraged by his great popularity among his immediate neighbors, he, the same year, ran for the legislature and was beaten – his own precinct, however, casting its votes 277 for and 7 against him. And this too while he was an avowed Clay man, and the precinct the autumn afterwards, giving a majority of 115 to Genl. Jackson over Mr Clay. This was the only time A. was ever beaten on a direct vote of the people. He was now without means and out of business, but was anxious to remain with his friends who had treated him with so much generosity, especially as he had nothing elsewhere to go to. He studied what he should do – thought of learning the blacksmith trade – thought of trying to study law – rather thought he could not succeed at that without a better education. Before long, strangely enough, a man offered to sell and did sell, to A. and another as poor as himself, an old stock of goods, upon credit. They opened as merchants; and he says that was *the* store. Of course they did nothing but get deeper

and deeper in debt. He was appointed postmaster at New Salem
– the office being too insignificant to make his politics an
objection. The store winked out. The surveyor of Sangamon
offered to depute to A. that portion of his work which was within
his part of the county. He accepted, procured a compass and
chain, studied Flint, and Gibson a little, and went at it. This
procured bread, and kept soul and body together. The election of
1834 came, and he was then elected to the legislature by the
highest vote cast for any candidate. Major John T. Stuart, then in
full practice of the law, was also elected. During the canvass, in a
private conversation he encouraged A. to study law. After the
election he borrowed books of Stuart, took them home with him,
and went at it in good earnest. He studied with nobody. He still
mixed in the surveying to pay board and clothing bills. When the
legislature met, the law books were dropped, but were taken up
again at the end of the session. He was re-elected in 1836, 1838,
and 1840. In the autumn of 1836 he obtained a law license, and
on 15th April 1837 removed to Springfield, and commenced the
practice, his old friend Stuart, taking him into partnership. March
3rd 1837, by a protest entered upon the Illinois House Journal of
that date, at pages 817, 818, A. with Dan Stone, another
representative of Sangamon, briefly defined his position on the
slavery question; and so far as it goes, it was then the same that it
is now. The protest is as follows – (here insert it).[1] In 1838, and
1840, Mr L.'s party in the legislature voted for him as speaker; but
being in the minority, he was not elected. After 1840 he declined a
re-election to the legislature. He was on the Harrison electoral

---

[1] Text of the protest, which was read before the House and ordered to be spread on the
Journal, is as follows:

'Resolutions upon the subject of domestic slavery having passed both branches of the
General Assembly at its present session, the undersigned hereby protest against the passage
of the same.

'They believe that the institution of slavery is founded on both injustice and bad policy;
but that the promulgation of abolition doctrines tends rather to increase than to abate its
evils.

'They believe that the Congress of the United States has no power, under the
Constitution, to interfere with the institution of slavery in the different states.

'They believe that the Congress of the United States has the power, under the
Constitution, to abolish slavery in the District of Columbia; but that the power ought not
to be exercised unless at the request of the people of said District.

'The difference between these opinions and those contained in the said resolutions, is
their reason for entering this protest.'

DAN STONE,
A. LINCOLN,
Representatives from the County of Sangamon.

ticket in 1840, and on that of Clay in 1844, and spent much time and labor in both those canvasses. In November 1842 he was married to Mary, daughter of Robert S. Todd, of Lexington, Kentucky. They have three living children, all sons – born in 1843, one in 1850, and one in 1853. They lost one, who was born in 1846. In 1846, he was elected to the lower House of Congress, and served one term only, commencing in December 1847 and ending with the inauguration of Gen. Taylor, in March 1849. All the battles of the Mexican War had been fought before Mr L. took his seat in Congress, but the American army was still in Mexico, and the treaty of peace was not fully and formally ratified till the June afterwards. Much has been said of his course in Congress in regard to this war. A careful examination of the Journals and Congressional Globe shows that he voted for all the supply measures which came up, and for all the measures in any way favorable to the officers, soldiers, and their families, who conducted the war through; with this exception that some of these measures passed without yeas and nays, leaving no record as to how particular men voted. The Journals and Globe also show him voting that the war was unnecessarily and unconstitutionally begun by the President of the United States. This is the language of Mr Ashmun's amendment, for which Mr L. and nearly or quite all other Whigs of the H.R. voted.

Mr L.'s reasons for the opinion expressed by this vote were briefly that the President had sent Genl. Taylor into an inhabited part of the country belonging to Mexico, and not to the US and thereby had provoked the first act of hostility – in fact the commencement of the war; that the place, being the country bordering on the east bank of the Rio Grande, was inhabited by native Mexicans, born there under the Mexican government; and had never submitted to, nor been conquered by Texas, or the US nor transferred to either by treaty – that although Texas claimed the Rio Grande as her boundary, Mexico had never recognized it, the people on the ground had never recognized it, and neither Texas nor the US had ever enforced it – that there was a broad desert between that and the country over which Texas had actual control – that the country where hostilities commenced, having once belonged to Mexico, must remain so, until it was somehow legally transferred, which had never been done.

Mr L. thought the act of sending an armed force among the Mexicans, was *unnecessary*, inasmuch as Mexico was in no way molesting or menacing the US or the people thereof; and that it was *unconstitutional*, because the power of levying war is vested in Congress, and not in the President. He thought the principal motive for the act was to divert public attention from the surrender of 'Fifty-four, forty, or fight' to Great Britain, on the Oregon boundary question.

Mr L. was not a candidate for re-election. This was determined upon and declared before he went to Washington, in accordance with an understanding among Whig friends, by which Col. Hardin, and Col. Baker had each previously served a single term in the same District.

In 1848, during his term in Congress, he advocated Gen. Taylor's nomination for the Presidency, in opposition to all others, and also took an active part for his election after his nomination — speaking a few times in Maryland, near Washington, several times in Massachusetts, and canvassing quite fully his own district in Illinois, which was followed by a majority in the district of over 1,500 for Gen. Taylor.

Upon his return from Congress he went to the practice of the law with greater earnestness than ever before. In 1852 he was upon the Scott electoral ticket, and did something in the way of canvassing, but owing to the hopelessness of the cause in Illinois, he did less than in previous presidential canvasses.

In 1854, his profession had almost superseded the thought of politics in his mind, when the repeal of the Missouri Compromise aroused him as he had never been before.

In the autumn of that year he took the stump with no broader practical aim or object than to secure, if possible, the re-election of Hon. Richard Yates to Congress. His speeches at once attracted a more marked attention than they had ever before done. As the canvass proceeded, he was drawn to different parts of the state, outside of Mr Yates's district. He did not abandon the law, but gave his attention, by turns, to that and politics. The state agricultural fair was at Springfield that year, and Douglas was announced to speak there.

In the canvass of 1856, Mr L. made over fifty speeches, no one of which, so far as he remembers, was put in print. One of them was made at Galena, but Mr L. has no recollection of any part of it being printed; nor does he remember whether in that speech he said anything about a Supreme Court decision. He may have spoken upon that subject; and some of the newspapers may have reported him as saying what is now ascribed to him; but he thinks he could not have expressed himself as represented.

Letter to Anson G. Henry, an old friend now living in Oregon Territory.

Springfield, 4 July 1860

My dear Doctor: Your very agreeable letter of 15th May was received three days ago. We are just now receiving the first sprinkling of your Oregon election returns — not enough, I think, to indicate the result. We should be too happy if both Logan and Baker should triumph.

Long before this you have learned who was nominated at Chicago. We know not what a day may bring forth; but to-day it looks as if the Chicago ticket will be elected. I think the chances were more than equal that we could have beaten the Democracy *united*. Divided as it is, its chance appears indeed very slim.[1] But great is Democracy in resources; and it may yet give its fortunes a turn. It is under great temptation to do something; but what can it do which was not thought of, and found impracticable, at Charleston and Baltimore? The signs now are that Douglas and Breckinridge will each have a ticket in every state. They are driven to this to keep up their bombastic claims of *nationality*, and to avoid the charge of *sectionalism* which they have so much lavished upon us.

It is an amusing fact, after all Douglas has said about *nationality*, and *sectionalism*, that I had more votes from the southern section at Chicago, than he had at Baltimore! In fact, there was more of the southern section represented in Chicago, than in the Douglas rump concern at Baltimore!

Our boy,[2] in his tenth year (the baby when you left), has just had a hard and tedious spell of scarlet-fever; and he is not yet beyond all danger. I have a headache, and a sore throat upon me now, inducing me to suspect that I have an inferior type of the same thing.

Our eldest boy, Bob, has been away from us nearly a year at

---

[1] The Democratic party had split into northern and southern wings, the former nominating Stephen A. Douglas and Herschel V. Johnson, the latter John C. Breckinridge and Joseph Lane. The Constitutional Union party (Whig and Know Nothing) further divided the field by nominating John Bell and Edward Everett.

[2] William Wallace Lincoln, born 21 December 1850.

school, and will enter Harvard University this month. He promises very well, considering we never controlled him much.

Write again when you receive this. Mary joins in sending our kindest regards to Mrs H., yourself, and all the family. Your friend, as ever

Letter to George C. Latham, a young man who had attended Phillips Exeter Academy with Robert Lincoln.

Springfield, 22 July 1860

My dear George: I have scarcely felt greater pain in my life than on learning yesterday from Bob's letter, that you had failed to enter Harvard University. And yet there is very little in it, if you will allow no feeling of *discouragement* to seize, and prey upon you. It is a *certain* truth, that you *can* enter, and graduate in, Harvard University; and having made the attempt, you *must* succeed in it. *Must* is the word.

I know not how to aid you, save in the assurance of one of mature age, and much severe experience, that you *can* not fail, if you resolutely determine, that you *will* not.

The President of the institution can scarcely be other than a kind man; and doubtless he would grant you an interview, and point out the readiest way to remove, or overcome, the obstacles which have thwarted you.

In your temporary failure there is no evidence that you may not yet be a better scholar, and a more successful man in the great struggle of life, than many others who have entered college more easily.

Again I say let no feeling of discouragement prey upon you, and in the end you are sure to succeed.

With more than a common interest I subscribe myself, Very truly your friend

Letter to George D. Prentice, editor of the Louisville, Kentucky, Journal.

29 October 1860

My dear Sir: Yours of the 26th is just received. Your suggestion that I, in a certain event, shall write a letter, setting forth my conservative views and intentions, is certainly a very worthy one. But would it do any good? If I were to labor a month, I could not express my conservative views and intentions more clearly and strongly than they are expressed in our platform, and in my many speeches already in print, and before the public. And yet even you, who do occasionally speak of me in terms of personal kindness, give no prominence to these oft-repeated expressions of conservative views and intentions; but busy yourself with appeals to all conservative men to vote for Douglas – vote any way which can possibly defeat me – thus impressing your readers that you think I am the very worst man living. If what I have already said has failed to convince you, no repetition of it would convince you. The writing of your letter, now before me, gives assurance that you would publish such a letter from me as you suggest; but, till now, what reason had I to suppose the *Louisville Journal*, even, would publish a *repetition* of that which is already at its command, and which it does not press upon the public attention?

And, now my friend – for such I esteem you personally – do not misunderstand me. I have not decided that I will not do substantially what you suggest. I will not forbear doing so, merely on *punctilio* and pluck. If I do finally abstain, it will be because of apprehension that it would do harm. For the good men of the South – and I regard the majority of them as such – I have no objection to repeat seventy and seven times. But I have *bad* men also to deal with, both North and South – men who are eager for something new upon which to base new misrepresentations – men who would like to frighten me, or, at least, to fix upon me the character of timidity and cowardice. They would seize upon almost any letter I could write, as being an 'awful coming down.' I intend keeping my eye upon these gentlemen, and to not unnecessarily put any weapons in their hands. Yours very truly

Letter to Lyman Trumbull, Republican Senator from Illinois.
Springfield, 10 December 1860

My dear Sir: Let there be no compromise on the question of *extending* slavery. If there be, all our labor is lost, and, ere long, must be done again. The dangerous ground – that into which some of our friends have a hankering to run – is Pop. Sov. Have none of it. Stand firm. The tug has to come, and better now, than any time hereafter. Yours as ever

To Alexander H. Stephens of Georgia, two days after South Carolina passed the Ordinance of Secession.

Springfield, 22 December 1860

My dear Sir: Your obliging answer to my short note is just received, and for which please accept my thanks. I fully appreciate the present peril the country is in, and the weight of responsibility on me.

Do the people of the South really entertain fears that a Republican administration would, *directly*, or *indirectly*, interfere with their slaves, or with them, about their slaves? If they do, I wish to assure you, as once a friend, and still, I hope, not an enemy, that there is no cause for such fears.

The South would be in no more danger in this respect, than it was in the days of Washington. I suppose, however, this does not meet the case. You think slavery is *right* and ought to be extended; while we think it is *wrong* and ought to be restricted. That I suppose is the rub. It certainly is the only substantial difference between us. Yours very truly

Farewell Address.

Springfield, 11 February 1861

My friends: No one, not in my situation, can appreciate my feeling of sadness at this parting. To this place, and the kindness of these people, I owe everything. Here I have lived a quarter of a century, and have passed from a young to an old man. Here my children have been born, and one is buried. I now leave, not knowing when, or whether ever, I may return, with a task before me greater than that which rested upon Washington. Without the assistance of that Divine Being, who ever attended him, I cannot succeed. With that assistance, I cannot fail. Trusting in Him, who can go with me, and remain with you and be everywhere for good, let us confidently hope that all will yet be well. To His care commending you, as I hope in your prayers you will commend me, I bid you an affectionate farewell.

Speech at Indianapolis, Indiana.

11 February 1861

It is not possible, in my journey to the national capital, to address assemblies like this which may do me the great honor to meet me as you have done, but very briefly. I should be entirely worn out if I were to attempt it. I appear before you now to thank you for this very magnificent welcome which you have given me, and still more for the very generous support which your state recently gave to the political cause of the whole country, and the whole world. Solomon has said, that there is a time to keep silence.[1] We know certain that they mean the same thing while using the same words now, and it perhaps would be as well if they would keep silence.

The words 'coercion' and 'invasion' are in great use about these days. Suppose we were simply to try if we can, and ascertain what is the meaning of these words. Let us get, if we can, the exact definitions of these words — not from dictionaries, but from the men who constantly repeat them — what things they mean to express by the words. What, then, is 'coercion'? What is 'invasion'? Would the marching of an army into South Carolina, for instance, without the consent of her people, and in hostility against them, be coercion or invasion? I very frankly say, I think it would be invasion, and it would be coercion too, if the people of that country were forced to submit. But if the government, for instance, but simply insists upon holding its own forts, or retaking those forts which belong to it — or the enforcement of the laws of the United States in the collection of duties upon foreign importations — or even the withdrawal of the mails from those portions of the country where the mails themselves are habitually violated; would any or all of these things be coercion? Do the lovers of the Union contend that they will resist coercion or invasion of any state, understanding that any or all of these would be coercing or invading a state? If they do, then it occurs to me that the means for the preservation of the Union they so greatly love, in their own estimation, is of a very thin and airy character. If sick, they would consider the little pills of the homoeopathist as already too large for them to swallow. In their view, the Union, as a family relation, would not be anything like a regular marriage at all, but only as a sort of free-love arrangement — to be maintained on what that sect calls passionate attraction. But, my friends, enough of this.

What is the particular sacredness of a state? I speak not of that position which is given to a state in and by the Constitution of the

---

[1] At this point the reporter apparently lost a passage.

United States, for that all of us agree to – we abide by; but that position assumed, that a state can carry with it out of the Union that which it holds in sacredness by virtue of its connection with the Union. I am speaking of that assumed right of a state, as a primary principle, that the Constitution should rule all that is less than itself, and ruin all that is bigger than itself. But, I ask, wherein does consist that right? If a state, in one instance, and a county in another, should be equal in extent of territory, and equal in the number of people, wherein is that state any better than the county? Can a change of name change the right? By what principle of original right is it that one-fiftieth or one-ninetieth of a great nation, by calling themselves a state, have the right to break up and ruin that nation as a matter of original principle? Now, I ask the question – I am not deciding anything – and with the request that you will think somewhat upon that subject and decide for yourselves, if you choose, when you get ready – where is the mysterious, original right, from principle, for a certain district of country with inhabitants, by merely being called a state, to play tyrant over all its own citizens, and deny the authority of everything greater than itself. I say I am deciding nothing, but simply giving something for you to reflect upon; and, with having said this much, and having declared, in the start, that I will make no long speeches, I thank you again for this magnificent welcome, and bid you an affectionate farewell.

Reply to Mayor Fernando Wood at New York City.
20 February 1861

... There is nothing that can ever bring me willingly to consent to the destruction of this Union, under which not only the commercial city of New York, but the whole country has acquired its greatness, unless it were to be that thing for which the Union itself was made. I understand a ship to be made for the carrying and preservation of the cargo, and so long as the ship can be saved, with the cargo, it should never be abandoned. This Union should likewise never be abandoned unless it fails and the probability of its preservation shall cease to exist without throwing the passengers and cargo overboard. So long, then, as it is possible that the prosperity and the liberties of the people can be preserved in the Union, it shall be my purpose at all times to preserve it ...

Address to the Senate of New Jersey.
                                    Trenton, 21 February 1861

Mr President and Gentlemen of the Senate of the State of New Jersey: I am very grateful to you for the honorable reception of which I have been the object. I cannot but remember the place that New Jersey holds in our early history. In the early revolutionary struggle, few of the states among the old Thirteen had more of the battle-fields of the country within their limits than old New Jersey. May I be pardoned if, upon this occasion, I mention that away back in my childhood, the earliest days of my being able to read, I got hold of a small book, such a one as few of the younger members have ever seen, Weems's *Life of Washington.* I remember all the accounts there given of the battle-fields and struggles for the liberties of the country, and none fixed themselves upon my imagination so deeply as the struggle here at Trenton, New Jersey. The crossing of the river, the contest with the Hessians, the great hardships endured at that time, all fixed themselves on my memory more than any single revolutionary event; and you all know, for you have all been boys, how these early impressions last longer than any others. I recollect thinking then, boy even though I was, that there must have been something more than common that those men struggled for. I am exceedingly anxious that that thing which they struggled for, that something even more than national independence, that something that held out a great promise to all the people of the world to all time to come; I am exceedingly anxious that this Union, the Constitution, and the liberties of the people shall be perpetuated in accordance with the original idea for which that struggle was made, and I shall be most happy indeed if I shall be an humble instrument in the hands of the Almighty, and of this, his almost chosen people, for perpetuating the object of that great struggle. You give me this reception, as I understand, without distinction of party. I learn that this body is composed of a majority of gentlemen who, in the exercise of their best judgment in the choice of a Chief Magistrate, did not think I was the man. I understand, nevertheless, that they came forward here to greet me as the constitutional President of the United States — as citizens of the United States, to meet the man who, for the time being, is the representative man of the nation, united by a purpose to perpetuate the Union and liberties of the people. As such, I accept this reception more gratefully than I could do did I believe it was tendered to me as an individual.

Speech in Independence Hall.
                              Philadelphia, 22 February 1861

Mr Cuyler: I am filled with deep emotion at finding myself standing here in the place where were collected together the wisdom, the patriotism, the devotion to principle, from which sprang the institutions under which we live. You have kindly suggested to me that in my hands is the task of restoring peace to our distracted country. I can say in return, sir, that all the political sentiments I entertain have been drawn, so far as I have been able to draw them, from the sentiments which originated, and were given to the world from this hall in which we stand. I have never had a feeling politically that did not spring from the sentiments embodied in the Declaration of Independence. I have often pondered over the dangers which were incurred by the men who assembled here and adopted that Declaration of Independence – I have pondered over the toils that were endured by the officers and soldiers of the army, who achieved that independence. I have often inquired of myself, what great principle or idea it was that kept this Confederacy so long together. It was not the mere matter of the separation of the colonies from the motherland; but something in that Declaration giving liberty not alone to the people of this country, but hope to the world for all future time. It was that which gave promise that in due time the weights should be lifted from the shoulders of all men, and that *all* should have an equal chance. This is the sentiment embodied in that Declaration of Independence.

Now, my friends, can this country be saved upon that basis? If it can, I will consider myself one of the happiest men in the world if I can help to save it. If it can't be saved upon that principle, it will be truly awful. But, if this country cannot be saved without giving up that principle – I was about to say I would rather be assassinated on this spot than to surrender it.

Now, in my view of the present aspect of affairs, there is no need of bloodshed and war. There is no necessity for it. I am not in favor of such a course, and I may say in advance, there will be no bloodshed unless it be forced upon the government. The government will not use force unless force is used against it.

My friends, this is a wholly unprepared speech. I did not expect to be called upon to say a word when I came here — I supposed I was merely to do something towards raising a flag. I may, therefore, have said something indiscreet, but I have said nothing but what I am willing to live by, and, in the pleasure of Almighty God, die by.

Chapter 6
Going to War
1861

The first six weeks of Lincoln's presidency were dominated by the issue of peace or war. Beset by conflicting advice, and even faced by a challenge to his authority from William H. Seward, his Secretary of State, Lincoln delayed any irreversible decision as long as he could. He was anxious that, if shots were to be fired, the Union side should not fire first. Fort Sumter, at the entrance to Charleston harbor, became the focal point of tension. The Confederate bombardment of Fort Sumter on 12–13 April signaled the outbreak of war. It was followed by the secession of four more slave states, and by hasty and massive mobilization on both sides.

The only major battle of 1861, at Bull Run in northern Virginia in July, ended in humiliating Northern defeat, and a short-lived threat to Washington itself. The most important strategic success for the North was to secure its hold on the border states of Maryland, Kentucky and Missouri (and on what was to become West Virginia). However, the fact that the dividing line between Union and Confederacy did not coincide with the line between free and slave states created political difficulties for Lincoln over the question of slavery. When General Fremont issued a proclamation emancipating slaves of disloyal owners in his military area, Lincoln felt obliged to revoke it, partly for fear of its effects in the border states.

Lincoln's inaugural address, and his message to Congress on 4 July, clearly rank among his great state papers – closely argued, wide ranging, finely judged in their attempt to appeal to some sections of opinion and appease others, and, in places, touching heights of deceptively simple eloquence. One of his main aims in 1861 was to win and keep the broadest possible support for the war for the Union. The task became harder as early enthusiasm faded, and it became clear that the war was not going to be over in a few weeks or months. The mood at the end of the year was one of growing impatience and frustration.

First Inaugural Address.

4 March 1861

Fellow-citizens of the United States: In compliance with a custom as old as the government itself, I appear before you to address you briefly, and to take, in your presence, the oath prescribed by the Constitution of the United States, to be taken by the President 'before he enters on the execution of his office.'

I do not consider it necessary at present, for me to discuss those matters of administration about which there is no special anxiety, or excitement.

Apprehension seems to exist among the people of the southern states, that by the accession of a Republican administration, their property, and their peace, and personal security, are to be endangered. There has never been any reasonable cause for such apprehension. Indeed, the most ample evidence to the contrary has all the while existed, and been open to their inspection. It is found in nearly all the published speeches of him who now addresses you. I do but quote from one of those speeches when I declare that 'I have no purpose, directly or indirectly, to interfere with the institution of slavery in the states where it exists. I believe I have no lawful right to do so, and I have no inclination to do so.' Those who nominated and elected me did so with full knowledge that I had made this, and many similar declarations, and had never recanted them. And more than this, they placed in the platform, for my acceptance, and as a law to themselves, and to me, the clear and emphatic resolution which I now read:

'*Resolved*, That the maintenance inviolate of the rights of the states, and especially the right of each state to order and control its own domestic institutions according to its own judgment exclusively, is essential to that balance of power on which the perfection and endurance of our political fabric depend; and we denounce the lawless invasion by armed force of the soil of any state or territory, no matter under what pretext, as among the gravest of crimes.'

I now reiterate these sentiments: and in doing so, I only press upon the public attention the most conclusive evidence of which the case is susceptible, that the property, peace, and security of no section are to be in any wise endangered by the now incoming administration. I add too, that all the protection which, consistently with the Constitution and the laws, can be given, will be cheerfully given to all the states when lawfully demanded, for whatever cause – as cheerfully to one section, as to another.

There is much controversy about the delivering up of fugitives from service or labor. The clause I now read is as plainly written in the Constitution as any other of its provisions:

'No person held to service or labor in one state, under the laws thereof, escaping into another, shall, in consequence of any law or regulation therein, be discharged from such service or labor, but shall be delivered up on claim of the party to whom such service or labor may be due.'

It is scarcely questioned that this provision was intended by those who make it, for the reclaiming of what we call fugitive slaves; and the intention of the lawgiver is the law. All members of Congress swear their support to the whole Constitution – to this provision as much as to any other. To the proposition, then, that slaves whose cases come within the terms of this clause, 'shall be delivered up,' their oaths are unanimous. Now, if they would make the effort in good temper, could they not, with nearly equal unanimity, frame and pass a law, by means of which to keep good that unanimous oath?

There is some difference of opinion whether this clause should be enforced by national or by state authority; but surely that difference is not a very material one. If the slave is to be surrendered, it can be of but little consequence to him, or to others, by which authority it is done. And should anyone, in any case, be content that his oath shall go unkept, on a merely unsubstantial controversy as to *how* it shall be kept?

Again, in any law upon this subject, ought not all the safeguards of liberty known in civilized and humane jurisprudence to be introduced, so that a free man be not, in any case, surrendered as a slave? And might it not be well, at the same time, to provide by law for the enforcement of that clause in the Constitution which guarantees that 'The citizens of each state shall be entitled to all privileges and immunities of citizens in the several states?'

I take the official oath to-day, with no mental reservations, and with no purpose to construe the Constitution or laws, by any hypercritical rules. And while I do not choose now to specify particular acts of Congress as proper to be enforced, I do suggest, that it will be much safer for all, both in official and private stations, to conform to, and abide by, all those acts which stand unrepealed, than to violate any of them, trusting to find impunity in having them held to be unconstitutional.

It is seventy-two years since the first inauguration of a President under our national Constitution. During that period fifteen different and greatly distinguished citizens, have, in succession, administered the executive branch of the government. They have conducted it through many perils; and, generally, with great success. Yet, with all this scope for precedent, I now enter upon the same task for the brief constitutional term of four years, under great and peculiar difficulty. A disruption of the Federal Union heretofore only menaced, is now formidably attempted.

I hold, that in contemplation of universal law, and of the Constitution, the Union of these states is perpetual. Perpetuity is implied, if not expressed, in the fundamental law of all national governments. It is safe to assert that no government proper, ever had a provision in its organic law for its own termination. Continue to execute all the express provisions of our national Constitution, and the Union will endure forever – it being impossible to destroy it, except by some action not provided for in the instrument itself.

Again, if the United States be not a government proper, but an association of states in the nature of contract merely, can it, as a contract, be peaceably unmade, by less than all the parties who made it? One party to a contract may violate it – break it, so to speak; but does it not require all to lawfully rescind it?

Descending from these general principles, we find the proposition that, in legal contemplation, the Union is perpetual, confirmed by the history of the Union itself. The Union is much older than the Constitution. It was formed in fact, by the Articles of Association in 1774. It was matured and continued by the Declaration of Independence in 1776. It was further matured and the faith of all the then thirteen states expressly plighted and engaged that it should be perpetual, by the Articles of Confederation in 1778. And finally, in 1787, one of the declared objects for ordaining and establishing the Constitution, was *'to form a more perfect union.'*

But if destruction of the Union, by one, or by a part only, of the states, be lawfully possible, the Union is *less* perfect than before the Constitution, having lost the vital element of perpetuity.

It follows from these views that no state, upon its own mere motion, can lawfully get out of the Union — that *resolves* and *ordinances* to that effect are legally void; and that acts of violence, within any state or states, against the authority of the United States, are insurrectionary or revolutionary, according to circumstances.

I therefore consider that, in view of the Constitution and the laws, the Union is unbroken; and, to the extent of my ability, I shall take care, as the Constitution itself expressly enjoins upon me, that the laws of the Union be faithfully executed in all the states. Doing this I deem to be only a simple duty on my part; and I shall perform it, so far as practicable, unless my rightful masters, the American people, shall withhold the requisite means, or, in some authoritative manner, direct the contrary. I trust this will not be regarded as a menace, but only as the declared purpose of the Union that it *will* constitutionally defend, and maintain itself.

In doing this there needs to be no bloodshed or violence; and there shall be none, unless it be forced upon the national authority. The power confided to me, will be used to hold, occupy, and possess the property, and places belonging to the government, and to collect the duties and imposts; but beyond what may be necessary for these objects, there will be no invasion — no using of force against, or among the people anywhere. Where hostility to the United States, in any interior locality, shall be so great and so universal, as to prevent competent resident citizens from holding the federal offices, there will be no attempt to force obnoxious strangers among the people for that object. While the strict legal right may exist in the government to enforce the exercise of these offices, the attempt to do so would be so irritating, and so nearly impracticable with all, that I deem it better to forgo, for the time, the uses of such offices.

The mails, unless repelled, will continue to be furnished in all parts of the Union. So far as possible, the people everywhere shall have that sense of perfect security which is most favorable to calm thought and reflection. The course here indicated will be followed, unless current events, and experience, shall show a modification, or change, to be proper; and in every case and exigency, my best direction will be exercised, according to circumstances actually existing, and with a view and a hope of a peaceful solution of the national troubles, and the restoration of fraternal sympathies and affections.

That there are persons in one section, or another who seek to destroy the Union at all events, and are glad of any pretext to do it, I will neither affirm nor deny; but if there be such, I need address no word to them. To those, however, who really love the Union, may I not speak?

Before entering upon so grave a matter as the destruction of our national fabric, with all its benefits, its memories, and its hopes, would it not be wise to ascertain precisely why we do it? Will you hazard so desperate a step, while there is any possibility that any portion of the ills you fly from, have no real existence? Will you, while the certain ills you fly to, are greater than all the real ones you fly from? Will you risk the commission of so fearful a mistake?

All profess to be content in the Union, if all constitutional rights can be maintained. Is it true, then, that any right, plainly written in the Constitution, has been denied? I think not. Happily the human mind is so constituted, that no party can reach to the audacity of doing this. Think, if you can, of a single instance in which a plainly written provision of the Constitution has ever been denied. If, by the mere force of numbers, a majority should deprive a minority of any clearly written constitutional right, it might, in a moral point of view, justify revolution – certainly would, if such right were a vital one. But such is not our case. All the vital rights of minorities, and of individuals, are so plainly assured to them, by affirmations and negations, guarantees and prohibitions, in the Constitution, that controversies never arise concerning them. But no organic law can ever be framed with a provision specifically applicable to every question which may occur in practical administration. No foresight can anticipate, nor any document of reasonable length contain express provisions for all possible questions. Shall fugitives from labor be surrendered by national or by state authority? The Constitution does not expressly say. *May* Congress prohibit slavery in the territories? The Constitution does not expressly say. *Must* Congress protect slavery in the territories? The Constitution does not expressly say.

From questions of this class spring all our constitutional controversies, and we divide upon them into majorities and minorities. If the minority will not acquiesce, the majority must, or the government must cease. There is no other alternative; for continuing the government is acquiescence on one side or the other. If a minority, in such case, will secede rather than acquiesce, they make a precedent which, in turn, will divide and ruin them; for a minority of their own will secede from them, whenever a majority refuses to be controlled by such minority. For instance, why may not any portion of a new confederacy, a year or two hence, arbitrarily secede again, precisely as portions of the present Union now claim to secede from it. All who cherish disunion sentiments, are now being educated to the exact temper of doing this. Is there such perfect identity of interests among the states to compose a new Union, as to produce harmony only, and prevent renewed secession?

Plainly, the central idea of secession, is the essence of anarchy. A majority, held in restraint by constitutional checks, and limitations, and always changing easily, with deliberate changes of popular opinions and sentiments, is the only true sovereign of a free people. Whoever rejects it, does, of necessity, fly to anarchy or to despotism. Unanimity is impossible; the rule of a minority, as a permanent arrangement, is wholly inadmissible; so that, rejecting the majority principle, anarchy, or despotism in some form, is all that is left.

I do not forget the position assumed by some, that constitutional questions are to be decided by the Supreme Court; nor do I deny that such decisions must be binding in any case, upon the parties to a suit, as to the object of that suit, while they are also entitled to very high respect and consideration, in all parallel cases, by all other departments of the government. And while it is obviously possible that such decision may be erroneous in any given case, still the evil effect following it, being limited to that particular case, with the chance that it may be overruled, and never become a precedent for other cases, can better be borne than could the evils of a different practice. At the same time the candid citizen must confess that if the policy of the government, upon vital questions, affecting the whole people, is to be irrevocably fixed by decisions of the Supreme Court, the instant they are made, in ordinary litigation between parties, in personal actions, the people will have ceased to be their own rulers, having, to that extent, practically resigned their government, into the hands of that eminent tribunal. Nor is there, in this view, any assault upon the court, or the judges. It is a duty, from which they may not shrink, to decide cases properly brought before them; and it is no fault of theirs if others seek to turn their decisions to political purposes.

One section of our country believes slavery is *right* and ought to be extended, while the other believes it is *wrong* and ought not to be extended. This is the only substantial dispute. The fugitive slave clause of the Constitution, and the law for the suppression of the foreign slave trade, are each as well enforced, perhaps, as any law can ever be in a community where the moral sense of the people imperfectly supports the law itself. The great body of the people abide by the dry legal obligation in both cases, and a few break over in each. This, I think, cannot be perfectly cured; and it would be worse in both cases *after* the separation of the sections, than before. The foreign slave trade, now imperfectly suppressed, would be ultimately revived without restriction, in one section; while fugitive slaves, now only partially surrendered, would not be surrendered at all, by the other.

Physically speaking, we cannot separate. We cannot remove our respective sections from each other, nor build an impassable wall between them. A husband and wife may be divorced, and go out of the presence, and beyond the reach of each other; but the different parts of our country cannot do this. They cannot but remain face to face; and intercourse, either amicable or hostile, must continue between them. Is it possible then to make that intercourse more advantageous, or more satisfactory, *after* separation than *before*? Can aliens make treaties easier than friends can make laws? Can treaties be more faithfully enforced between aliens, than laws can among friends? Suppose you go to war, you cannot fight always; and when, after much loss on both sides, and no gain on either, you cease fighting, the identical old questions, as to terms of intercourse, are again upon you.

This country, with its institutions, belongs to the people who inhabit it. Whenever they shall grow weary of the existing government, they can exercise their *constitutional* right of amending it, or their *revolutionary* right to dismember, or overthrow it. I cannot be ignorant of the fact that many worthy, and patriotic citizens are desirous of having the national constitution amended. While I make no recommendation of amendments, I fully recognize the rightful authority of the people over the whole subject, to be exercised in either of the modes prescribed in the instrument itself; and I should, under existing circumstances, favor, rather than oppose, a fair opportunity being afforded the people to act upon it.

I will venture to add that, to me, the convention mode seems preferable, in that it allows amendments to originate with the people themselves, instead of only permitting them to take, or reject, propositions originated by others, not especially chosen for the purpose, and which might not be precisely such, as they would wish to either accept or refuse. I understand a proposed amendment to the Constitution – which amendment, however, I have not seen, has passed Congress, to the effect that the federal government shall never interfere with the domestic institutions of the states, including that of persons held to service. To avoid misconstruction of what I have said, I depart from my purpose not to speak of particular amendments, so far as to say that, holding such a provision to now be implied constitutional law, I have no objection to its being made express and irrevocable.

The Chief Magistrate derives all his authority from the people, and they have conferred none upon him to fix terms for the separation of the states. The people themselves can do this also if they choose; but the executive, as such, has nothing to do with it. His duty is to administer the present government, as it came to his hands, and to transmit it, unimpaired by him, to his successor.

Why should there not be a patient confidence in the ultimate justice of the people? Is there any better, or equal hope, in the world? In our present differences, is either party without faith of being in the right? If the Almighty Ruler of nations, with his eternal truth and justice, be on your side of the North, or on yours of the South, that truth, and that justice, will surely prevail, by the judgment of this great tribunal, the American people.

By the frame of the government under which we live, this same people have wisely given their public servants but little power for mischief; and have, with equal wisdom, provided for the return of that little to their own hands at very short intervals.

While the people retain their virtue and vigilance, no administration, by any extreme of wickedness or folly, can very seriously injure the government, in the short space of four years.

My countrymen, one and all, think calmly and *well*, upon this whole subject. Nothing valuable can be lost by taking time. If there be an object to *hurry* any of you, in hot haste, to a step which you would never take *deliberately*, that object will be frustrated by taking time; but no good object can be frustrated by it. Such of you as are now dissatisfied, still have the old Constitution unimpaired, and, on the sensitive point, the laws of your own framing under it; while the new administration will have no immediate power, if it would, to change either. If it were admitted that you who are dissatisfied, hold the right side in the dispute, there still is no single good reason for precipitate action. Intelligence, patriotism, Christianity, and a firm reliance on Him, who has never yet forsaken this favored land, are still competent to adjust, in the best way, all our present difficulty.

In *your* hands, my dissatisfied fellow countrymen, and not in *mine*, is the momentous issue of civil war. The government will not assail *you*. You can have no conflict, without being yourselves the aggressors. *You* have no oath registered in Heaven to destroy the government, while *I* shall have the most solemn one to 'preserve, protect, and defend' it.

I am loth to close. We are not enemies, but friends. We must not be enemies. Though passion may have strained, it must not break our bonds of affection. The mystic chords of memory, stretching from every battle-field, and patriot grave, to every living heart and hearthstone, all over this broad land, will yet swell the chorus of the Union, when again touched, as surely they will be, by the better angels of our nature.

To William H. Seward, Secretary of State: a letter which may not have been sent.

1 April 1861

My dear Sir: Since parting with you I have been considering your paper dated this day, and entitled 'Some thoughts for the President's consideration.' The first proposition in it is, '1st. We are at the end of a month's administration, and yet without a policy, either domestic or foreign.'

At the *beginning* of that month, in the inaugural, I said: 'The power confided to me will be used to hold, occupy, and possess the property and places belonging to the government, and to collect the duties, and imposts.' This had your distinct approval at the time; and, taken in connection with the order I immediately gave General Scott, directing him to employ every means in his power to strengthen and hold the forts, comprises the exact domestic policy you now urge, with the single exception, that it does not propose to abandon Fort Sumter.

Again, I do not perceive how the reinforcement of Fort Sumter would be done on a slavery, or party issue, while that of Fort Pickens would be on a more national, and patriotic one.

The news received yesterday in regard to St Domingo, certainly brings a new item within the range of our foreign policy, but up to that time we have been preparing circulars, and instructions to ministers, and the like, all in perfect harmony, without even a suggestion that we had no foreign policy.

Upon your closing propositions, that 'whatever policy we adopt, there must be an energetic prosecution of it';

'For this purpose it must be somebody's business to pursue and direct it incessantly';

'Either the President must do it himself, and be all the while active in it, or';

'Devolve it on some member of his cabinet';

'Once adopted, debates on it must end, and all agree and abide'; I remark that if this must be done, *I* must do it. When a general line of policy is adopted, I apprehend there is no danger of its being changed without good reason, or continuing to be a subject of unnecessary debate; still, upon points arising in its progress, I wish, and suppose I am entitled to have the advice of all the cabinet. Your Obt. Servt.

Proclamation calling up militia and convening Congress.

15 April 1861

By the President of the United States
A Proclamation

Whereas the laws of the United States have been for some time past, and now are opposed, and the execution thereof obstructed, in the States of South Carolina, Georgia, Alabama, Florida, Mississippi, Louisiana, and Texas, by combinations too powerful to be suppressed by the ordinary course of judicial proceedings, or by the powers vested in the Marshals by law,

Now therefore, I, Abraham Lincoln, President of the United States, in virtue of the power in me vested by the Constitution, and the laws, have thought fit to call forth, and hereby do call forth, the militia of the several States of the Union, to the aggregate number of seventy-five thousand, in order to suppress said combinations, and to cause the laws to be duly executed. The details, for this object, will be immediately communicated to the State authorities through the War Department.

I appeal to all loyal citizens to favor, facilitate, and aid this effort to maintain the honor, the integrity, and the existence of our National Union, and the perpetuity of popular government; and to redress wrongs already long enough endured.

I deem it proper to say that the first service assigned to the forces hereby called forth will probably be to repossess the forts, places, and property which have been seized from the Union; and in every event, the utmost care will be observed, consistently with the objects aforesaid, to avoid any devastation, any destruction of, or interference with, property, or any disturbance of peaceful citizens in any part of the country.

And I hereby command the persons composing the combinations aforesaid to disperse, and retire peaceably to their respective abodes within twenty days from this date.

Deeming that the present condition of public affairs presents an extraordinary occasion, I do hereby, in virtue of the power in me vested by the Constitution, convene both Houses of Congress. Senators and Representatives are therefore summoned to assemble at their respective chambers, at twelve o'clock, noon, on Thursday, the fourth day of July, next, then and there to consider and determine such measures, as, in their wisdom, the public safety, and interest may seem to demand.

In Witness Whereof I have hereunto set my hand, and caused the Seal of the United States to be affixed.

> Done at the city of Washington this fifteenth day of April in the year of our Lord One thousand, Eight hundred and Sixty-one, and of the Independence of the United States the Eighty-fifth.

ABRAHAM LINCOLN.

By the President
  WILLIAM H. SEWARD, Secretary of State.

Reply to a Baltimore Committee.

22 April 1861

You, gentlemen, come here to me and ask for peace on any terms, and yet have no word of condemnation for those who are making war on us. You express great horror of bloodshed, and yet would not lay a straw in the way of those who are organizing in Virginia and elsewhere to capture this city. The rebels attack Fort Sumter, and your citizens attack troops sent to the defense of the government,[1] and the lives and property in Washington, and yet you would have me break my oath and surrender the government without a blow. There is no Washington in that — no Jackson in that — no manhood nor honor in that. I have no desire to invade the South; but I must have troops to defend this Capital. Geographically it lies surrounded by the soil of Maryland; and mathematically the necessity exists that they should come over her territory. Our men are not moles, and can't dig under the earth; they are not birds, and can't fly through the air. There is no way but to march across, and that they must do. But in doing this there is no need of collision. Keep your rowdies in Baltimore, and there will be no bloodshed. Go home and tell your people that if they will not attack us, we will not attack them; but if they do attack us, we will return it, and that severely.

Letter to Gustavus V. Fox, who had commanded the Fort Sumter expedition.

1 May 1861

My dear Sir: I sincerely regret that the failure of the late attempt to provision Fort Sumter, should be the source of any annoyance to you. The practicability of your plan was not, in fact, brought to a test. By reason of a gale, well known in advance to be possible, and not improbable, the tugs, an essential part of the plan, never reached the ground; while, by an accident, for which you were in no wise responsible, and possibly I, to some extent was, you were deprived of a war vessel with her men, which you deemed of great importance to the enterprise.

I most cheerfully and truly declare that the failure of the undertaking has not lowered you a particle, while the qualities you developed in the effort, have greatly heightened you, in my estimation. For a daring and dangerous enterprise, of a similar character, you would, to-day, be the man, of all my acquaintances, whom I would select.

You and I both anticipated that the cause of the country would

---

[1] On 19 April a secessionist mob had attacked the 6th Massachusetts Regiment as it passed through Baltimore, killing several soldiers.

be advanced by making the attempt to provision Fort Sumter, even if it should fail; and it is no small consolation now to feel that our anticipation is justified by the result. Very truly your friend

Letter to the parents of Col. Elmer E. Ellsworth, killed at Alexandria, Virginia, on the preceding day.

25 May 1861

My dear Sir and Madam: In the untimely loss of your noble son, our affliction here, is scarcely less than your own. So much of promised usefulness to one's country, and of bright hopes for one's self and friends, have rarely been so suddenly dashed, as in his fall. In size, in years, and in youthful appearance, a boy only, his power to command men, was surpassingly great. This power, combined with a fine intellect, an indomitable energy, and a taste altogether military, constituted in him, as seemed to me, the best natural talent, in that department, I ever knew. And yet he was singularly modest and deferential in social intercourse. My acquaintance with him began less than two years ago; yet through the latter half of the intervening period, it was as intimate as the disparity of our ages, and my engrossing engagements, would permit. To me, he appeared to have no indulgences or pastimes; and I never heard him utter a profane, or an intemperate word. What was conclusive of his good heart, he never forgot his parents. The honors he labored for so laudably, and, in the sad end, so gallantly gave his life, he meant for them, no less than for himself.

In the hope that it may be no intrusion upon the sacredness of your sorrow, I have ventured to address you this tribute to the memory of my young friend, and your brave and early fallen child.

May God give you that consolation which is beyond all earthly power. Sincerely your friend in a common affliction

From the President's message to Congress in special session.

4 July 1861

Fellow-citizens of the Senate and House of Representatives: Having been convened on an extraordinary occasion, as authorized by the Constitution, your attention is not called to any ordinary subject of legislation.

At the beginning of the present presidential term, four months ago, the functions of the federal government were found to be generally suspended within the several states of South Carolina, Georgia, Alabama, Mississippi, Louisiana, and Florida, excepting only those of the Post Office Department.

Within these states, all the forts, arsenals, dockyards, custom-houses, and the like, including the movable and stationary property in and about them, had been seized, and were held in open hostility to this government, excepting only Forts Pickens, Taylor, and Jefferson, on, and near the Florida coast, and Fort Sumter, in Charleston harbor, South Carolina. The forts thus seized had been put in improved condition; new ones had been built; and armed forces had been organized, and were organizing, all avowedly with the same hostile purpose.

The forts remaining in the possession of the federal government, in, and near, these states, were either besieged or menaced by warlike preparations; and especially Fort Sumter was nearly surrounded by well-protected hostile batteries, with guns equal in quality to the best of its own, and outnumbering the latter as perhaps ten to one. A disproportionate share of the federal muskets and rifles had somehow found their way into these states, and had been seized, to be used against the government. Accumulations of the public revenue, lying within them, had been seized for the same object. The Navy was scattered in distant seas; leaving but a very small part of it within the immediate reach of the government. Officers of the Federal Army and Navy, had resigned in great numbers; and, of those resigning, a large proportion had taken up arms against the government. Simultaneously, and in connection with all this, the purpose to sever the Federal Union was openly avowed. In accordance with this purpose, an ordinance had been adopted in each of these states, declaring the states, respectively, to be separated from the national Union. A formula for instituting a combined government of these states had been promulgated; and this illegal organization, in the character of Confederate States, was already invoking recognition, aid, and intervention, from foreign powers.

Finding this condition of things, and believing it to be an imperative duty upon the incoming Executive to prevent, if possible, the consummation of such attempt to destroy the Federal Union, a choice of means to that end became indispensable. This choice was made; and was declared in the inaugural address. The policy chosen looked to the exhaustion of all peaceful measures, before a resort to any stronger ones. It sought only to hold the public places and property, not already wrested from the government, and to collect the revenue; relying for the rest on time, discussion, and the ballot-box. It promised a continuance of the mails, at government expense, to the very people who were resisting the government; and it gave repeated pledges against any disturbance to any of the people, or any of their rights. Of all that which a president might constitutionally, and justifiably, do in such a case, everything was forborne, without which it was believed possible to keep the government on foot.

On the 5th of March (the present incumbent's first full day in office) a letter of Major Anderson, commanding at Fort Sumter, written on the 28th of February, and received at the War Department on the 4th of March, was, by that department, placed in his hands. This letter expressed the professional opinion of the writer, that reinforcements could not be thrown into that fort within the time for his relief, rendered necessary by the limited supply of provisions, and with a view of holding possession of the same, with a force of less than twenty thousand good, and well-disciplined men. This opinion was concurred in by all the officers of his command; and their *memoranda* on the subject, were made enclosures of Major Anderson's letter. The whole was immediately laid before Lieutenant-General Scott, who at once concurred with Major Anderson in opinion. On reflection, however, he took full time, consulting with other officers, both of the Army and the Navy; and, at the end of four days, came reluctantly, but decidedly, to the same conclusion as before. He also stated at the same time that no such sufficient force was then at the control of the government, or could be raised, and brought to the ground, within the time when the provisions in the fort would be exhausted. In a purely military point of view, this reduced the duty of the administration, in the case, to the mere matter of getting the garrison safely out of the fort.

It was believed, however, that to so abandon that position, under the circumstances, would be utterly ruinous; that the *necessity* under which it was to be done, would not be fully understood – that, by many, it would be construed as a part of a *voluntary* policy – that, at home, it would discourage the friends of the Union, embolden its adversaries, and go far to insure to the latter, a recognition abroad – that, in fact, it would be our national destruction consummated. This could not be allowed. Starvation was not yet upon the garrison; and ere it would be reached, *Fort Pickens* might be reinforced. This last would be a clear indication of *policy*, and would better enable the country to accept the evacuation of Fort Sumter, as a military *necessity*. An order was at once directed to be sent for the landing of the troops from the Steamship *Brooklyn*, into Fort Pickens. This order could not go by land, but must take the longer and slower route by sea. The first return news from the order was received just one week before the fall of Fort Sumter. The news itself was, that the officer commanding the *Sabine*, to which vessel the troops had been transferred from the *Brooklyn*, acting upon some *quasi* armistice of the late administration (and of the existence of which, the present administration, up to the time the order was dispatched, had only too vague and uncertain rumors, to fix attention), had refused to land the troops. To now reinforce Fort Pickens, before a crisis would be reached at Fort Sumter, was impossible – rendered so by the near exhaustion of provisions in the latter-named fort. In precaution against such a conjuncture, the government had, a few days before, commenced preparing an expedition, as well adapted as might be, to relieve Fort Sumter, which expedition was intended to be ultimately used, or not, according to circumstances. The strongest anticipated case for using it was now presented; and it was resolved to send it forward. As had been intended, in this contingency, it was also resolved to notify the Governor of South Carolina, that he might expect an attempt would be made to provision the fort; and that, if the attempt should not be resisted, there would be no effort to throw in men, arms, or ammunition, without further notice, or in case of an attack upon the fort. This notice was accordingly given; whereupon the fort was attacked, and bombarded to its fall, without even awaiting the arrival of the provisioning expedition.

It is thus seen that the assault upon, and reduction of, Fort Sumter, was in no sense a matter of self-defence on the part of the assailants. They well knew that the garrison in the fort could, by no possibility, commit aggression upon them. They knew – they were expressly notified – that the giving of bread to the few brave and hungry men of the garrison, was all which would on that occasion be attempted, unless themselves by resisting so much, should provoke more. They knew that this government desired to keep the garrison in the fort, not to assail them, but merely to maintain visible possession, and thus to preserve the Union from actual and immediate dissolution – trusting, as hereinbefore stated, to time, discussion, and the ballot-box, for final adjustment; and they assailed, and reduced the fort, for precisely the reverse object – to drive out the visible authority of the Federal Union, and thus force it to immediate dissolution.

That this was their object, the Executive well understood; and having said to them in the inaugural address: 'You can have no conflict without being yourself the aggressors,' he took pains, not only to keep this declaration good, but also to keep the case so free from the power of ingenious sophistry, as that the world should not be able to misunderstand it. By the affair at Fort Sumter, with its surrounding circumstances, that point was reached. Then, and thereby, the assailants of the government, began the conflict of arms, without a gun in sight, or in expectancy, to return their fire, save only the few in the fort, sent to that harbor years before for their own protection, and still ready to give that protection, in whatever was lawful. In this act, discarding all else, they have forced upon the country the distinct issue: 'Immediate dissolution, or blood.'

And this issue embraces more than the fate of these United States. It presents to the whole family of man the question, whether a constitutional republic, or a democracy – a government of the people, by the same people – can, or cannot, maintain its territorial integrity against its own domestic foes. It presents the question, whether discontented individuals, too few in numbers to control administration according to organic law, in any case, can always, upon the pretenses made in this case, or on any other pretenses, or arbitrarily, without any pretense, break up their government, and thus practically put an end to free government upon the earth. It forces us to ask: 'Is there, in all republics, this inherent, and fatal weakness?' 'Must a government, of necessity, be too *strong* for the liberties of its own people, or too *weak* to maintain its own existence?'

So viewing the issue, no choice was left but to call out the war power of the government; and so to resist force employed for its destruction, by force for its preservation.

The call was made; and the response of the country was most gratifying; surpassing, in unanimity and spirit, the most sanguine expectation. Yet none of the states commonly called slave-states, except Delaware, gave a regiment through regular state organization. A few regiments have been organized within some others of those states, by individual enterprise and received into the government service. Of course the seceded states, so-called (and to which Texas had been joined about the time of the inauguration), gave no troops to the cause of the Union. The border states, so-called, were not uniform in their actions; some of them being almost *for* the Union, while in others – as Virginia, North Carolina, Tennessee, and Arkansas – the Union sentiment was nearly repressed and silenced. The course taken in Virginia was the most remarkable – perhaps the most important. A convention, elected by the people of that state, to consider this very question of disrupting the Federal Union, was in session at the capital of Virginia when Fort Sumter fell. To this body the people had chosen a large majority of professed Union men. Almost immediately after the fall of Sumter, many members of that majority went over to the original disunion minority, and, with them, adopted an ordinance for withdrawing the state from the Union. Whether this change was wrought by their great approval of the assault upon Sumter, or their great resentment at the government's resistance to that assault, is not definitely known. Although they submitted the ordinance, for ratification, to a vote of the people, to be taken on a day then somewhat more than a month distant, the convention, and the legislature (which was also in session at the same time and place), with leading men of the state, not members of either, immediately commenced acting as if the state were already out of the Union. They pushed military preparations vigorously forward all over the state. They seized the United States Armory at Harper's Ferry, and the navy-yard at Gosport, near Norfolk. They received – perhaps invited – into their state large bodies of troops, with their warlike appointments, from the so-called seceded states. They formally entered into a treaty of temporary alliance and co-operation with the so-called 'Confederate States,' and sent members to their Congress at Montgomery. And, finally, they permitted the insurrectionary government to be transferred to their capital at Richmond.

The people of Virginia have thus allowed this giant insurrection to make its nest within her borders; and this government has no choice left but to deal with it, *where* it finds it. And it has the less regret, as the loyal citizens have, in due form, claimed its protection. Those loyal citizens this government is bound to recognize, and protect, as being Virginia.

In the border states, so-called – in fact, the middle states – there are those who favor a policy which they call 'armed neutrality' – that is, an arming of those states to prevent the Union forces passing one way, or the disunion, the other, over their soil. This would be disunion completed. Figuratively speaking, it would be the building of an impassable wall along the line of separation. And yet, not quite an impassable one; for, under the guise of neutrality, it would tie the hands of the Union men, and freely pass supplies from among them to the insurrectionists, which it could not do as an open enemy. At a stroke, it would take all the trouble off the hands of secession, except only what proceeds from the external blockade. It would do for the disunionists that which, of all things, they most desire – feed them well, and give them disunion without a struggle of their own. It recognizes no fidelity to the Constitution, no obligation to maintain the Union; and while very many who have favored it are, doubtless, loyal citizens, it is, nevertheless, treason in effect . . .

Soon after the first call for militia, it was considered a duty to authorize the Commanding General, in proper cases, according to his discretion, to suspend the privilege of the writ of habeas corpus; or, in other words, to arrest, and detain, without resort to the ordinary processes and form of law, such individuals as he might deem dangerous to the public safety. This authority has purposely been exercised but very sparingly. Nevertheless, the legality and propriety of what has been done under it are questioned; and the attention of the country has been called to the proposition that one who is sworn to 'take care that the laws be faithfully executed,' should not himself violate them. Of course some consideration was given to the questions of power and propriety before this matter was acted upon. The whole of the laws which were required to be faithfully executed, were being resisted, and failing of execution, in nearly one-third of the states. Must they be allowed to finally fail of execution, even had it been perfectly clear, that by the use of the means necessary to their execution, some single law, made in such extreme tenderness of the citizen's liberty, that practically, it relieves more of the guilty, than of the innocent, should, to a very limited extent, be violated? To state the question more directly, are all the laws *but one* to go unexecuted, and the government itself go to pieces, lest that one be violated? Even in such a case, would not the official oath be broken if the government should be overthrown, when it was believed that disregarding the single law would tend to preserve it? But it was not believed that this question was presented. It was not believed that any law was violated. The provision of the Constitution that 'The privilege of the writ of habeas corpus, shall not be suspended unless when, in cases of rebellion or invasion, the public safety may require it,' is equivalent to a provision – is a provision – that such privilege may be suspended when, in cases of rebellion or invasion, the public safety *does* require it. It was decided that we have a case of rebellion, and that the public safety does require the qualified suspension of the privilege of the writ which was authorized to be made. Now it is insisted that Congress, and not the Executive, is vested with this power. But the Constitution itself is silent as to which, or who, is to exercise the power; and as the provision was plainly made for a dangerous emergency, it cannot be believed the framers of the instrument intended that in every case the danger should run its course, until Congress could be called together; the very assembling of which might be prevented, as was intended in this case, by the rebellion . . .

It might seem, at first thought, to be of little difference whether the present movement at the South be called 'secession' or 'rebellion.' The movers, however, well understand the difference. At the beginning, they knew they could never raise their treason to any respectable magnitude, by any name which implies *violation* of law. They knew their people possessed as much of moral sense, as much of devotion to law and order, and as much pride in, and reverence for, the history and government of their common country, as any other civilized and patriotic people. They knew they could make no advancement directly in the teeth of these strong and noble sentiments. Accordingly they commenced by an insidious debauching of the public mind. They invented an ingenious sophism, which, if conceded, was followed by perfectly logical steps, through all the incidents, to the complete destruction of the Union. The sophism itself is, that any state of the Union may, *consistently* with the national Constitution, and therefore *lawfully*, and *peacefully* withdraw from the Union, without the consent of the Union, or of any other state. The little disguise that the supposed right is to be exercised only for just cause, themselves to ɔe the sole judge of its justice, is too thin to merit any notice.

With rebellion thus sugar-coated, they have been drugging the public mind of their section for more than thirty years; and, until at length, they have brought many good men to a willingness to take up arms against the government the day *after* some assemblage of men have enacted the farcical pretense of taking their state out of the Union, who could have been brought to no such thing the day *before*.

This sophism derives much – perhaps the whole – of its currency from the assumption that there is some omnipotent and sacred supremacy pertaining to a *state* – to each state of our Federal Union. Our states have neither more nor less power, than that reserved to them, in the Union, by the Constitution – no one of them ever having been a state *out* of the Union. The original ones passed into the Union even *before* they cast off their British colonial dependence; and the new ones each came into the Union directly from a condition of dependence, excepting Texas. And even Texas, in its temporary independence, was never designated a state. The new ones only took the designation of states, on coming into the Union, while that name was first adopted for the old ones, in, and by, the Declaration of Independence. Therein the 'United Colonies' were declared to be 'Free and Independent States'; but, even then, the object plainly was not to declare their independence of *one another*, or of the *Union*; but directly the contrary, as their mutual pledge, and their mutual action, before, at the time, and afterwards, abundantly show. The express plighting of faith, by each and all of the original thirteen, in the Articles of Confederation, two years later, that the Union shall be perpetual, is most conclusive. Having never been states, either in substance, or in name, *outside* of the Union, whence this magical omnipotence of 'state rights,' asserting a claim of power to lawfully destroy the Union itself? Much is said about the 'sovereignty' of the states; but the word, even, is not in the national Constitution; nor, as is believed, in any of the state constitutions. What is 'sovereignty,' in the political sense of the term? Would it be far wrong to define it 'A political community, without a political superior'? Tested by this, no one of our states, except Texas, ever was a sovereignty. And even Texas gave up the character on coming into the Union; by which act, she acknowledged the Constitution of the United States, and the laws and treaties of the United States made in pursuance of the Constitution, to be, for her, the supreme law of the land. The states have their *status* IN the Union, and they have no other *legal status*. If they break from this, they can only do so against law and by revolution. The Union, and not themselves separately, procured their independence and their liberty. By conquest, or purchase, the Union gave each of them whatever of independence, and liberty, it has. The Union is older than any of the states; and, in fact, it created them as states. Originally, some dependent colonies made the Union; and, in turn, the Union threw off their old dependence for them, and made them states, such as they are. Not one of them ever had a state constitution independent of the Union. Of course, it is not forgotten that all the new states framed their constitutions before they entered the Union; nevertheless, dependent upon and preparatory to, coming into the Union.

Unquestionably the states have the powers, and rights, reserved to them in and by the national Constitution; but among these, surely, are not included all conceivable powers, however mischievous or destructive; but, at most, such only as were known in the world, at the time, as governmental powers; and certainly, a power to destroy the government itself, had never been known as a governmental – as a merely administrative power. This relative matter of national power, and state rights, as a principle, is no other than the principle of *generality*, and *locality*. Whatever concerns the whole, should be confided to the whole – to the general government; while, whatever concerns *only* the state, should be left exclusively to the state. This is all there is of original principle about it. Whether the national Constitution, in defining boundaries between the two, has applied the principle with exact accuracy, is not to be questioned. We are all bound by that defining, without question . . .

The seceders insist that our Constitution admits of secession. They have assumed to make a national Constitution of their own, in which, of necessity, they have either *discarded* or *retained* the right of secession, as they insist it exists in ours. If they have discarded it, they thereby admit that, on principle, it ought not to be in ours. If they have retained it, by their own construction of ours they show that to be consistent they must secede from one another, whenever they shall find it the easiest way of settling their debts, or effecting any other selfish or unjust object. The principle itself is one of disintegration, and upon which no government can possibly endure.

If all the states, save one, should assert the power to *drive* that one out of the Union, it is presumed the whole class of seceder politicians would at once deny the power, and denounce the act as the greatest outrage upon state rights. But suppose that precisely the same act, instead of being called 'driving the one out,' should be called 'the seceding of the others from that one,' it would be exactly what the seceders claim to do; unless, indeed, they make the point, that the one, because it is a minority, may rightfully do what the others, because they are a majority, may not rightfully do. These politicians are subtle and profound on the rights of minorities. They are not partial to that power which made the Constitution, and speaks from the preamble, calling itself 'We, the People.'

It may well be questioned whether there is, to-day, a majority of the legally qualified voters of any state, except perhaps South Carolina, in favor of disunion. There is much reason to believe that the Union men are the majority in many, if not in every other one, of the so-called seceded states. The contrary has not been demonstrated in any one of them. It is ventured to affirm this, even of Virginia and Tennessee; for the result of an election, held in military camps, where the bayonets are all on one side of the question voted upon, can scarcely be considered as demonstrating popular sentiment. At such an election, all that large class who are, at once, *for* the Union, and *against* coercion would be coerced to vote against the Union.

It may be affirmed, without extravagance, that the free institutions we enjoy, have developed the powers, and improved the condition of our whole people, beyond any example in the world. Of this we now have a striking and an impressive illustration. So large an army as the government has now on foot, was never before known without a soldier in it but who had taken his place there of his own free choice. But more than this: there are many single regiments whose members, one and another, possess full practical knowledge of all the arts, sciences, professions, and whatever else, whether useful or elegant, is known in the world; and there is scarcely one from which there could not be selected a president, a cabinet, a congress, and perhaps a court, abundantly competent to administer the government itself. Nor do I say this is not true, also, in the army of our late friends, now adversaries, in this contest; but if it is, so much better the reason why the government, which has conferred such benefits on both them and us, should not be broken up. Whoever, in any section, proposes to abandon such a government, would do well to consider, in deference to what principle it is that he does it – what better he is likely to get in its stead – whether the substitute will give, or be intended to give, so much of good to the people. There are some foreshadowings on this subject. Our adversaries have adopted some declarations of independence; in which, unlike the good old one, penned by Jefferson, they omit the words 'all men are created equal.' Why? They have adopted a temporary national constitution, in the preamble of which, unlike our good old one, signed by Washington, they omit 'We, the People,' and substitute 'We, the deputies of the sovereign and independent states.' Why? Why this deliberate pressing out of view, the rights of men and the authority of the people?

This is essentially a people's contest. On the side of the Union, it is a struggle for maintaining in the world, that form and substance of government, whose leading object is to elevate the condition of men – to lift artificial weights from all shoulders – to clear the paths of laudable pursuit for all – to afford all an unfettered start and a fair chance in the race of life. Yielding to partial and temporary departures, from necessity, this is the leading object of the government for whose existence we contend.

I am most happy to believe that the plain people understand and appreciate this. It is worthy of note, that while in this, the government's hour of trial, large numbers of those in the Army and Navy who have been favored with the offices have resigned, and proved false to the hand which had pampered them, not one common soldier or common sailor is known to have deserted his flag.

Great honor is due to those officers who remain true, despite the example of their treacherous associates; but the greatest honor, and most important fact of all, is the unanimous firmness of the common soldiers and common sailors. To the last man, so far as known, they have successfully resisted the traitorous efforts of those, whose commands, but an hour before, they obeyed as absolute law. This is the patriotic instinct of the plain people. They understand, without an argument, that destroying the government, which was made by Washington, means no good to them.

Our popular government has often been called an experiment. Two points in it our people have already settled – the successful *establishing*, and the successful *administering* of it. One still remains — its successful *maintenance* against a formidable attempt to overthrow it. It is now for them to demonstrate to the world, that those who can fairly carry an election, can also suppress a rebellion — that ballots are the rightful, and peaceful, successors of bullets; and that when ballots have fairly, and constitutionally, decided, there can be no successful appeal back to bullets; that there can be no successful appeal except to ballots themselves, at succeeding elections. Such will be a great lesson of peace; teaching men that what they cannot take by an election, neither can they take it by a war — teaching all the folly of being the beginners of a war.

Lest there be some uneasiness in the minds of candid men, as to what is to be the course of the government towards the southern states *after* the rebellion shall have been suppressed, the Executive deems it proper to say, it will be his purpose then, as ever, to be guided by the Constitution and the laws; and that he probably will have no different understanding of the powers and duties of the federal government, relatively to the rights of the states and the people under the Constitution, than that expressed in the inaugural address.

He desires to preserve the government, that it may be administered for all, as it was administered by the men who made it. Loyal citizens everywhere, have the right to claim this of their government; and the government has no right to withhold or neglect it. It is not perceived that, in giving it, there is any coercion, any conquest, or any subjugation, in any just sense of those terms.

The Constitution provides, and all the states have accepted the provision, that 'The United States shall guarantee to every state in this Union a republican form of government.' But, if a state may lawfully go out of the Union, having done so it may also discard the republican form of government; so that to prevent its going out is an indispensable *means* to the *end* of maintaining the guarantee mentioned; and when an end is lawful and obligatory, the indispensable means to it are also lawful and obligatory.

It was with the deepest regret that the Executive found the duty of employing the war-power, in defense of the government, forced upon him. He could but perform this duty, or surrender the existence of the government. No compromise by public servants, could, in this case, be a cure; not that compromises are not often proper, but that no popular government can long survive a marked precedent, that those who carry an election, can only save the government from immediate destruction, by giving up the main point upon which the people gave the election. The people themselves, and not their servants, can safely reverse their own deliberate decisions. As a private citizen, the Executive could not have consented that these institutions shall perish; much less could he, in betrayal of so vast, and so sacred a trust, as these free people had confided to him. He felt that he had no moral right to shrink; nor even to count the chances of his own life, in what might follow. In full view of his great responsibility, he has, so far, done what he has deemed his duty. You will now, according to your own judgment, perform yours. He sincerely hopes that your views, and your action, may so accord with his as to assure all faithful citizens, who have been disturbed in their rights, of a certain and speedy restoration to them, under the Constitution, and the laws.

And having thus chosen our course, without guile and with pure purpose, let us renew our trust in God, and go forward without fear, and with manly hearts.

Letter to Beriah Magoffin, Governor of Kentucky.
24 August 1861

Sir: Your letter of the 19th inst. in which you '*urge the removal from the limits of Kentucky of the military force now organized, and in camp within said State*' is received.

I may not possess full and precisely accurate knowledge upon this subject; but I believe it is true that there is a military force in camp within Kentucky, acting by authority of the United States, which force is not very large, and is not now being augmented.

I also believe that some arms have been furnished to this force by the United States.

I also believe this force consists exclusively of Kentuckians, having their camp in the immediate vicinity of their own homes, and not assailing, or menacing, any of the good people of Kentucky.

In all I have done in the premises, I have acted upon the urgent solicitation of many Kentuckians, and in accordance with what I believed, and still believe, to be the wish of a majority of all the Union-loving people of Kentucky.

While I have conversed on this subject with many eminent men of Kentucky, including a large majority of her Members of

Congress, I do not remember that any one of them, or any other person, except your Excellency and the bearers of your Excellency's letter, has urged me to remove the military force from Kentucky, or to disband it. One other very worthy citizen of Kentucky did solicit me to have the augmenting of the force suspended for a time.

Taking all the means within my reach to form a judgment, I do not believe it is the popular wish of Kentucky that this force shall be removed beyond her limits; and, with this impression, I must respectfully decline to so remove it.

I most cordially sympathize with your Excellency, in the wish to preserve the peace of my own native state, Kentucky, but it is with regret I search, and cannot find, in your not very short letter, any declaration or intimation that you entertain any desire for the preservation of the Federal Union. Your obedient servant

Letter to Senator Orville H. Browning, who had been appointed to serve the unexpired term of Stephen A. Douglas, deceased.

22 September 1861

My dear Sir: Yours of the 17th is just received; and coming from you, I confess it astonishes me. That you should object to my adhering to a law, which you had assisted in making, and presenting to me, less than a month before, is odd enough. But this is a very small part. Genl. Fremont's proclamation, as to confiscation of property, and the liberation of slaves, is *purely political*, and not within the range of *military* law, or necessity.[1] If a commanding general finds a necessity to seize the farm of a private owner, for a pasture, an encampment, or a fortification, he has the right to do so, and to so hold it, as long as the necessity lasts; and this is within military law, because within military necessity. But to say the farm shall no longer belong to the owner, or his heirs forever; and this as well when the farm is not needed for military purposes as when it is, is purely political, without the savor of military law about it. And the same is true of slaves. If the General needs them, he can seize them, and use them; but when the need is past, it is not for him to fix their permanent future

---

[1] On 30 August 1861 General John C. Fremont, commanding the Union forces in Missouri, had issued a proclamation declaring the property of Missourians in rebellion confiscated and their slaves emancipated. Lincoln asked Fremont to modify the proclamation; the general refused. Lincoln then ordered modifications which had the practical effect of rescinding the document.

condition. That must be settled according to laws made by lawmakers, and not by military proclamations. The proclamation in the point in question, is simply 'dictatorship.' It assumes that the General may do *anything* he pleases – confiscate the lands and free the slaves of *loyal* people as well as of disloyal ones. And going the whole figure I have no doubt would be more popular with some thoughtless people, than that which has been done! But I cannot assume this reckless position; nor allow others to assume it on my responsibility. You speak of it as being the only means of *saving* the government. On the contrary it is itself the surrender of the government. Can it be pretended that it is any longer the government of the US – any government of Constitution and laws – wherein a General, or a President, may make permanent rules of property by proclamation?

I do not say Congress might not with propriety pass a law on the point, just such as General Fremont proclaimed. I do not say I might not, as a member of Congress, vote for it. What I object to is, that I as President shall expressly or impliedly seize and exercise the permanent legislative functions of the government.

So much as to principle. Now as to policy. No doubt the thing was popular in some quarters, and would have been more so if it had been a general declaration of emancipation. The Kentucky legislature would not budge till that proclamation was modified; and Gen. Anderson telegraphed me that on the news of Gen. Fremont having actually issued deeds of manumission, a whole company of our volunteers threw down their arms and disbanded. I was so assured, as to think it probable, that the very arms we had furnished Kentucky would be turned against us. I think to lose Kentucky is nearly the same as to lose the whole game. Kentucky gone, we cannot hold Missouri, nor, as I think, Maryland. These all against us, and the job on our hands is too large for us. We would as well consent to separation at once, including the surrender of this capital. On the contrary, if you will give up your restlessness for new positions, and back me manfully on the grounds upon which you and other kind friends gave me the election, and have approved in my public documents, we shall go through triumphantly.

You must not understand I took my course on the proclamation *because* of Kentucky. I took the same ground in a private letter to General Fremont before I heard from Kentucky.

You think I am inconsistent because I did not also forbid Gen.

Fremont to shoot men under the proclamation. I understand that part to be within military law; but I also think, and so privately wrote Gen. Fremont, that it is impolitic in this, that our adversaries have the power, and will certainly exercise it, to shoot as many of our men as we shoot of theirs. I did not say this in the public letter, because it is a subject I prefer not to discuss in the hearing of our enemies.

There has been no thought of removing Gen. Fremont on any ground connected with his proclamation; and if there has been any wish for his removal on any ground, our mutual friend Sam. Glover can probably tell you what it was. I hope no real necessity for it exists on any ground . . . Your friend as ever

Letter to Major George D. Ramsay about a widow with six children.

17 October 1861

My dear Sir: The lady — bearer of this — says she has two sons who want to work. Set them at it, if possible. Wanting to work is so rare a merit, that it should be encouraged. Yours truly

From the Annual Message to Congress.

3 December 1861

. . . The inaugural address at the beginning of the administration, and the message to Congress at the late special session, were both mainly devoted to the domestic controversy out of which the insurrection and consequent war have sprung. Nothing now occurs to add or subtract, to or from, the principles or general purposes stated and expressed in those documents.

The last ray of hope for preserving the Union peaceably, expired at the assault upon Fort Sumter; and a general review of what has occurred since may not be unprofitable. What was painfully uncertain then, is much better defined and more distinct now; and the progress of events is plainly in the right direction. The insurgents confidently claimed a strong support from north of Mason and Dixon's line; and the friends of the Union were not free from apprehension on the point. This, however, was soon settled definitely and on the right side. South of the line, noble little Delaware led off right from the first. Maryland was made to *seem* against the Union. Our soldiers were assaulted, bridges were burned, and railroads torn up, within her limits; and we were many days, at one time, without the ability to bring a single regiment over her soil to the capital. Now, her bridges and railroads are repaired and open to the government; she already gives seven regiments to the cause of the Union and none to the enemy; and her people, at a regular election, have sustained the Union by a larger majority and a larger aggregate vote than they ever before gave to any candidate, or any question. Kentucky, too, for some time in doubt, is now decidedly, and I think unchangeably, ranged on the side of the Union. Missouri is comparatively quiet; and I believe cannot again be overrun by the insurrectionists. These three states of Maryland, Kentucky, and Missouri, neither of which would promise a single soldier at first, have now an aggregate of not less than forty thousand in the field, for the Union; while, of their citizens, certainly not more than a third of that number, and they of doubtful whereabouts, and doubtful existence, are in arms against it. After a somewhat bloody struggle of months, winter closes on the Union people of western Virginia, leaving them masters of their own country.

An insurgent force of about fifteen hundred, for months dominating the narrow peninsular region, constituting the counties of Accomac and Northampton, and known as eastern shore of Virginia, together with some contiguous parts of Maryland, have laid down their arms; and the people there have renewed their allegiance to, and accepted the protection of, the old flag. This leaves no armed insurrectionist north of the Potomac, or east of the Chesapeake.

Also we have obtained a footing at each of the isolated points, on the southern coast, of Hatteras, Port Royal, Tybee Island, near Savannah, and Ship Island; and we likewise have some general accounts of popular movements, in behalf of the Union, in North Carolina and Tennessee.

These things demonstrate that the cause of the Union is advancing steadily and certainly southward.

Since your last adjournment, Lieutenant General Scott has retired from the head of the army. During his long life, the nation has not been unmindful of his merit; yet, on calling to mind how faithfully, ably, and brilliantly he has served the country, from a time far back in our history, when few of the now living had been born, and thenceforward continually, I cannot but think we are still his debtors. I submit therefore, for your consideration, what further mark of recognition is due to him, and to ourselves, as a grateful people.

With the retirement of General Scott came the executive duty of appointing, in his stead, a general-in-chief of the army. It is a fortunate circumstance that neither in council nor country was there, so far as I know, any difference of opinion as to the proper person to be selected. The retiring chief repeatedly expressed his judgment in favor of General McClellan for the position; and in this the nation seemed to give a unanimous concurrence. The designation of General McClellan is therefore in considerable degree, the selection of the country as well as of the Executive; and hence there is better reason to hope there will be given him, the confidence and cordial support thus, by fair implication promised, and without which, he cannot, with so full efficiency, serve the country.

It has been said that one bad general is better than two good ones; and the saying is true, if taken to mean no more than that an army is better directed by a single mind, though inferior, than by two superior ones, at variance and cross-purposes with each other.

And the same is true, in all joint operations wherein those engaged *can* have none but a common end in view, and *can* differ only as to the choice of means. In a storm at sea, no one on board *can* wish the ship to sink; and yet, not unfrequently, all go down together, because too many will direct, and no single mind can be allowed to control.

It continues to develop that the insurrection is largely, if not exclusively, a war upon the first principle of popular government – the rights of the people. Conclusive evidence of this is found in the most grave and maturely considered public documents, as well as in the general tone of the insurgents. In those documents we find the abridgment of the existing right of suffrage and the denial to the people of all right to participate in the selection of public officers, except the legislative boldly advocated, with labored arguments to prove that large control of the people in government, is the source of all political evil. Monarchy itself is something hinted at as a possible refuge from the power of the people.

In my present position, I could scarcely be justified were I to omit raising a warning voice against this approach of returning despotism.

It is not needed, nor fitting here, that a general argument should be made in favor of popular institutions; but there is one point, with its connections, not so hackneyed as most others, to which I ask a brief attention. It is the effort to place *capital* on an equal footing with, if not above *labor*, in the structure of government. It is assumed that labor is available only in connection with capital; that nobody labors unless somebody else, owning capital, somehow by the use of it, induces him to labor. This assumed, it is next considered whether it is best that capital shall *hire* laborers, and thus induce them to work by their own consent, or *buy* them, and drive them to it without their consent. Having proceeded so far, it is naturally concluded that all laborers are either *hired* laborers, or what we call slaves. And further it is assumed that whoever is once a hired laborer, is fixed in that condition for life.

Now, there is no such relation between capital and labor as assumed; nor is there any such thing as a free man being fixed for life in the condition of a hired laborer. Both these assumptions are false, and all inferences from them are groundless.

Labor is prior to, and independent of, capital. Capital is only the fruit of labor, and could never have existed if labor had not first existed. Labor is the superior of capital, and deserves much the higher consideration. Capital has its rights, which are as worthy of protection as any other rights. Nor is it denied that there is, and probably always will be, a relation between labor and capital, producing mutual benefits. The error is in assuming that the whole labor of community exists within that relation. A few men own capital, and that few avoid labor themselves and, with their capital, hire or buy another few to labor for them. A large majority belong to neither class — neither work for others nor have others working for them. In most of the southern states, a majority of the whole people of all colors are neither slaves nor masters; while in the northern a large majority are neither hirers nor hired. Men with their families — wives, sons, and daughters — work for themselves, on their farms, in their houses, and in their shops, taking the whole product to themselves, and asking no favors of capital on the one hand nor of hired laborers or slaves on the other. It is not forgotten that a considerable number of persons mingle their own labor with capital — that is, they labor with their own hands, and also buy or hire others to labor for them; but this is only a mixed, and not a distinct class. No principle stated is disturbed by the existence of this mixed class.

Again: as has already been said, there is not, of necessity, any such thing as the free hired laborer being fixed to that condition for life. Many independent men everywhere in these states, a few years back in their lives, were hired laborers. The prudent, penniless beginner in the world, labors for wages awhile, saves a surplus with which to buy tools or land for himself; then labors on his own account another while, and at length hires another new beginner to help him. This is the just, and generous, and prosperous system, which opens the way to all – gives hope to all, and consequent energy, and progress, and improvement of condition to all. No men living are more worthy to be trusted than those who toil up from poverty – none less inclined to take, or touch, aught which they have not honestly earned. Let them beware of surrendering a political power which they already possess, and which, if surrendered, will surely be used to close the door of advancement against such as they, and to fix new disabilities and burdens upon them, till all of liberty shall be lost.

From the first taking of our national census to the last are seventy years; and we find our population at the end of the period eight times as great as it was at the beginning. The increase of those other things which men deem desirable has been even greater. We thus have at one view what the popular principle applied to government, through the machinery of the states and the Union, has produced in a given time; and also what, if firmly maintained, it promises for the future. There are already among us those, who, if the Union be preserved, will live to see it contain two hundred and fifty millions. The struggle of to-day is not altogether for to-day – it is for a vast future also. With a reliance on Providence, all the more firm and earnest, let us proceed in the great task which events have devolved upon us.

Letter to Major-General David Hunter, a disgruntled officer.
31 December 1861

Dear Sir: Yours of the 23rd is received; and I am constrained to say it is difficult to answer so ugly a letter in good temper. I am, as you intimate, losing much of the great confidence I placed in you, not from any act or omission of yours touching the public service, up to the time you were sent to Leavenworth, but from the flood of grumbling dispatches and letters I have seen from you since. I knew you were being ordered to Leavenworth at the time it was done; and I aver that with as tender a regard for your honor and your sensibilities as I had for my own, it never occurred to me that you were being 'humiliated, insulted, and disgraced'; nor have I, up to this day, heard an intimation that you have been wronged, coming from anyone but yourself. No one has blamed you for the retrograde movement from Springfield, nor for the information you gave Gen. Cameron; and this you could readily understand, if it were not for your unwarranted assumption that the ordering you to Leavenworth must necessarily have been done as a *punishment* for some *fault*. I thought then, and think yet, the position assigned to you is as responsible, and as honorable, as that assigned to Buell. I know that Gen. McClellan expected more important results from it. My impression is that at the time you were assigned to the new Western Department, it had not been determined to replace Gen. Sherman in Kentucky; but of this I am not certain, because the idea that a command in Kentucky was very desirable, and one in the farther West, very undesirable, had never occurred to me. You constantly speak of being placed in command of only 3,000. Now tell me, is not this mere impatience? Have you not known all the while that you are to command four or five times that many?

I have been, and am sincerely your friend; and if, as such, I dare to make a suggestion, I would say you are adopting the best possible way to ruin yourself. 'Act well your part, there all the honor lies.' He who does *something* at the head of one regiment, will eclipse him who does *nothing* at the head of a hundred. Your friend as ever

Chapter 7
Battlefield Setbacks and the Politics of Emancipation
1862-3

For much of the year 1862, the war went badly for the North, apart from one or two major successes, such as the capture of New Orleans. In the eastern theater, Lincoln was increasingly at odds with his military commander, George B. McClellan, who, he complained, had 'got the slows'. Lincoln's letters and dispatches to McClellan set the pattern of his remarkably frank and intensely personal correspondence with his generals, and reveal a growing confidence in his own military judgment.

After the failure of McClellan's peninsular campaign, Robert E. Lee won a second Confederate victory at Bull Run, and invaded Maryland. In the early autumn, the Confederates also marched deep into Kentucky. Both invasions were eventually repelled – Lee's in Maryland after the battle of Antietam, the bloodiest single day of the war. Lincoln finally dismissed McClellan in November, but his successor, Ambrose Burnside, suffered an appalling defeat at Fredericksburg in December.

Lincoln's claim to the title of Great Emancipator rests as much on his mastery of political tactics, subtle sense of timing, and sensitivity to public opinion, as on his growing moral commitment. Having tried in vain to win support in the border states for a plan of gradual, compensated emancipation, Lincoln turned in July to the more direct approach set out in the Emancipation Proclamations. For fear that it would be regarded as a panic measure, he put off publication of the first Proclamation until after the half-victory at Antietam in September. In the meantime, he concealed his intentions, and used various audiences as sounding-boards to test objections to emancipation. Between the first and second Proclamations, he did not waver, despite military failures, sagging morale, severe setbacks for the Republicans in the mid-term congressional elections in November, and a cabinet crisis in December.

After the second Proclamation on 1 January 1863, the war for the Union became also a war to free the slaves.

Letter to Major-General Don Carlos Buell.

13 January 1862

. . . For my own views, I have not offered, and do not now offer them as orders; and while I am glad to have them respectfully considered, I would blame you to follow them contrary to your own clear judgment – unless I should put them in the form of orders . . . I state my general idea of this war to be that we have the greater numbers, and the enemy has the greater facility of concentrating forces upon points of collision; that we must fail, unless we can find some way of making our advantage an over-match for his; and that this can only be done by menacing him with superior forces at different points, at the same time; so that we can safely attack one, or both, if he makes no change; and if he weakens one to strengthen the other, forbear to attack the strengthened one, but seize and hold the weakened one, gaining so much. . .

To Queen Victoria: a letter of condolence on the death of Prince Albert.

1 February 1862

Abraham Lincoln,
President of the United States of America.

To Her Majesty Victoria,
Queen of the United Kingdom
of Great Britain and Ireland,
etc., etc., etc., Sendeth Greeting!

Great and Good Friend: By a letter from your son, His Royal Highness, the Prince of Wales, which has just been received, I am informed of the overwhelming affliction which has fallen upon Your Majesty, by the untimely death of His Royal Highness the late Prince Consort, Prince Albert of Saxe Coburg.

The offer of condolence in such cases is a customary ceremony, which has its good uses, though it is conventional, and may sometimes be even insincere. But I would fain have Your Majesty apprehend, on this occasion, that real sympathy can exist, as real truthfulness can be practiced, in the intercourse of nations. The people of the United States are kindred of the people of Great Britain. With all our distinct national interests, objects, and aspirations, we are conscious that our moral strength is largely derived from that relationship, and we think we do not deceive ourselves when we suppose that, by constantly cherishing cordial friendship and sympathy with the other branches of the family to which we belong, we impart to them not less strength than we derive from the same connection. Accidents, however, incidental to all states, and passions, common to all nations, often tend to disturb the harmony so necessary and so proper between countries, and to convert them into enemies. It was reserved for Your Majesty in sending your son, the Heir Apparent of the British throne, on a visit among us, to inaugurate a policy destined to counteract these injurious tendencies, as it has been Your Majesty's manifest endeavor, through a reign already of considerable length and of distinguished success, to cultivate the friendship on our part so earnestly desired. It is for this reason that you are honored on this side of the Atlantic as a friend of the American people. The late Prince Consort was with sufficient evidence regarded as your counsellor in the same friendly relation. The American people, therefore, deplore his death and sympathize in Your Majesty's irreparable bereavement with an unaffected sorrow. This condolence may not be altogether ineffectual, since we are sure it emanates from only virtuous motives and natural affection. I do not dwell upon it, however, because I know that the Divine hand that has wounded, is the only one that can heal: And so, commending Your Majesty and the Prince Royal, the Heir Apparent, and all your afflicted family to the tender mercies of God, I remain Your Good Friend,

ABRAHAM LINCOLN.

Washington, 1st Feby. 1862.

By the President:

WILLIAM H. SEWARD, Secretary of State.

To the King of Siam: a letter of thanks and good will.

3 February 1862

Abraham Lincoln,
President of the United States of America.

To His Majesty Somdetch Phra Paramendr Maha Mongut,
King of Siam, etc., etc.

Great and Good Friend: I have received Your Majesty's two letters of the date of February 14th, 1861.

I have also received in good condition the royal gifts which accompanied those letters – namely, a sword of costly materials and exquisite workmanship; a photographic likeness of Your Majesty and of Your Majesty's beloved daughter; and also two elephants' tusks of length and magnitude such as indicate that they could have belonged only to an animal which was a native of Siam.

Your Majesty's letters show an understanding that our laws forbid the President from receiving these rich presents as personal treasures. They are therefore accepted in accordance with Your Majesty's desire as tokens of your good will and friendship for the American people. Congress being now in session at this capital, I have had great pleasure in making known to them this manifestation of Your Majesty's munificence and kind consideration.

Under their directions the gifts will be placed among the archives of the government, where they will remain perpetually as tokens of mutual esteem and pacific dispositions more honorable to both nations than any trophies of conquest could be.

I appreciate most highly Your Majesty's tender of good offices in forwarding to this government a stock from which a supply of elephants might be raised on our own soil. This government would not hesitate to avail itself of so generous an offer if the object were one which could be made practically useful in the present condition of the United States.

Our political jurisdiction, however, does not reach a latitude so low as to favor the multiplication of the elephant, and steam on land, as well as on water, has been our best and most efficient agent of transportation in internal commerce.

I shall have occasion at no distant day to transmit to Your Majesty some token of indication of the high sense which this government entertains of Your Majesty's friendship.

Meantime, wishing for Your Majesty a long and happy life, and for the generous and emulous people of Siam the highest possible prosperity, I commend both to the blessing of Almighty God. Your Good Friend,

ABRAHAM LINCOLN.

Washington, 3 February 1862.
By the President:
WILLIAM H. SEWARD, Secretary of State.

Letter, with a memorandum, to General George B. McClellan, commanding the Army of the Potomac.

3 February 1862

My dear Sir: You and I have distinct, and different plans for a movement of the Army of the Potomac – yours to be down the Chesapeake, up the Rappahannock to Urbana, and across land to the terminus of the railroad on the York River – mine to move directly to a point on the railroad south-west of Manassas.

If you will give me satisfactory answers to the following questions, I shall gladly yield my plan to yours.

1st. Does not your plan involve a greatly larger expenditure of *time*, and *money* than mine?

2nd. Wherein is a victory *more certain* by your plan than mine?

3rd. Wherein is a victory *more valuable* by your plan than mine?

4th. In fact, would it not be *less* valuable, in this, that it would break no great line of the enemy's communications, while mine would?

5th. In case of disaster, would not a safe retreat be more difficult by your plan than by mine? Yours truly

[*Memorandum accompanying letter of President to General McClellan, dated 3 February 1862*]

1. Suppose the enemy should attack us in force *before* we reach the Ocoquan, what? In view of the possibility of this, might it not be safest to have our entire force to move together from above the Ocoquan?

2. Suppose the enemy, in force, shall dispute the crossing of the Ocoquan, what? In view of this, might it not be safest for us to cross the Ocoquan at Colchester rather than at the village of

Ocoquan? This would cost the enemy two miles more of travel to meet us, but would, on the contrary, leave us two miles further from our ultimate destination.

3. Suppose we reach Maple valley without an attack, will we not be attacked there, in force, by the enemy marching by the several roads from Manassas? and if so, what?

Message to Congress on the compensated emancipation of slaves.
6 March 1862

Fellow-citizens of the Senate, and House of Representatives: I recommend the adoption of a Joint Resolution by your honorable bodies which shall be substantially as follows:

'Resolved that the United States ought to co-operate with any state which may adopt gradual abolishment of slavery, giving to such state pecuniary aid, to be used by such state in its discretion, to compensate for the inconveniences public and private, produced by such change of system.'

If the proposition contained in the resolution does not meet the approval of Congress and the country, there is the end; but if it does command such approval, I deem it of importance that the states and people immediately interested should be at once distinctly notified of the fact, so that they may begin to consider whether to accept or reject it. The federal government would find its highest interest in such a measure as one of the most efficient means of self-preservation. The leaders of the existing insurrection entertain the hope that this government will ultimately be forced to acknowledge the independence of some part of the disaffected region, and that all the slave states north of such part will then say 'the Union, for which we have struggled, being already gone, we now choose to go with the southern section.' To deprive them of this hope, substantially ends the rebellion; and the initiation of emancipation completely deprives them of it, as to all the states initiating it. The point is not that *all* the states tolerating slavery would very soon, if at all, initiate emancipation; but that, while the offer is equally made to all, the more northern shall, by such initiation, make it certain to the more southern, that in no event, will the former ever join the latter, in their proposed confederacy. I say 'initiation' because, in my judgment, gradual, and not sudden emancipation, is better for all. In the mere financial or pecuniary view, any member of Congress, with the census-tables and Treasury reports before him, can readily see for himself how very soon the current expenditures of this war would purchase, at fair valuation, all the slaves in any named state. Such a proposition, on the part of the general government, sets up no claim of a right, by federal authority, to interfere with slavery within state limits, referring, as it does, the absolute control of the subject, in each case, to the state and its people immediately interested. It is proposed as a matter of perfectly free choice with them.

In the annual message last December, I thought fit to say 'The Union must be preserved; and hence all indispensable means must be employed.' I said this, not hastily, but deliberately. War has been made, and continues to be an indispensable means to this end. A practical re-acknowledgment of the national authority would render the war unnecessary, and it would at once cease. If, however, resistance continues, the war must also continue; and it is impossible to foresee all the incidents which may attend and all the ruin which may follow it. Such as may seem indispensable, or may obviously promise great efficiency towards ending the struggle, must and will come.

The proposition now made, though an offer only, I hope it may be esteemed no offense to ask whether the pecuniary consideration tendered would not be of more value to the states and private persons concerned, than are the institution, and property in it, in the present aspect of affairs.

While it is true that the adoption of the proposed resolution would be merely initiatory, and not within itself a practical measure, it is recommended in the hope that it would soon lead to important practical results. In full view of my great responsibility to my God, and to my country, I earnestly beg the attention of Congress and the people to the subject.

Letter to General George B. McClellan, now embarked on his campaign to take Richmond by way of the peninsula between the York and James rivers.

9 April 1862

My dear Sir: Your dispatches complaining that you are not properly sustained, while they do not offend me, do pain me very much.

Blencker's Division was withdrawn from you before you left here; and you knew the pressure under which I did it, and, as I thought, acquiesced in it — certainly not without reluctance.

After you left, I ascertained that less than twenty thousand unorganized men, without a single field battery, were all you designed to be left for the defense of Washington and Manassas Junction; and part of this even, was to go to Gen. Hooker's old position. Gen. Banks's corps, once designed for Manassas Junction, was diverted, and tied up on the line of Winchester and Strasburg, and could not leave it without again exposing the upper Potomac, and the Baltimore and Ohio Railroad. This presented (or would present, when McDowell and Sumner should be gone) a great temptation to the enemy to turn back from the Rappahannock, and sack Washington. My explicit order that Washington should, by the judgment of *all* the commanders of army corps, be left entirely secure, had been neglected. It was precisely this that drove me to detain McDowell.

I do not forget that I was satisfied with your arrangement to leave Banks at Manassas Junction; but when that arrangement was broken up and *nothing* was substituted for it, of course I was not satisfied. I was constrained to substitute something for it myself. And now allow me to ask: 'Do you really think I should permit the line from Richmond, via Manassas Junction, to this city to be entirely open, except what resistance could be presented by less than twenty thousand unorganized troops?' This is a question which the country will not allow me to evade.

There is a curious mystery about the *number* of the troops now with you. When I telegraphed you on the 6th saying you had over a hundred thousand with you, I had just obtained from the Secretary of War a statement, taken as he said, from your own returns, making 108,000 then with you, and *en route* to you. You now say you will have but 85,000, when all *en route* to you shall have reached you. How can the discrepancy of 23,000 be accounted for?

As to Gen. Wool's command, I understand it is doing for you precisely what a like number of your own would have to do, if that command was away.

I suppose the whole force which has gone forward for you is with you by this time; and if so, I think it is the precise time for you to strike a blow. By delay the enemy will relatively gain upon you — that is, he will gain faster, by *fortifications* and *reinforcements*, than you can by reinforcements alone.

And, once more let me tell you, it is indispensable to *you* that you strike a blow. *I* am powerless to help this. You will do me the justice to remember I always insisted, that going down the Bay in search of a field, instead of fighting at or near Manassas, was only shifting, and not surmounting, a difficulty – that we would find the same enemy, and the same, or equal, intrenchments, at either place. The country will not fail to note – is now noting – that the present hesitation to move upon an intrenched enemy, is but the story of Manassas repeated.

I beg to assure you that I have never written you, or spoken to you, in greater kindness of feeling than now, nor with a fuller purpose to sustain you, so far as in my most anxious judgment, I consistently can. *But you must act.* Yours very truly

Letter to General George B. McClellan.
Fort Monroe, Virginia, 9 May 1862

My dear Sir: I have just assisted the Secretary of War in framing the part of a dispatch to you, relating to army corps, which dispatch of course will have reached you long before this will. I wish to say a few words to you privately on this subject. I ordered the army corps organization not only on the unanimous opinion of the twelve generals whom you had selected and assigned as Generals of Division, but also on the unanimous opinion of every *military man* I could get an opinion from, and every modern military book, yourself only excepted. Of course, I did not, on my own judgment, pretend to understand the subject. I now think it indispensable for you to know how your struggle against it is received in quarters which we cannot entirely disregard. It is looked upon as merely an effort to pamper one or two pets, and to persecute and degrade their supposed rivals. I have had no word from Sumner, Heintzelman, or Keyes. The commanders of these corps are of course the three highest officers with you, but I am constantly told that you have no consultation or communication with them; that you consult and communicate with nobody but General Fitz John Porter, and perhaps General Franklin. I do not say these complaints are true or just; but at all events it is proper you should know of their existence. Do the commanders of corps disobey your orders in anything?

When you relieved General Hamilton of his command the other day, you thereby lost the confidence of at least one of your best friends in the Senate. And here let me say, not as applicable to you personally, that Senators and Representatives speak of me in their places as they please, without question; and that officers of the army must cease addressing insulting letters to them for taking no greater liberty with them.

But, to return, are you strong enough – are you strong enough, even with my help – to set your foot upon the necks of Sumner, Heintzelman, and Keyes all at once? This is a practical and very serious question for you.

The success of your army and the cause of the country are the same; and of course I only desire the good of the cause. Yours truly

Letter to Edwin M. Stanton, Secretary of War.

5 June 1862

My dear Sir: Herewith I return you the papers in relation to the proposed reappointment of William Kellogg, Jr, to a cadetship. Upon Gen. Totten's statement of the case I think it is natural that he should feel as he expresses himself. And yet the case comes upon me in the very strongest way to be painful to me. Hon. William Kellogg, the father, is not only a member of Congress from my state, but he is my personal friend of more than twenty years' standing, and of whom I had many personal kindnesses. This matter touches him very deeply – the feelings of a father for a child – as he thinks, all the future of his child. I cannot be the instrument to crush his heart. According to strict rule he has the right to make the renomination. Let the appointment be made. It needs not to become a precedent. Hereafter let no resignation be accepted under demerit amounting to cause for dismissal, unless upon express stipulation in writing that the cadet resigning shall not be renominated. In this I mean no censure upon Gen. Totten; and although I have marked this note '*private*' I am quite willing for him to see it. Yours truly

Telegram to General John C. Fremont, commanding the Mountain Department in western Virginia.

16 June 1862

Your dispatch of yesterday reminding me of a supposed understanding that I would furnish you a corps of thirty-five thousand men, and asking of me 'the fulfilment of this understanding' is received. I am ready to come to a fair settlement of accounts with you on the fulfilment of understandings.

Early in March last, when I assigned you to the command of the Mountain Department, I did tell you I would give you all the force I could, and that I hoped to make it reach thirty-five thousand. You, at the same time told me that, within a reasonable time, you would seize the railroad at, or east of, Knoxville, Tennessee, if you could. There was then in the Department a force supposed to be twenty-five thousand – the exact number as well known to you as to me. After looking about two or three days you called and distinctly told me that if I would add the Blenker division to the force already in the Department, you would undertake the job. The Blenker division contained ten thousand; and at the expense of great dissatisfaction to Gen. McClellan, I took it from his army, and gave it to you. My promise was literally fulfilled. I had given you all I could, and I had given you very nearly if not quite thirty-five thousand.

Now for yours. On the 23rd of May, largely over two months afterwards, you were at Franklin, Virginia, not within three hundred miles of Knoxville, nor within eighty miles of any part of the railroad east of it – and not moving forward, but telegraphing here that you could not move for lack of everything. Now, do not misunderstand me. I do not say you have not done all you could. I presume you met unexpected difficulties; and I beg you to believe that as surely as you have done your best, so have I. I have not the power now to fill up your corps to thirty-five thousand. I am not demanding of you to do the work of thirty-five thousand. I am only asking of you to stand cautiously on the defensive, get your force in order, and give such protection as you can to the valley of the Shenandoah, and to Western Virginia. Have you received the orders? and will you act upon them?

Telegram to General George B. McClellan, now engaged in the Seven Days Battles before Richmond.

26 June 1862

Your three dispatches of yesterday in relation to the affair, ending with the statement that you completely succeeded in making your point, are very gratifying. The later one of 6.15 p.m., suggesting the probability of your being overwhelmed by 200,000, and talking of where the responsibility will belong, pains me very much. I give you all I can, and act on the presumption that you will do the best you can with what you have, while you continue, ungenerously I think, to assume that I could give you more if I would. I have omitted and shall omit no opportunity to send you reinforcements whenever I possibly can.

Letter to Quintin Campbell, who had just entered West Point.
28 June 1862

My dear Sir: Your good mother tells me you are feeling very badly in your new situation. Allow me to assure you it is a perfect certainty that you will, very soon, feel better – quite happy – if you only stick to the resolution you have taken to procure a military education. I am older than you, have felt badly myself, and *know* what I tell you is true. Adhere to your purpose and you will soon feel as well as you ever did. On the contrary, if you falter and give up, you will lose the power of keeping any resolution, and will regret it all your life. Take the advice of a friend, who, though he never saw you, deeply sympathizes with you, and stick to your purpose. Sincerely your friend

Telegram to General George B. McClellan, whose army was taking heavy casualties in the Seven Days Battles.
28 June 1862

Save your army at all events. Will send reinforcements as fast as we can. Of course they cannot reach you to-day, to-morrow, or next day. I have not said you were ungenerous for saying you needed reinforcement. I thought you were ungenerous in assuming that I did not send them as fast as I could. I feel any misfortune to you and your army quite as keenly as you feel it yourself. If you have had a drawn battle, or a repulse, it is the price we pay for the enemy not being in Washington. We protected Washington, and the enemy concentrated on you; had we stripped Washington, he would have been upon us before the troops sent could have got to you. Less than a week ago you notified us that reinforcements were leaving Richmond to come in front of us. It is the nature of the case, and neither you or the government that is to blame. Please tell at once the present condition and aspect of things.
    P.S. Gen. Pope thinks if you fall back it would be much better

towards York River, than towards the James. As Pope now has charge of the Capital, please confer with him through the telegraph.

Telegram to General B. McClellan, at the end of the Seven Days Battles.

2 July 1862

Your dispatch of Tuesday morning induces me to hope your army is having some rest. In this hope, allow me to reason with you a moment. When you ask for fifty thousand men to be promptly sent you, you surely labor under some gross mistake of fact. Recently you sent papers showing your disposal of forces, made last spring, for the defense of Washington, and advising a return to that plan. I find it included in and about Washington seventy-five thousand men. Now please be assured, I have not men enough to fill that very plan by fifteen thousand. All of Fremont in the valley, all of Banks, all of McDowell, not with you, and all in Washington, taken together do not exceed, if they reach sixty thousand. With Wool and Dix added to those mentioned, I have not, outside of your army, seventy-five thousand men east of the mountains. Thus, the idea of sending you fifty thousand, or any other considerable force promptly, is simply absurd. If in your frequent mention of responsibility, you have the impression that I blame you for not doing more than you can, please be relieved of such impression. I only beg that in like manner, you will not ask impossibilities of me. If you think you are not strong enough to take Richmond just now, I do not ask you to try just now. Save the army, material and personal; and I will strengthen it for the offensive again as fast as I can. The governors of eighteen states offer me a new levy of three hundred thousand, which I accept.

Telegram to General George B. McClellan.

4 July 1862

I understand your position as stated in your letter, and by Gen. Marcy. To reinforce you so as to enable you to resume the offensive within a month, or even six weeks, is impossible. In addition to that arrived, and now arriving from the Potomac (about ten thousand, I suppose) and about ten thousand I hope you will have from Burnside very soon, and about five thousand from Hunter a little later, I do not see how I can send you another man within a month. Under these circumstances the defensive, for the present, must be your only care. Save the army — first, where you are, if you *can*; and secondly, by removal, if you must. You, on the ground, must be the judge as to which you will attempt, and of the means for effecting it. I but give it as opinion, that with the aid of the gunboats, and the reinforcements mentioned above, you can hold your present position, provided, and so long as, you can keep the James River open below you. If you are not tolerably confident you can keep the James River open, you had better remove as soon as possible. I do not remember that you have expressed any apprehension as to the danger of having your communication cut on the river below you; yet I do not suppose it can have escaped your attention. Yours very truly

P.S. If, at any time, you feel able to take the offensive, you are not restrained from doing so.

Telegram to General George B. McClellan.

5 July 1862

A thousand thanks for the relief your two dispatches of 12 and 1 p.m. yesterday give me. Be assured the heroism and skill of yourself, officers, and men, are, and forever will be appreciated. If you can hold your present position, we shall 'hive' the enemy yet.

To a delegation of Border State Congressmen.

12 July 1862

Gentlemen: After the adjournment of Congress, now very near, I shall have no opportunity of seeing you for several months. Believing that you of the border states hold more power for good than any other equal number of members, I feel it a duty which I cannot justifiably waive, to make this appeal to you. I intend no reproach or complaint when I assure you that in my opinion if you all had voted for the resolution in the gradual emancipation message of last March, the war would now be substantially ended. And the plan therein proposed is yet one of the most potent and swift means of ending it. Let the states which are in rebellion see, definitely and certainly, that, in no event, will the states you represent ever join their proposed Confederacy, and they cannot much longer maintain the contest. But you cannot divest them of their hope to ultimately have you with them so long as you show a determination to perpetuate the institution within your own states. Beat them at elections, as you have overwhelmingly done, and, nothing daunted, they still claim you as their own. You and I know what the lever of their power is. Break that lever before their faces, and they can shake you no more forever.

Most of you have treated me with kindness and consideration; and I trust you will not now think I improperly touch what is exclusively your own, when, for the sake of the whole country I ask, 'Can you, for your states, do better than to take the course I urge?' Discarding *punctilio*, and maxims adapted to more manageable times, and looking only to the unprecedentedly stern facts of our case, can you do better in any possible event? You prefer that the constitutional relation of the states to the nation shall be practically restored, without disturbance of the institution; and if this were done, my whole duty, in this respect, under the Constitution, and my oath of office, would be performed. But it is not done, and we are trying to accomplish it by war. The incidents of the war cannot be avoided. If the war continue long, as it must, if the object be not sooner attained, the institution in your states will be extinguished by mere friction and abrasion – by the mere incidents of the war. It will be gone, and you will have nothing valuable in lieu of it. Much of its value is gone already. How much better for you, and for your people, to take the step which, at once, shortens the war, and secures substantial compensation for that which is sure to be wholly lost in any other event. How much better to thus save the money which else we sink forever in the war. How much better to do it while we can, lest the war ere long render us pecuniarily unable to do it. How much better for you, as seller, and the nation as buyer, to sell out, and buy out, that without which the war could never have been, than to sink both the thing to be sold, and the price of it, in cutting one another's throats.

I do not speak of emancipation *at once*, but of a *decision* at once to emancipate *gradually*. Room in South America for colonization can be obtained cheaply and in abundance; and when numbers shall be large enough to be company and encouragement for one another, the freed people will not be so reluctant to go.

I am pressed with a difficulty not yet mentioned – one which threatens division among those who, united, are none too strong.

An instance of it is known to you. Gen. Hunter is an honest man. He was, and I hope, still is, my friend. I valued him none the less for his agreeing with me in the general wish that all men everywhere could be free. He proclaimed all men free within certain states, and I repudiated the proclamation. He expected more good, and less harm from the measure, than I could believe would follow. Yet in repudiating it, I gave dissatisfaction, if not offense, to many whose support the country cannot afford to lose. And this is not the end of it. The pressure, in this direction, is still upon me, and is increasing. By conceding what I now ask, you can relieve me, and much more, can relieve the country, in this important point. Upon these considerations I have again begged your attention to the message of March last. Before leaving the Capital, consider and discuss it among yourselves. You are patriots and statesmen; and, as such, I pray you, consider this proposition; and, at the least, commend it to the consideration of your states and people. As you would perpetuate popular government for the best people in the world, I beseech you that you do in no wise omit this. Our common country is in great peril, demanding the loftiest views, and boldest action to bring it speedy relief. Once relieved, its form of government is saved to the world; its beloved history, and cherished memories, are vindicated; and its happy future fully assured, and rendered inconceivably grand. To you, more than to any others, the privilege is given, to assure that happiness, and swell that grandeur, and to link your own names therewith forever.

Letter to Reverdy Johnson, who had reported on conditions in New Orleans under the Union occupation.

26 July 1862

My dear Sir: Yours of the 16th by the hand of Governor Shepley is received. It seems the Union feeling in Louisiana is being crushed out by the course of General Phelps. Please pardon me for believing that is a false pretense. The people of Louisiana — all intelligent people everywhere — know full well that I never had a wish to touch the foundations of their society, or any right of theirs. With perfect knowledge of this, they forced a necessity upon me to send armies among them, and it is their own fault, not mine, that they are annoyed by the presence of General Phelps. They also know the remedy — know how to be cured of General

Phelps. Remove the necessity of his presence. And might it not be well for them to consider whether they have not already had *time* enough to do this? If they can conceive of anything worse than General Phelps, within my power, would they not better be looking out for it? They very well know the way to avert all this is simply to take their place in the Union upon the old terms. If they will not do this, should they not receive harder blows rather than lighter ones?

You are ready to say I apply to *friends* what is due only to *enemies*. I distrust the *wisdom* if not the *sincerity* of friends, who would hold my hands while my enemies stab me. This appeal of professed friends has paralysed me more in this struggle than any other one thing. You remember telling me the day after the Baltimore mob in April 1861, that it would crush all Union feeling in Maryland for me to attempt bringing troops over Maryland soil to Washington. I brought the troops notwithstanding, and yet there was Union feeling enough left to elect a legislature the next autumn which in turn elected a very excellent Union US Senator!

I am a patient man – always willing to forgive on the Christian terms of repentance; and also to give ample *time* for repentance. Still I must save this government if possible. What I *cannot* do, of course I *will* not do; but it may as well be understood, once for all, that I shall not surrender this game leaving any available card unplayed. Yours truly

Letter to Cuthbert Bullitt, a New Orleans loyalist.

28 July 1862

Sir: The copy of a letter addressed to yourself by Mr Thomas J. Durant, has been shown to me. The writer appears to be an able, a dispassionate, and an entirely sincere man.[1] The first part of the letter is devoted to an effort to show that the Secession Ordinance of Louisiana was adopted against the will of a majority of the people. This is probably true; and in that fact may be found some instruction. Why did they allow the Ordinance to go into effect? Why did they not assert themselves? Why stand passive and allow themselves to be trodden down by a minority? Why did they not hold popular meetings, and have a convention of their own, to

---

[1] Durant was a New Orleans lawyer who had remained loyal to the Union. At the time of this letter he was the acknowledged leader of a movement to organize Louisiana as a free state.

express and enforce the true sentiment of the state? If pre-organization was against them *then*, why not do this *now*, that the United States Army is present to protect them? The paralysis – the dead palsy – of the government in this whole struggle is, that this class of men will do nothing for the government, nothing for themselves, except demanding that the government shall not strike its open enemies, lest they be struck by accident!

Mr Durant complains that in various ways the relation of master and slave is disturbed by the presence of our army; and he considers it particularly vexatious that this, in part, is done under cover of an act of Congress, while constitutional guarantees are suspended on the plea of military necessity. The truth is, that what is done and omitted about slaves, is done and omitted on the same military necessity. It is a military necessity to have men and money; and we can get neither in sufficient numbers, or amounts, if we keep from, or drive from, our lines, slaves coming to them. Mr Durant cannot be ignorant of the pressure in this direction; nor of my efforts to hold it within bounds till he, and such as he shall have time to help themselves.

I am not posted to speak understandingly on all the police regulations of which Mr Durant complains. If experience shows any one of them to be wrong, let them be set right. I think I can perceive, in the freedom of trade, which Mr Durant urges, that he would relieve both friends and enemies from the pressure of the blockade. By this he would serve the enemy more effectively than the enemy is able to serve himself. I do not say or believe that to serve the enemy is the purpose of Mr Durant; or that he is conscious of any purpose, other than national and patriotic ones. Still, if there were a class of men who, having no choice of sides in the contest, were anxious only to have quiet and comfort for themselves while it rages, and to fall in with the victorious side at the end of it, without loss to themselves, their advice as to the mode of conducting the contest would be precisely such as his is. He speaks of no duty – apparently thinks of none – resting upon Union men. He even thinks it injurious to the Union cause that they should be restrained in trade and passage without taking sides. They are to touch neither a sail nor a pump, but to be merely passengers – dead-heads at that – to be carried snug and dry, throughout the storm, and safely landed right side up. Nay, more; even a mutineer is to go untouched lest these sacred passengers receive an accidental wound.

Of course the rebellion will never be suppressed in Louisiana, if the professed Union men there will neither help to do it, nor permit the government to do it without their help.

Now, I think the true remedy is very different from what is suggested by Mr Durant. It does not lie in rounding the rough angles of the war, but in removing the necessity for the war. The people of Louisiana who wish protection to person and property, have but to reach forth their hands and take it. Let them, in good faith, reinaugurate the national authority, and set up a state government conforming thereto under the Constitution. They know how to do it, and can have the protection of the army while doing it. The army will be withdrawn so soon as such state government can dispense with its presence; and the people of the state can then upon the old constitutional terms, govern themselves to their own liking. This is very simple and easy.

If they will not do this, if they prefer to hazard all for the sake of destroying the government, it is for them to consider whether it is probable I will surrender the government to save them from losing all. If they decline what I suggest, you scarcely need to ask what I will do. What would you do in my position? Would you drop the war where it is? Or, would you prosecute it in future, with elder-stalk squirts, charged with rose-water? Would you deal lighter blows rather than heavier ones? Would you give up the contest, leaving any available means unapplied?

I am in no boastful mood. I shall not do *more* than I can, and I shall do *all* I can to save the government, which is my sworn duty as well as my personal inclination. I shall do nothing in malice. What I deal with is too vast for malicious dealing. Yours truly

Address on Colonization to a Deputation of Free Blacks.

14 August 1862

. . . You and we are different races. We have between us a broader difference than exists between almost any other two races. Whether it is right or wrong I need not discuss, but this physical difference is a great disadvantage to us both, as I think your race suffer very greatly, many of them by living among us, while ours suffer from your presence. In a word we suffer on each side. If this is admitted, it affords a reason at least why we should be separated . . .

Your race are suffering, in my judgment, the greatest wrong

inflicted on any people. But even when you cease to be slaves, you are yet far removed from being placed on an equality with the white race. You are cut off from many of the advantages which the other race enjoy. The aspiration of men is to enjoy equality with the best when free, but on this broad continent, not a single man of your race is made the equal of a single man of ours. Go where you are treated the best, and the ban is still upon you.

I do not propose to discuss this, but to present it as a fact with which we have to deal. I cannot alter it if I would. It is a fact, about which we all think and feel alike, I and you. We look to our condition, owing to the existence of the two races on this continent. I need not recount to you the effects upon white men, growing out of the institution of slavery. I believe in its general evil effects on the white race. See our present condition — the country engaged in war! — our white men cutting one another's throats, none knowing how far it will extend; and then consider what we know to be the truth. But for your race among us there could not be war, although many men engaged on either side do not care for you one way or the other. Nevertheless, I repeat, without the institution of slavery and the colored race as a basis, the war could not have an existence.

It is better for us both, therefore, to be separated . . .

Letter to Horace Greeley, editor of the New York Tribune.
22 August 1862

Dear Sir: I have just read yours of the 19th addressed to myself through the *New York Tribune*. If there be in it any statements, or assumptions of fact, which I may know to be erroneous, I do not, now and here, controvert them. If there be in it any inferences which I may believe to be falsely drawn, I do not now and here argue against them. If there be perceptible in it an impatient and dictatorial tone, I waive it in deference to an old friend, whose heart I have always supposed to be right.

As to the policy I 'seem to be pursuing' as you say, I have not meant to leave anyone in doubt.

I would save the Union. I would save it the shortest way under the Constitution. The sooner the national authority can be restored, the nearer the Union will be 'the Union as it was.' If there be those who would not save the Union, unless they could at the same time *save* slavery, I do not agree with them. If there be those who would not save the Union unless they could at the same time *destroy* slavery, I do not agree with them. My paramount object in this struggle *is* to save the Union, and is *not* either to save or to destroy slavery. If I could save the Union without freeing *any* slave I would do it, and if I could save it by freeing *all* the slaves I would do it; and if I could save it by freeing some and leaving others alone I would also do that. What I do about slavery, and the colored race, I do because I believe it helps to save the Union; and what I forbear, I forbear because I do *not* believe it would help to save the Union. I shall do *less* whenever I shall believe what I am doing hurts the cause, and I shall do *more* whenever I shall believe doing more will help the cause. I shall try to correct errors when shown to be errors; and I shall adopt new views so fast as they shall appear to be true views.

I have here stated my purpose according to my view of *official* duty; and I intend no modification of my oft-expressed *personal* wish that all men everywhere could be free. Yours

Meditation on the Divine Will.

[2 September 1862?]

The will of God prevails. In great contests each party claims to act in accordance with the will of God. Both *may* be, and one *must* be wrong. God cannot be *for*, and *against* the same thing at the same time. In the present civil war it is quite possible that God's purpose is something different from the purpose of either party – and yet the human instrumentalities, working just as they do, are of the best adaptation to effect His purpose. I am almost ready to say this is probably true – that God wills this contest, and wills that it shall not end yet. By his mere quiet power, on the minds of the now contestants, He could have either *saved* or *destroyed* the Union without a human contest. Yet the contest began. And having begun He could give the final victory to either side any day. Yet the contest proceeds.

Reply to Emancipation Memorial Presented by Chicago Christians of All Denominations (in which Lincoln offers a searching critique of the Emancipation Proclamation which he issued nine days later).

13 September 1862

... What good would a proclamation of emancipation from me

do, especially as we are now situated? I do not want to issue a document that the whole world will see must necessarily be inoperative, like the Pope's bull against the comet! Would my word free the slaves, when I cannot even enforce the Constitution in the rebel states? Is there a single court, or magistrate, or individual that would be influenced by it there? And what reason is there to think it would have any greater effect upon the slaves than the late law of Congress, which I approved, and which offers protection and freedom to the slaves of rebel masters who come within our lines? Yet I cannot learn that that law has caused a single slave to come over to us. And suppose they could be induced by a proclamation of freedom from me to throw themselves upon us, what should we do with them? How can we feed and care for such a multitude? . . .

I admit that slavery is the root of the rebellion, or at least its *sine qua non*. The ambition of politicians may have instigated them to act, but they would have been impotent without slavery as their instrument. I will also concede that emancipation would help us in Europe, and convince them that we are incited by something more than ambition. I grant further that it would help somewhat at the North, though not so much, I fear, as you and those you represent would imagine. Still, some additional strength would be added in that way to the war. And then unquestionably it would weaken the rebels by drawing off their laborers, which is of great importance. But I am not so sure we could do much with the blacks. If we were to arm them, I fear that in a few weeks the arms would be in the hands of the rebels; and indeed thus far we have not had arms enough to equip our white troops. I will mention another thing, though it meet only your scorn and contempt. There are fifty thousand bayonets in the Union armies from the Border Slave States. It would be a serious matter if, in consequence of a proclamation such as you desire, they should go over to the rebels. I do not think they all would—not so many indeed as a year ago, or as six months ago — not so many to-day as yesterday. Every day increases their Union feeling. They are also getting their pride enlisted, and want to beat the rebels. Let me say one thing more. I think you should admit that we already have an important principle to rally and unite the people in the fact that constitutional government is at stake. This is a fundamental idea, going down about as deep as any thing . . .

Do not misunderstand me, because I have mentioned these

objections. They indicate the difficulties that have thus far prevented my action in some such way as you desire. I have not decided against a proclamation of liberty to the slaves, but hold the matter under advisement. And I can assure you that the subject is on my mind, by day and night, more than any other. Whatever shall appear to be God's will I will do. I trust that, in the freedom with which I have canvassed your views, I have not in any respect injured your feelings.

First Proclamation of Emancipation.

22 September 1862

By the President of the
United States of America
A Proclamation

I, Abraham Lincoln, President of the United States of America, and Commander-in-Chief of the Army and Navy thereof, do hereby proclaim and declare that hereafter, as heretofore, the war will be prosecuted for the object of practically restoring the constitutional relation between the United States, and each of the states, and the people thereof, in which states that relation is, or may be suspended, or disturbed.

That it is my purpose, upon the next meeting of Congress to again recommend the adoption of a practical measure tendering pecuniary aid to the free acceptance or rejection of all slave-states, so-called, the people whereof may not then be in rebellion against the United States, and which states may then have voluntarily adopted, or thereafter may voluntarily adopt, immediate or gradual abolishment of slavery within their respective limits; and that the effort to colonize persons of African descent, with their consent, upon this continent, or elsewhere, with the previously obtained consent of the governments existing there, will be continued.

That on the first day of January in the year of our Lord, one thousand eight hundred and sixty-three, all persons held as slaves within any state, or designated part of a state, the people whereof shall then be in rebellion against the United States shall be then, thenceforward, and forever free; and the executive government of the United States, including the military and naval authority thereof, will recognize and maintain the freedom of such persons, and will do no act or acts to repress such persons, or any of them, in any efforts they may make for their actual freedom.

That the Executive will, on the first day of January aforesaid, by proclamation, designate the states, and parts of states, if any, in which the people thereof respectively, shall then be in rebellion against the United States; and the fact that any state, or the people thereof shall, on that day be, in good faith represented in the Congress of the United States, by members chosen thereto, at elections wherein a majority of the qualified voters of such state shall have participated, shall, in the absence of strong countervailing testimony, be deemed conclusive evidence that such state and the people thereof, are not then in rebellion against the United States.

That attention is hereby called to an act of Congress entitled 'An act to make an additional Article of War,' approved 13th March 1862, and which act is in the words and figure following:

'*Be it enacted by the Senate and House of Representatives of the United States of America in Congress assembled*, That hereafter the following shall be promulgated as an additional article of war for the government of the army of the United States, and shall be obeyed and observed as such:

'Article – All officers or persons in the military or naval service of the United States are prohibited from employing any of the forces under their respective commands for the purpose of returning fugitives from service or labor, who may have escaped from any persons to whom such service or labor is claimed to be due, and any officer who shall be found guilty by a court-martial of violating this article shall be dismissed from the service.

'SEC. 2. *And be it further enacted*, That this act shall take effect from and after its passage.'

Also to the ninth and tenth sections of an act entitled 'An Act to suppress Insurrection, to punish Treason and Rebellion, to seize and confiscate property of rebels, and for other purposes,' approved 17th July 1862, and which sections are in the words and figures following:

'SEC. 9. *And be it further enacted*, That all slaves of persons who shall hereafter be engaged in rebellion against the government of the United States, or who shall in any way give aid or comfort thereto, escaping from such persons and taking refuge within the lines of the army; and all slaves captured from such persons or deserted by them and coming under the control of the government of the United States; and all slaves of such persons found *on* (or) being within any place occupied by rebel forces and afterwards occupied by the forces of the United States, shall be deemed captives of war, and shall be forever free of their servitude and not again held as slaves.

'SEC. 10. *And be it further enacted*, That no slave escaping into any state, territory, or the District of Columbia, from any other state, shall be delivered up, or in any way impeded or hindered of his liberty, except for crime, or some offence against the laws, unless the person claiming said fugitive shall first make oath that the person to whom the labor or service of such fugitive is alleged to be due is his lawful owner, and has not borne arms against the United States in the present rebellion, nor in any way given aid and comfort thereto; and no person engaged in the military or naval service of the United States shall, under any pretense whatever, assume to decide on the validity of the claim of any person to the service or labor of any other person, or surrender up any such person to the claimant, on pain of being dismissed from the service.'

And I do hereby enjoin upon and order all persons engaged in the military and naval service of the United States to observe, obey, and enforce, within their respective spheres of service, the act, and sections above recited.

And the executive will in due time recommend that all citizens of the United States who shall have remained loyal thereto throughout the rebellion, shall (upon the restoration of the constitutional relation between the United States, and their respective states, and people, if that relation shall have been suspended or disturbed) be compensated for all losses by acts of the United States, including the loss of slaves.

In witness whereof, I have hereunto set my hand, and caused the seal of the United States to be affixed.

Done at the City of Washington, this twenty-second day of September, in the year of our Lord, one thousand eight hundred and sixty-two, and of the Independence of the United States, the eighty-seventh.

By the President: ABRAHAM LINCOLN.
WILLIAM H. SEWARD, Secretary of State.

Letter to General George B. McClellan, nearly a month after he had repulsed Lee at Antietam.

13 October 1862

My dear Sir: You remember my speaking to you of what I called your over-cautiousness. Are you not over-cautious when you assume that you cannot do what the enemy is constantly doing? Should you not claim to be at least his equal in prowess, and act upon the claim?

As I understand, you telegraph Gen. Halleck that you cannot subsist your army at Winchester unless the railroad from Harper's Ferry to that point be put in working order. But the enemy does now subsist his army at Winchester at a distance nearly twice as great from railroad transportation as you would have to do without the railroad last named. He now wagons from Culpeper C.H. which is just about twice as far as you would have to do from Harper's Ferry. He is certainly not more than half as well provided with wagons as you are. I certainly should be pleased for you to have the advantage of the railroad from Harper's Ferry to Winchester, but it wastes all the remainder of autumn to give it to you; and, in fact ignores the question of *time*, which cannot, and must not be ignored.

Again, one of the standard maxims of war, as you know, is 'to operate upon the enemy's communications as much as possible without exposing your own.' You seem to act as if this applies *against* you, but cannot apply in your *favor*. Change positions with the enemy, and think you not he would break your communication with Richmond within the next twenty-four hours? You dread his going into Pennsylvania. But if he does so in full force, he gives up his communications to you absolutely, and you have nothing to do but to follow, and ruin him; if he does so with less than full force, fall upon, and beat what is left behind all the easier.

Exclusive of the water-line, you are now nearer Richmond than the enemy is by the route that you *can*, and he *must* take. Why can you not reach there before him, unless you admit that he is more than your equal on a march. His route is the arc of a circle, while yours is the chord. The roads are as good on yours as on his.

You know I desired, but did not order, you to cross the Potomac below, instead of above the Shenandoah and Blue Ridge. My idea was that this would at once menace the enemy's communications, which I would seize if he would permit. If he should move northward I would follow him closely, holding his communications. If he should prevent our seizing his communications and move towards Richmond, I would press closely to him, fight him if a favorable opportunity should present, and, at least, try to beat him to Richmond on the inside track. I say 'try'; if we never try, we shall never succeed. If he make a stand at Winchester, moving neither north or south, I would fight him there, on the idea that if we cannot beat him when he bears the wastage of coming to us, we never can when we bear the wastage of going to him. This proposition is a simple truth, and is too important to be lost sight of for a moment. In coming to us, he tenders us an advantage which we should not waive. We should not so operate as to merely drive him away. As we must beat him somewhere, or fail finally, we can do it, if at all, easier near to us, than far away. If we cannot beat the enemy where he now is, we never can, he again being within the entrenchments of Richmond.

Recurring to the idea of going to Richmond on the inside track, the facility of supplying from the side away from the enemy is remarkable − as it were, by the different spokes of a wheel extending from the hub towards the rim − and this whether you move directly by the chord, or on the inside arc, hugging the Blue Ridge more closely. The chord-line, as you see, carries you by Aldie, Hay-Market, and Fredericksburg; and you see how turnpikes, railroads, and finally, the Potomac by Acquia Creek, meet you at all points from Washington. The same, only the lines lengthened a little, if you press closer to the Blue Ridge part of the way. The gaps through the Blue Ridge I understand to be about the following distances from Harper's Ferry, to wit: Vestal's five miles; Gregorie's, thirteen, Snicker's eighteen, Ashby's, twenty-eight, Manassas, thirty-eight, Chester, forty-five, and Thornton's fifty-three. I should think it preferable to take the route nearest the enemy, disabling him to make an important move without your knowledge, and compelling him to keep his forces together, for dread of you. The gaps would enable you to attack if you should wish. For a great part of the way you would be practically between the enemy and both Washington and Richmond, enabling us to spare you the greatest number of troops from here. When at length, running for Richmond ahead of him enables him to move this way; if he does so, turn and attack him in rear. But I think he should be engaged long before such point is reached. It is all easy if our troops march as well as the enemy; and it is unmanly to say they cannot do it.

This letter is in no sense an order. Yours truly

Telegram to General George B. McClellan.

24 October 1862

I have just read your dispatch about sore-tongued and fatigued horses. Will you pardon me for asking what the horses of your army have done since the Battle of Antietam that fatigue anything?

Telegram to General George B. McClellan.

27 October 1862

Yours of yesterday received. Most certainly I intend no injustice to any; and if I have done any, I deeply regret it. To be told after more than five weeks total inaction of the army, and during which period we had sent to that army every fresh horse we possibly could, amounting in the whole to 7,918 that the cavalry horses were too much fatigued to move, presented a very cheerless, almost hopeless, prospect for the future; and it may have forced something of impatience into my dispatches. If not recruited, and rested then, when could they ever be? I suppose the river is rising, and I am glad to believe you are crossing.[1]

Letter to Samuel Treat, a federal judge at St Louis.

19 November 1862

My dear Sir: Your very patriotic and judicious letter, addressed to Judge Davis, in relation to the Mississipi, has been left with me by him for perusal. You do not estimate the value of the object you press, more highly than it is estimated here. It is now the object of particular attention. It has not been neglected, as you seem to think, because the West was divided into different military departments. The cause is much deeper. The country will not allow us to send our whole western force down the Mississippi, while the enemy sacks Louisville and Cincinnati. Possibly it

[1] On 5 November 1862 Lincoln relieved McClellan of command of the Army of the Potomac, replacing him with General Ambrose E. Burnside.

would be better if the country would allow this, but it will not. I confidently believed, last September, that we could end the war by allowing the enemy to go to Harrisburg and Philadelphia, only that we could not keep down mutiny, and utter demoralization among the Pennsylvanians. And this, though very unhandy sometimes, is not at all strange. I presume if an army was starting to-day for New Orleans, and you confidently believed that St Louis would be sacked in consequence, you would be in favor of stopping such army.

We are compelled to watch all these things. With great respect Your Obt. Servt.

Letter to Brigadier General Carl Schurz, in civil life a leader of the German-American wing of the Republican party.

24 November 1862

My dear Sir: I have just received, and read, your letter of the 20th. The purport of it is that we lost the late elections, and the administration is failing, because the war is unsuccessful; and that I must not flatter myself that I am not justly to blame for it. I certainly know that if the war fails, the administration fails, and that I *will* be blamed for it, whether I deserve it or not. And I ought to be blamed, if I could do better. You think I could do better; therefore you blame me already. I think I could not do better; therefore I blame you for blaming me. I understand you *now* to be willing to accept the help of men, who are not Republicans, provided they have 'heart in it.' Agreed. I want no others. But who is to be the judge of hearts, or of 'heart in it'? If I must discard my own judgment, and take yours, I must also take that of others; and by the time I should reject all I should be advised to reject, I should have none left, Republicans, or others – not even yourself. For, be assured, my dear sir, there are men who have 'heart in it' that think you are performing your part as poorly as you think I am performing mine. I certainly have been dissatisfied with the slowness of Buell and McClellan; but before I relieved them I had great fears I should not find successors to them, who would do better; and I am sorry to add, that I have seen little since to relieve those fears. I do not clearly see the prospect of any more rapid movements. I fear we shall at last find out that the difficulty is in our case, rather than in particular generals. I wish to disparage no one – certainly not those who sympathize with me; but I must say

I need success more than I need sympathy, and that I have not seen the so much greater evidence of getting success from my sympathizers, than from those who are denounced as the contrary. It does seem to me that in the field the two classes have been very much alike, in what they have done, and what they have failed to do. In sealing their faith with their blood, Baker, and Lyon, and Bohlen, and Richardson, Republicans, did all that men could do; but did they any more than Kearney, and Stevens, and Reno, and Mansfield, none of whom were Republicans, and some at least of whom have been bitterly, and repeatedly, denounced to me as secession sympathizers? I will not perform the ungrateful task of comparing cases of failure.

In answer to your question 'Has it not been publicly stated in the newspapers, and apparently proved as a fact, that from the commencement of the war the enemy was continually supplied with information by some of the confidential subordinates of as important an officer as Adjutant General Thomas?' I must say 'no' so far as my knowledge extends. And I add that if you can give any tangible evidence upon that subject, I will thank you to come to the City and do so. Very truly Your friend

From the Annual Message to Congress.

1 December 1862

. . . On the twenty-second day of September last a proclamation was issued by the Executive, a copy of which is herewith submitted.

In accordance with the purpose expressed in the second paragraph of that paper, I now respectfully recall your attention to what may be called 'compensated emancipation.'

A nation may be said to consist of its territory, its people, and its laws. The territory is the only part which is of certain durability. 'One generation passeth away, and another generation cometh, but the earth abideth forever.' It is of the first importance to duly consider, and estimate, this ever-enduring part. That portion of the earth's surface which is owned and inhabited by the people of the United States, is well adapted to be the home of one national family; and it is not well adapted for two, or more. Its vast extent, and its variety of climate and productions, are of advantage, in this age, for one people, whatever they might have been in former ages. Steam, telegraphs, and intelligence, have brought these to be an advantageous combination for one united people . . .

There is no line, straight or crooked, suitable for a national boundary, upon which to divide. Trace through, from east to west, upon the line between the free and slave country, and we shall find a little more than one-third of its length are rivers, easy to be crossed, and populated, or soon to be populated, thickly upon both sides; while nearly all its remaining length, are merely surveyors' lines, over which people may walk back and forth without any consciousness of their presence. No part of this line can be made any more difficult to pass, by writing it down on paper, or parchment, as a national boundary. The fact of separation, if it comes, gives up, on the part of the seceding section, the fugitive slave clause, along with all other constitutional obligations upon the section seceded from, while I should expect no treaty stipulation would ever be made to take its place.

But there is another difficulty. The great interior region, bounded east by the Alleghanies, north by the British dominions, west by the Rocky Mountains, and south by the line along which the culture of corn and cotton meets, and which includes part of Virginia, part of Tennessee, all of Kentucky, Ohio, Indiana, Michigan, Wisconsin, Illinois, Missouri, Kansas, Iowa, Minnesota, and the Territories of Dakota, Nebraska, and part of Colorado, already has above ten millions of people, and will have fifty millions within fifty years, if not prevented by any political folly or mistake. It contains more than one-third of the country owned by the United States — certainly more than one million of square miles. Once half as populous as Massachusetts already is, it would have more than seventy-five millions of people. A glance at the map shows that, territorially speaking, it is the great body of the republic. The other parts are but marginal borders to it, the magnificent region sloping west from the Rocky Mountains to the Pacific, being the deepest, and also the richest, in undeveloped resources. In the production of provisions, grains, grasses, and all which proceed from them, this great interior region is naturally one of the most important in the world. Ascertain from the statistics the small proportion of the region which has, as yet, been brought into cultivation, and also the large and rapidly increasing amount of its products, and we shall be overwhelmed with the magnitude of the prospect presented. And yet this region has no sea-coast, touches no ocean anywhere. As part of one nation, its people now find and may forever find, their way to Europe by New York, to South America and Africa by New Orleans, and to Asia by San Francisco. But separate our common country into two nations, as designed by the present rebellion, and every man of this great interior region is thereby cut off from some one or more of these outlets, not, perhaps, by a physical barrier, but by embarrassing and onerous trade regulations.

And this is true, *wherever* a dividing, or boundary line, may be fixed. Place it between the now free and slave country, or place it south of Kentucky, or north of Ohio, and still the truth remains, that none south of it can trade to any port or place north of it, and none north of it can trade to any port or place south of it, except upon terms dictated by a government foreign to them. These outlets, east, west, and south, are indispensable to the well-being of the people inhabiting, and to inhabit, this vast interior region. *Which* of the three may be the best, is no proper question. All are better than either, and all, of right, belong to that people, and to their successors forever. True to themselves, they will not ask *where* a line of separation shall be, but will vow, rather, that there shall be no such line. Nor are the marginal regions less interested in these communications to, and through them, to the great outside world. They too, and each of them, must have access to this Egypt of the West, without paying toll at the crossing of any national boundary.

Our national strife springs not from our permanent part; not from the land we inhabit; not from our national homestead. There is no possible severing of this, but would multiply, and not mitigate, evils among us. In all its adaptations and aptitudes, it demands union, and abhors separation. In fact, it would, ere long, force reunion, however much of blood and treasure the separation might have cost.

Our strife pertains to ourselves – to the passing generations of men; and it can, without convulsion, be hushed forever with the passing of one generation.

In this view, I recommend the adoption of the following resolution and articles amendatory to the Constitution of the United States:

'*Resolved by the Senate and House of Representatives of the United States of America in Congress assembled* (two-thirds of both houses concurring), That the following articles be proposed to the legislatures (or conventions) of the several states as amendments to the Constitution of the United States, all or any of which articles when ratified by three-fourths of the said legislatures (or conventions) to be valid as part or parts of the said Constitution, viz.:

'Article –

'every state, wherein slavery now exists, which shall abolish the same therein, at any time, or times, before the first day of January, in the year of our Lord one thousand and nine hundred, shall receive compensation from the United States as follows, to wit:

'The President of the United States shall deliver to every such state, bonds of the United States, bearing interest at the rate of — per cent, per annum, to an amount equal to the aggregate sum of   for each slave shown to have been therein, by the eighth census of the United States, said bonds to be delivered to such state by instalments, or in one parcel, at the completion of the abolishment, accordingly as the same shall have been gradual, or at one time, within such state; and interest shall begin to run upon any such bond, only from the proper time of its delivery as aforesaid. Any state having received bonds as aforesaid, and afterwards reintroducing or tolerating slavery therein, shall refund to the United States the bonds so received, or the value thereof, and all interest paid thereon.

'Article –

'all slaves who shall have enjoyed actual freedom by the chances of the war, at any time before the end of the rebellion, shall be forever free; but all owners of such, who shall not have been disloyal, shall be compensated for them, at the same rates as is provided for states adopting abolishment of slavery, but in such way that no slave shall be twice accounted for.

'Article –

'congress may appropriate money, and otherwise provide, for colonizing free colored persons, with their own consent, at any place or places without the United States.'

I beg indulgence to discuss these proposed articles at some length. Without slavery the rebellion could never have existed; without slavery it could not continue.

Among the friends of the Union there is great diversity, of sentiment, and of policy, in regard to slavery, and the African race amongst us. Some would perpetuate slavery; some would abolish it suddenly, and without compensation; some would abolish it gradually, and with compensation; some would remove the freed people from us, and some would retain them with us; and there are yet other minor diversities. Because of these diversities, we waste much strength in struggles among ourselves. By mutual concession we should harmonize, and act together. This would be compromise; but it would be compromise among the friends, and not with the enemies of the Union. These articles are intended to embody a plan of such mutual concessions. If the plan shall be adopted, it is assumed that emancipation will follow, at least in several of the states.

As to the first article, the main points are: first, the emancipation; secondly, the length of time for consummating it — thirty-seven years; and thirdly, the compensation.

The emancipation will be unsatisfactory to the advocates of perpetual slavery; but the length of time should greatly mitigate their dissatisfaction. The time spares both races from the evils of sudden derangement — in fact, from the necessity of any derangement — while most of those whose habitual course of thought will be disturbed by the measure will have passed away before its consummation. They will never see it. Another class will hail the prospect of emancipation, but will deprecate the length of time. They will feel that it gives too little to the now living slaves. But it really gives them much. It saves them from the vagrant destitution which must largely attend immediate emancipation in localities where their numbers are very great; and it gives the inspiring assurance that their posterity shall be free forever. The plan leaves to each state, choosing to act under it, to abolish slavery now, or at the end of the century, or at any intermediate time, or by degrees, extending over the whole or any part of the period; and it obliges no two states to proceed alike. It also provides for compensation, and generally the mode of making it. This, it would seem, must further mitigate the dissatisfaction of those who favor perpetual slavery, and especially of those who are to receive the compensation. Doubtless some of those who are to pay and not to receive will object. Yet the measure is both just and economical. In a certain sense the liberation of slaves is the destruction of property — property acquired by descent, or by purchase, the same as any other property. It is no less true for having been often said, that the people of the South are not more responsible for the original introduction of this property, than are the people of the North; and when it is remembered how unhesitatingly we all use cotton and sugar, and share the profits of dealing in them, it may not be quite safe to say, that the South has been more responsible than the North for its continuance. If then, for a common object, this property is to be sacrificed is it not just that it be done at a common charge?

And if, with less money, or money more easily paid, we can preserve the benefits of the Union by this means, than we can by the war alone, is it not also economical to do it? Let us consider it then. Let us ascertain the sum we have expended in the war since compensated emancipation was proposed last March, and consider whether, if that measure had been promptly accepted, by even some of the slave states, the same sum would not have done more to close the war, than has been otherwise done. If so the measure would save money, and, in that view, would be a prudent and economical measure. Certainly it is not so easy to pay *something* as it is to pay *nothing*; but it is easier to pay a *large* sum than it is to pay a larger one. And it is easier to pay any sum *when* we are able, than it is to pay it *before* we are able. The war requires large sums, and requires them at once. The aggregate sum necessary for compensated emancipation, of course, would be large. But it would require no ready cash; nor the bonds even, any faster than the emancipation progresses. This might not, and probably would not, close before the end of the thirty-seven years. At that time we shall probably have a hundred millions of people to share the burden, instead of thirty-one millions, as now . . .

The proposed emancipation would shorten the war, perpetuate peace, insure this increase of population, and proportionately the wealth of the country. With these, we should pay all the emancipation would cost, together with our other debt, easier than we should pay our other debt without it. If we had allowed our old national debt to run at 6 per cent per annum, simple interest, from the end of our revolutionary struggle until to-day, without paying anything on either principal or interest, each man of us would owe less upon that debt now, than each man owed upon it then; and this because our increase of men, through the whole period, has been greater than 6 per cent; has run faster than the interest upon the debt. Thus, time alone relieves a debtor nation, so long as its population increases faster than unpaid interest accumulates on its debt.

This fact would be no excuse for delaying payment of what is justly due; but it shows the great importance of time in this connection – the great advantage of a policy by which we shall not have to pay until we number a hundred millions, what, by a different policy, we would have to pay now, when we number but thirty-one millions. In a word, it shows that a dollar will be much harder to pay for the war than will be a dollar for emancipation on the proposed plan. And then the latter will cost no blood, no precious life. It will be a saving of both.

As to the second article, I think it would be impracticable to return to bondage the class of persons therein contemplated. Some of them, doubtless, in the property sense, belong to loyal owners; and hence, provision is made in this article for compensating such.

The third article relates to the future of the freed people. It does not oblige, but merely authorizes, Congress to aid in colonizing such as may consent. This ought not to be regarded as objectionable, on the one hand, or on the other, in so much as it comes to nothing, unless by the mutual consent of the people to be deported, and the American voters, through their representatives in Congress.

I cannot make it better known than it already is, that I strongly favor colonization. And yet I wish to say there is an objection urged against free colored persons remaining in the country, which is largely imaginary, if not sometimes malicious.

It is insisted that their presence would injure and displace white labor and white laborers. If there ever could be a proper time for mere catch arguments, that time surely is not now. In times like the present, men should utter nothing for which they would not willingly be responsible through time and in eternity. Is it true, then, that colored people can displace any more white labor, by being free, than by remaining slaves? If they stay in their old places, they jostle no white laborers; if they leave their old places, they leave them open to white laborers. Logically, there is neither more nor less of it. Emancipation, even without deportation, would probably enhance the wages of white labor, and, very surely, would not reduce them. Thus, the customary amount of labor would still have to be performed; the freed people would surely not do more than their old proportion of it, and very probably, for a time, would do less, leaving an increased part to white laborers, bringing their labor into greater demand, and, consequently, enhancing the wages of it. With deportation, even to a limited extent, enhanced wages to white labor is mathematically certain. Labor is like any other commodity in the market — increase the demand for it, and you increase the price for it. Reduce the supply of black labor, by colonizing the black laborer out of the country, and, by precisely so much, you increase the demand for, and wages of, white labor.

But it is dreaded that the freed people will swarm forth, and cover the whole land. Are they not already in the land? Will liberation make them any more numerous? Equally distributed among the whites of the whole country, and there would be but one colored to seven whites. Could the one, in any way, greatly disturb the seven? There are many communities now, having more than one free colored person, to seven whites; and this, without any apparent consciousness of evil from it. The District of Columbia, and the states of Maryland and Delaware, are all in this condition. The District has more than one free colored to six whites; and yet, in its frequent petitions to Congress, I believe it has never presented the presence of free colored persons as one of its grievances. But why should emancipation south, send the free people north? People, of any color, seldom run, unless there be something to run from. *Heretofore* colored people, to some extent, have fled north from bondage; and *now*, perhaps, from both bondage and destitution. But if gradual emancipation and deportation be adopted, they will have neither to flee from. Their old masters will give them wages at least until new laborers can be procured; and the freed men, in turn, will gladly give their labor for the wages, till new homes can be found for them, in congenial climes, and with people of their own blood and race. This proposition can be trusted on the mutual interests involved. And, in any event, cannot the North decide for itself whether to receive them?

Again, as practice proves more than theory in any case, has there been any irruption of colored people northward, because of the abolishment of slavery in this District last spring?

What I have said of the proportion of free colored persons to the whites, in the District, is from the census of 1860, having no reference to persons called contrabands, nor to those made free by the act of Congress abolishing slavery here.

The plan consisting of these articles is recommended, not but that a restoration of the national authority would be accepted without its adoption.

Nor will the war, nor proceedings under the proclamation of 22nd September 1862, be stayed because of the *recommendation* of this plan. Its timely *adoption*, I doubt not, would bring restoration and thereby stay both.

And, notwithstanding this plan, the recommendation that Congress provide by law for compensating any state which may adopt emancipation, before this plan shall have been acted upon, is hereby earnestly renewed. Such would be only an advance part of the plan, and the same arguments apply to both.

This plan is recommended as a means, not in exclusion of, but additional to, all others for restoring and preserving the national authority throughout the Union. The subject is presented exclusively in its economical aspect. The plan would, I am confident, secure peace more speedily, and maintain it more permanently, than can be done by force alone; while all it would cost, considering amounts, and manner of payment, and times of payment, would be easier paid than will be the additional cost of the war if we rely solely upon force. It is much – very much – that it would cost no blood at all.

The plan is proposed as permanent constitutional law. It cannot become such without the concurrence of, first, two-thirds of Congress, and, afterwards, three-fourths of the states. The requisite three-fourths of the states will necessarily include seven of the slave states. Their concurrence, if obtained, will give assurance of their severally adopting emancipation, at no very distant day, upon the new constitutional terms. This assurance would end the struggle now, and save the Union forever.

I do not forget the gravity which should characterize a paper addressed to the Congress of the nation by the Chief Magistrate of the nation. Nor do I forget that some of you are my seniors, nor that many of you have more experience than I, in the conduct of public affairs. Yet I trust that in view of the great responsibility resting upon me, you will perceive no want of respect to yourselves, in any undue earnestness I may seem to display.

Is it doubted, then, that the plan I propose, if adopted, would shorten the war, and thus lessen its expenditure of money and of blood? Is it doubted that it would restore the national authority and national prosperity, and perpetuate both indefinitely? Is it doubted that we here – Congress and Executive – can secure its adoption? Will not the good people respond to a united, and earnest appeal from us? Can we, can they, by any other means, so certainly, or so speedily, assure these vital objects? We can succeed only by concert. It is not 'can *any* of us *imagine* better?' but 'can we *all* do better?' Object whatsoever is possible, still the question recurs 'can we do better?' The dogmas of the quiet past, are inadequate to the stormy present. The occasion is piled high with difficulty, and we must rise with the occasion. As our case is new, so we must think anew and act anew. We must disenthral ourselves, and then we shall save our country.

Fellow-citizens, *we* cannot escape history. We of this Congress and this administration, will be remembered in spite of ourselves. No personal significance, or insignificance, can spare one or another of us. The fiery trial through which we pass, will light us down, in honor or dishonor, to the latest generation. We *say* we are for the Union. The world will not forget that we say this. We know how to save the Union. The world knows we do know how to save it. We – even *we here* – hold the power, and bear the responsibility. In *giving* freedom to the *slave*, we *assure* freedom to the *free* – honorable alike in what we give, and what we preserve. We shall nobly save, or meanly lose, the last best, hope of earth. Other means may succeed; this could not fail. The way is plain, peaceful, generous, just – a way which, if followed, the world will forever applaud, and God must forever bless.

Letter to Fanny McCullough, whose father, a friend of Lincoln's, had recently been killed in battle.

23 December 1862

Dear Fanny: It is with deep grief that I learn of the death of your kind and brave father; and, especially, that it is affecting your young heart beyond what is common in such cases. In this sad world of ours, sorrow comes to all; and, to the young, it comes with bitterest agony, because it takes them unawares. The older have learned to ever expect it. I am anxious to afford some alleviation of your present distress. Perfect relief is not possible, except with time. You cannot now realize that you will ever feel better. Is not this so? And yet it is a mistake. You are sure to be happy again. To know this, which is certainly true, will make you some less miserable now. I have had experience enough to know what I say; and you need only to believe it, to feel better at once. The memory of your dear father, instead of an agony, will yet be a sad sweet feeling in your heart, of a purer, and holier sort than you have known before.

Please present my kind regards to your afflicted mother. Your sincere friend

The Proclamation of Emancipation.   1 January 1863

By the President of the United States of America:
A Proclamation.

Whereas, on the twenty-second day of September, in the year of our Lord one thousand eight hundred and sixty-two, a proclamation was issued by the President of the United States, containing among other things, the following, to wit:

'That on the first day of January, in the year of our Lord one thousand eight hundred and sixty-three, all persons held as slaves within any State or designated part of a State, the people whereof shall then be in rebellion against the United States, shall be then, thenceforward, and forever free; and the Executive Government of the United States, including the military and naval authority thereof, will recognize and maintain the freedom of such persons, and will do no act or acts to repress such persons, or any of them, in any efforts they may make for their actual freedom.

'That the Executive will, on the first day of January aforesaid, by proclamation, designate the States and parts of States, if any, in which the people thereof, respectively, shall then be in rebellion against the United States; and the fact that any State, or the people thereof, shall on that day be, in good faith, represented in the Congress of the United States by members chosen thereto at elections wherein a majority of the qualified voters of such State shall have participated, shall, in the absence of strong countervailing testimony, be deemed conclusive evidence that such State, and the people thereof, are not then in rebellion against the United States.'

Now, therefore I, Abraham Lincoln, President of the United States, by virtue of the power in me vested as Commander-in-Chief, of the Army and Navy of the United States in time of actual armed rebellion against authority and government of the United States, and as a fit and necessary war measure for suppressing said rebellion, do, on this first day of January, in the year of our Lord one thousand eight hundred and sixty-three, and in accordance with my purpose, so to do publicly proclaimed for the full period of one hundred days, from the day first above mentioned, order and designate as the States and parts of States wherein the people thereof respectively, are this day in rebellion against the United States, the following, to wit:

Arkansas, Texas, Louisiana (except the Parishes of St Bernard, Plaquemines, Jefferson, St Johns, St Charles, St James, Ascension, Assumption, Terrebonne, Lafourche, St Mary, St Martin, and Orleans, including the City of New Orleans), Mississippi, Alabama, Florida, Georgia, South Carolina, North Carolina, and Virginia (except the forty-eight counties designated as West Virginia, and also the counties of Berkley, Accomac, Northampton, Elizabeth-City, York, Princess Ann, and Norfolk, including the cities of Norfolk and Portsmouth); and which excepted parts are, for the present, left precisely as if this proclamation were not issued.

And by virtue of the power, and for the purpose aforesaid, I do order and declare that all persons held as slaves within said designated States, and parts of States, are, and henceforward shall be free; and that the Executive Government of the United States, including the military and naval authorities thereof, will recognize and maintain the freedom of said persons.

And I hereby enjoin upon the people so declared to be free to abstain from all violence, unless in necessary self-defense; and I recommend to them that, in all cases when allowed, they labor faithfully for reasonable wages.

And I further declare and make known, that such persons of suitable condition will be received into the armed service of the United States to garrison forts, positions, stations, and other places, and to man vessels of all sorts in said service.

And upon this act, sincerely believed to be an act of justice, warranted by the Constitution, upon military necessity, I invoke the considerate judgment of mankind, and the gracious favor of Almighty God.

In witness whereof, I have hereunto set my hand and caused the seal of the United States to be affixed.

> Done at the City of Washington, this first day of January, in the year of our Lord one thousand eight hundred and sixty-three, and of the Independence of the United States of America the eighty-seventh.   ABRAHAM LINCOLN.

By the President:
WILLIAM H. SEWARD, Secretary of State.

Chapter 8
A President
in His Prime
1863

The Emancipation Proclamations enabled Lincoln to unite his passion for the Union with his commitment to freedom for the slaves. A new confidence and authority can be discerned in his writings during 1863. This is nowhere clearer than in his masterly letters of 12 June and 26 August 1863, in reply to his Democratic critics, to whom he is courteous but merciless.

The year began with more military disappointments and delays, and one more humiliating defeat, at Chancellorsville in May. Lincoln's letters to General Hooker, whose confidence considerably outstripped his proven performance, can have few parallels in the history of civil-military relations. Hooker described the letter appointing him to command the Army of the Potomac, but containing severe words of warning and rebuke, as the kind of letter which a father might write to his son.

In June Lee, seeking a spectacular victory on Northern soil, launched his invasion of Pennsylvania. On the first three days of July, at Gettysburg, a new Union commander, General Meade, successfully withstood Lee's assaults. On the next day, far away to the south-west, Grant's long campaign in Mississippi ended in triumph with the capture of Vicksburg. These two victories were the turning-point in the war, but, in an unrelenting struggle to the death of this kind, the end did not come for another twenty-one months. Lincoln bitterly regretted the failure to follow up the successes of midsummer 1863 – as his letter to Meade of 14 July (never actually sent) amply illustrates.

Lincoln showed an ever deeper understanding of the underlying and universal issues at stake in the war. His letter of

19 January to the working men of Manchester addresses these issues. However, they are most succinctly and sublimely expressed in the words of the Gettysburg Address in November – a speech often dismissed and ridiculed at the time, but clearly appreciated by Edward Everett, the formal orator for the occasion.

Letter to General Samuel R. Curtis, commanding the Department of the Missouri.

2 January 1863

My dear Sir: Yours of 29th Dec. by the hand of Mr Strong is just received. The day I telegraphed you suspending the order in relation to Dr McPheeters, he, with Mr Bates, the Attorney-General, appeared before me, and left with me a copy of the order mentioned. The doctor also showed me the copy of an oath which he said he had taken, which is, indeed, very strong and specific. He also verbally assured me that he had constantly prayed in church for the President and government, as he had always done before the present war. In looking over the recitals in your order, I do not see that this matter of the prayer, as he states it, is negatived; nor that any violation of his oath is charged; nor, in fact, that anything specific is alleged against him. The charges are all general – that he has a rebel wife and rebel relations, that he sympathizes with rebels, and that he exercises rebel influence. Now, after talking with him, I tell you frankly, I believe he does sympathize with the rebels; but the question remains whether such a man, of unquestioned good moral character, who has taken such an oath as he has, and cannot even be charged of violating it, and who can be charged with no other specific act or omission, can, with safety to the government be exiled, upon the suspicion of his secret sympathies. But I agree that this must be left to you who are on the spot; and if, after all, you think the public good requires his removal, my suspension of the order is withdrawn, only with this qualification that the time during the suspension, is not to be counted against him. I have promised him this.

But I must add that the US government must not, as by this order, undertake to run the churches. When an individual, in a church or out of it, becomes dangerous to the public interest, he must be checked; but let the churches as such take care of themselves. It will not do for the US to appoint trustees, supervisors, or other agents for the churches. Yours very truly

P.S. The committee composed of Messrs Yeatman and Filley (Mr Brodhead not attending) has presented your letter and the memorial of sundry citizens. On the whole subject embraced, exercise your best judgment, with a sole view to the public interest, and I will not interfere without hearing you.

Letter to General John A. McClernand.

8 January 1863

My dear Sir: Your interesting communication by the hand of Major Scates is received.[1] I never did ask more, nor ever was willing to accept less, than for all the states, and the people thereof, to take and hold their places, and their rights, in the Union, under the Constitution of the United States. For this alone have I felt authorized to struggle; and I seek neither more nor less now. Still, to use a coarse but an expressive figure, broken eggs cannot be mended. I have issued the emancipation proclamation, and I cannot retract it.

After the commencement of hostilities I struggled nearly a year and a half to get along without touching the 'institution'; and when finally I conditionally determined to touch it, I gave a hundred days' fair notice of my purpose, to all the states and people, within which time they could have turned it wholly aside, by simply again becoming good citizens of the United States. They chose to disregard it, and I made the peremptory proclamation on what appeared to me to be a military necessity. And being made, it must stand. As to the states not included in it, of course they can have their rights in the Union as of old. Even the people of the states included, if they choose, need not to be hurt by it. Let them adopt systems of apprenticeship for the colored people, conforming substantially to the most approved plans of gradual emancipation; and, with the aid they can have from the general government, they may be nearly as well off, in this respect, as if the present trouble had not occurred, and much better off than they can possibly be if the contest continues persistently.

---

[1] McClernand had written that Confederate officers, formerly his personal and political friends, 'desire the restoration of peace and are represented to be willing to wheel their columns into the line of that policy. They admit that the South-west and the North-west are geographically and commercially identified . . .'

As to any dread of my having a 'purpose to enslave, or exterminate, the whites of the South,' I can scarcely believe that such dread exists. It is too absurd. I believe you can be my personal witness that no man is less to be dreaded for undue severity, in any case.

If the friends you mention really wish to have peace upon the old terms, they should act at once. Every day makes the case more difficult. They can so act, with entire safety, so far as I am concerned.

I think you would better not make this letter public; but you may rely confidently on my standing by whatever I have said in it. Please write me if anything more comes to light. Yours very truly

Letter to the working men of Manchester, England.

19 January 1863

I have the honor to acknowledge the receipt of the address and resolutions which you sent to me on the eve of the new year.

When I came, on the fourth day of March 1861, through a free and constitutional election, to preside in the government of the United States, the country was found at the verge of civil war. Whatever might have been the cause, or whosesoever the fault, one duty paramount to all others was before me, namely, to maintain and preserve at once the Constitution and the integrity of the federal republic. A conscientious purpose to perform this duty is a key to all the measures of administration which have been, and to all which will hereafter be pursued. Under our form of government, and my official oath, I could not depart from this purpose if I would. It is not always in the power of governments to enlarge or restrict the scope of moral results which follow the policies that they may deem it necessary for the public safety, from time to time, to adopt.

I have understood well that the duty of self-preservation rests solely with the American people. But I have at the same time been aware that favor or disfavor of foreign nations might have a material influence in enlarging and prolonging the struggle with disloyal men in which the country is engaged. A fair examination of history has seemed to authorize a belief that the past action and influences of the United States were generally regarded as having been beneficent towards mankind. I have therefore reckoned upon the forbearance of nations. Circumstances, to some of which you kindly allude, induced me especially to expect that if justice and good faith should be practiced by the United States, they would encounter no hostile influence on the part of Great Britain. It is now a pleasant duty to acknowledge the demonstration you have given of your desire that a spirit of peace and amity towards this country may prevail in the councils of your Queen, who is respected and esteemed in your own country only more than she is by the kindred nation which has its home on this side of the Atlantic.

I know and deeply deplore the sufferings which the working men at Manchester and in all Europe are called to endure in this crisis. It has been often and studiously represented that the attempt to overthrow this government, which was built upon the foundation of human rights, and to substitute for it one which should rest exclusively on the basis of human slavery, was likely to obtain the favor of Europe. Through the actions of our disloyal citizens the working men of Europe have been subjected to a severe trial, for the purpose of forcing their sanction to that attempt. Under these circumstances, I cannot but regard your decisive utterance upon the question as an instance of sublime Christian heroism which has not been surpassed in any age or in any country. It is, indeed, an energetic and reinspiring assurance of the inherent power of truth and of the ultimate and universal triumph of justice, humanity, and freedom. I do not doubt that the sentiments you have expressed will be sustained by your great nation, and, on the other hand, I have no hesitation in assuring you that they will excite admiration, esteem, and the most reciprocal feelings of friendship among the American people. I hail this interchange of sentiment, therefore, as an augury that, whatever else may happen, whatever misfortune may befall your country or my own, the peace and friendship which now exist between the two nations will be, as it shall be my desire to make them, perpetual.[1]

---

[1] On 31 December 1862 a public meeting of the working men of Manchester had adopted an address to the President of the United States which read in part:

'We honour your free States, as a singular, happy abode for the working millions . . . One thing alone has, in the past, lessened our sympathy with your country and our confidence in it; we mean the ascendancy of politicians who not merely maintained Negro slavery, but desired to extend and root it more firmly. Since we have discerned, however, that the victory of the free north, in the war which has so sorely distressed us as well as afflicted you, will strike off the fetters of the slave, you have attracted our warm and earnest sympathy.

'We joyfully honour you, as the President, and the Congress with you, for the many decisive steps towards practically exemplifying your belief in the words of your great founders, "All men are created free and equal." '

Letter to General Joseph Hooker.

26 January 1863

I have placed you at the head of the Army of the Potomac. Of course I have done this upon what appear to me to be sufficient reasons. And yet I think it best for you to know that there are some things in regard to which, I am not quite satisfied with you. I believe you to be a brave and a skilful soldier, which, of course, I like. I also believe you do not mix politics with your profession, in which you are right. You have confidence in yourself, which is a valuable, if not an indispensable quality. You are ambitious, which, within reasonable bounds, does good rather than harm. But I think that during Gen. Burnside's command of the Army, you have taken counsel of your ambition, and thwarted him as much as you could, in which you did a great wrong to the country, and to a most meritorious and honorable brother officer. I have heard, in such way as to believe it, of your recently saying that both the Army and the government needed a dictator. Of course it was not *for* this, but in spite of it, that I have given you the command. Only those generals who gain successes, can set up dictators. What I now ask of you is military success, and I will risk the dictatorship. The government will support you to the utmost of its ability, which is neither more nor less than it has done and will do for all commanders. I much fear that the spirit which you have aided to infuse into the Army, of criticizing their commander, and withholding confidence from him, will now turn upon you. I shall assist you as far as I can, to put it down. Neither you, nor Napoleon, if he were alive again, could get any good out of an army, while such a spirit prevails in it.

And now, beware of rashness. Beware of rashness, but with energy, and sleepless vigilance, go forward, and give us victories. Yours very truly

Letter to Mrs L. H. Phipps, seeking a government post for her husband.

9 March 1863

Yours of the 8th is received. It is difficult for you to understand, what is, nevertheless true, that the bare reading of a letter of that length requires more than any one person's share of my time. And when read, what is it but an evidence that you intend to importune me for one thing, and another, and another, until, in self-defence, I must drop all and devote myself to find a place, even though I remove somebody else to do it, and thereby turn him and his friends upon me for indefinite future importunity, and hindrance from the legitimate duties for which I am supposed to be placed here? Yours etc.

Letter to Andrew Johnson, military governor of Tennessee.

26 March 1863

I am told you have at least thought of raising a Negro military force. In my opinion, the country now needs no specific thing so much as some man of your ability and position, to go to this work. When I speak of your position, I mean that of an eminent citizen of a slave state, and himself a slave-holder. The colored population is the great available, and yet unavailed of, force for restoring the Union. The bare sight of fifty thousand armed and drilled black soldiers on the banks of the Mississippi, would end the rebellion at once. And who doubts that we can present that sight, if we but take hold in earnest? If you have been thinking of it please do not dismiss the thought.

Letter to General John M. Schofield.

27 May 1863

My dear Sir: Having relieved Gen. Curtis and assigned you to the command of the Department of the Missouri—I think it may be of some advantage for me to state to you why I did it. I did not relieve Gen. Curtis because of any full conviction that he had done wrong by commission or omission. I did it because of a conviction in my mind that the Union men of Missouri, constituting, when united, a vast majority of the whole people, have entered into a pestilent factional quarrel among themselves, Gen. Curtis, perhaps not of choice, being the head of one faction, and Gov. Gamble that of the other. After months of labor to reconcile the difficulty, it seemed to grow worse and worse until I felt it my duty to break it up somehow; and as I could not remove Gov. Gamble, I had to remove Gen. Curtis. Now that you are in the position, I wish you to undo nothing merely because Gen. Curtis or Gov. Gamble did it; but to exercise your own judgment, and do *right* for the public interest. Let your military measures be strong enough to repel the invader and keep the peace, and not so strong as to unnecessarily harass and persecute the people. It is a difficult role, and so much greater will be the honor if you perform it well. If both factions, or neither, shall abuse you, you will probably be about right. Beware of being assailed by one, and praised by the other. Yours truly

Telegram to General Joseph Hooker, facing Lee and the Army of Northern Virginia.

5 June 1863

Yours of to-day was received an hour ago. So much of professional military skill is requisite to answer it, that I have turned the task over to Gen. Halleck. He promises to perform it with his utmost care. I have but one idea which I think worth suggesting to you, and that is in case you find Lee coming to the north of the Rappahannock, I would by no means cross to the south of it. If he should leave a rear force at Fredericksburg, tempting you to fall upon it, it would fight in intrenchments, and have you at disadvantage, and so, man for man, worst you at that point, while his main force would in some way be getting an advantage of you northward. In one word, I would not take any risk of being entangled upon the river, like an ox jumped half over a fence and liable to be torn by dogs, front and rear, without a fair chance to gore one way or kick the other. If Lee would come to my side of the river I would keep on the same side and fight him, or act on the defence, according as might be my estimate of his strength relatively to my own. But these are mere suggestions which I desire to be controlled by the judgment of yourself and Gen. Halleck.

Telegram to General Joseph Hooker.

10 June 1863

Your long dispatch of to-day is just received. If left to me, I would not go south of the Rappahannock, upon Lee's moving north of it. If you had Richmond invested to-day, you would not be able to take it in twenty days; meanwhile, your communications, and with them, your army, would be ruined. I think *Lee*'s army, and not *Richmond*, is your true objective point. If he comes towards the Upper Potomac, follow on his flank, and on the inside track, shortening your lines, whilst he lengthens his. Fight him when opportunity offers. If he stays where he is, fret him, and fret him.

To Erastus Corning and others, Democratic critics of the administration.

[12 June] 1863

Gentlemen: Your letter of 19th May inclosing the resolutions of a public meeting held at Albany, New York, on the 16th of the same month, was received several days ago.

The resolutions, as I understand them, are resolvable into two propositions — first, the expression of a purpose to sustain the cause of the Union, to secure peace through victory, and to support the administration in every constitutional and lawful measure to suppress the rebellion; and secondly, a declaration of censure upon the administration for supposed unconstitutional action such as the making of military arrests.

And, from the two propositions a third is deduced, which is, that the gentlemen composing the meeting are resolved on doing their part to maintain our common government and country, despite the folly or wickedness, as they may conceive, of any administration. This position is eminently patriotic, and as such, I thank the meeting, and congratulate the nation for it. My own purpose is the same; so that the meeting and myself have a common object, and can have no difference, except in the choice of means or measures, for effecting that object.

And here I ought to close this paper, and would close it, if there were no apprehension that more injurious consequences, than any merely personal to myself, might follow the censures systematically cast upon me for doing what, in my view of duty, I could not forbear. The resolutions promise to support me in every constitutional and lawful measure to suppress the rebellion; and I have not knowingly employed, nor shall knowingly employ, any other. But the meeting, by their resolutions, assert and argue, that certain military arrests and proceedings following them for which I am ultimately responsible, are unconstitutional. I think they are not. The resolutions quote from the Constitution the definition of treason; and also the limiting safeguards and guarantees therein provided for the citizen, on trials for treason, and on his being held to answer for capital or otherwise infamous crimes, and, in criminal prosecutions, his right to a speedy and public trial by an impartial jury. They proceed to resolve 'That these safeguards of the rights of the citizen against the pretensions of arbitrary power, were intended more *especially* for his protection in times of civil commotion.' And, apparently, to demonstrate the proposition, the resolutions proceed 'They were secured substantially to the English people, *after* years of protracted civil war, and were adopted into our constitution at the *close* of the Revolution.' Would not the demonstration have been better, if it could have been truly said that these safeguards had been adopted, and applied *during* the civil wars and *during* our Revolution, instead of *after* the one, and at the *close* of the other? I too am devotedly for them *after* civil war, and *before* civil war, and at all times 'except when, in cases of rebellion or invasion, the public safety may require' their suspension. The resolutions proceed to tell us that these safeguards 'have stood the test of seventy-six years of trial, under our republican system, under circumstances which show that while they constitute the foundation of all free government, they are the elements of the enduring stability of the Republic.' No one denies that they have so stood the test up to the beginning of the present rebellion if we except a certain matter at New Orleans hereafter to be mentioned; nor does anyone question that they will stand the same test much longer after the rebellion closes. But these provisions of the Constitution have no application to the case we have in hand, because the arrests complained of were not made for treason – that is, not for *the* treason defined in the Constitution, and upon the conviction of which, the punishment is death – nor yet were they made to hold persons to answer for any capital, or otherwise infamous crimes; nor were the proceedings following, in any constitutional or legal sense, 'criminal prosecutions.' The arrests were made on totally different grounds, and the proceedings following accorded with the grounds of the arrests. Let us consider the real case with which we are dealing, and apply to it the parts of the Constitution plainly made for such cases.

Prior to my installation here it had been inculcated that any state had a lawful right to secede from the national Union; and that it would be expedient to exercise the right, whenever the devotees of the doctrine should fail to elect a President to their own liking. I was elected contrary to their liking; and accordingly, so far as it was legally possible, they had taken seven states out of the Union, had seized many of the United States forts, and had fired upon the United States flag, all before I was inaugurated, and, of course, before I had done any official act whatever. The rebellion, thus began, soon ran into the present civil war; and, in certain respects, it began on very unequal terms between the parties. The insurgents had been preparing for it more than thirty years, while the government had taken no steps to resist them. The former had carefully considered all the means which could be turned to their account. It undoubtedly was a well-pondered reliance with them that in their own unrestricted effort to destroy Union, Constitution, and law, all together, the government would, in great degree, be restrained by the same Constitution and law, from arresting their progress. Their sympathizers pervaded all departments of the government, and nearly all communities of the people. From this material, under cover of 'Liberty of speech,' 'Liberty of the press,' and 'Habeas corpus' they hoped to keep on foot amongst us a most efficient corps of spies, informers, suppliers, and aiders and abettors of their cause in a thousand ways. They knew that in times such as they were inaugurating, by the Constitution itself, the 'Habeas corpus' might be suspended; but they also knew they had friends who would make a question as to *who* was to suspend it; meanwhile their spies and others might remain at large to help on their cause. Or if, as has happened, the executive should suspend the writ, without ruinous waste of time, instances of arresting innocent persons might occur, as are always likely to occur in such cases; and then a clamor could be raised in regard to this, which might be, at least, of some service to the insurgent cause. It needed no very keen perception to discover this part of the enemies' program, so soon as by open hostilities their machinery was fairly put in motion. Yet, thoroughly imbued with a reverence for the guaranteed rights of individuals, I was slow to adopt the strong measures, which by degrees I have been forced to regard as being within the exceptions of the Constitution, and as indispensable to the public safety. Nothing is better known to history than that courts of justice are utterly incompetent to such cases. Civil courts are organized chiefly for trials of individuals, or, at most, a few individuals acting in concert; and this in quiet times, and on charges of crimes well defined in the law. Even in times of peace, bands of horse-thieves and robbers frequently grow too numerous and powerful for the ordinary courts of justice. But what comparison, in numbers, have such bands ever borne to the insurgent sympathizers even in many of the loyal states? Again, a jury too frequently have at least one member, more ready to hang the panel than to hang the traitor. And yet again, he who dissuades one man from volunteering, or induces one soldier to desert, weakens the Union cause as much as he who kills a Union soldier in battle. Yet this dissuasion, or inducement, may be so conducted as to be no defined crime of which any civil court would take cognizance.

Ours is a case of rebellion – so called by the resolutions before me – in fact, a clear, flagrant, and gigantic case of rebellion; and the provision of the Constitution that 'The privilege of the writ of habeas corpus shall not be suspended, unless when in cases of rebellion or invasion, the public safety may require it' is *the* provision which specially applies to our present case. This provision plainly attests the understanding of those who made the Constitution that ordinary courts of justice are inadequate to 'cases of rebellion' – attests their purpose that in such cases, men may be held in custody whom the courts acting on ordinary rules, would discharge. Habeas corpus does not discharge men who are proved to be guilty of defined crime; and its suspension is allowed by the Constitution on purpose that men may be arrested, and held, who cannot be proved to be guilty of defined crime, 'when, in cases of rebellion or invasion the public safety may require it.' This is precisely our present case – a case of rebellion, wherein the public safety does require the suspension. Indeed, arrests by process of courts, and arrests in cases of rebellion, do not proceed altogether upon the same basis. The former is directed at the small percentage of ordinary and continuous perpetration of crime; while the latter is directed at sudden and extensive uprisings against the government, which, at most, will succeed or fail, in no great length of time. In the latter case, arrests are made, not so much for what has been done, as for what probably would be done. The latter is more for the preventive, and less for the vindictive, than the former. In such cases the purposes of men are much more easily understood, than in cases of ordinary crime. The man who stands by and says nothing, when the peril of his government is discussed, cannot be misunderstood. If not hindered, he is sure to help the enemy. Much more, if he talks ambiguously – talks for his country with 'buts' and 'ifs' and 'ands.' Of how little value the constitutional provision I have quoted will be rendered, if arrests shall never be made until defined crimes shall have been committed, may be illustrated by a few notable examples. Gen. John C. Breckinridge, Gen. Robert E. Lee, Gen. Joseph E. Johnston, Gen. John B. Magruder, Gen. William B. Preston, Gen. Simon B. Buckner, and Commodore Buchanan, now occupying the very highest places in the rebel war service, were all within the power of the government since the rebellion began, and were nearly as well known to be traitors then as now. Unquestionably if we had seized and held them, the insurgent cause would be much weaker. But no one of them had then committed any crime defined in the law. Every one of them if arrested would have been discharged on habeas corpus, were the writ allowed to operate. In view of these and similar cases, I think the time not unlikely to come when I shall be blamed for having made too few arrests rather than too many.

By the third resolution the meeting indicate their opinion that military arrests may be constitutional in localities where rebellion actually exists; but that such arrests are unconstitutional in localities where rebellion, or insurrection, does not actually exist. They insist that such arrests shall not be made 'outside of the lines of necessary military occupation, and the scenes of insurrection.' Inasmuch, however, as the Constitution itself makes no such distinction, I am unable to believe that there is any such constitutional distinction. I concede that the class of arrests complained of, can be constitutional only when, in cases of rebellion or invasion, the public safety may require them; and I insist that in such cases, they are constitutional *wherever* the public safety does require them – as well in places to which they may prevent the rebellion extending, as in those where it may be already prevailing – as well where they may restrain mischievous interference with the raising and supplying of armies, to suppress the rebellion, as where the rebellion may actually be – as well where they may restrain the enticing men out of the army, as where they would prevent mutiny in the army – equally constitutional at all places where they will conduce to the public safety, as against the dangers of rebellion or invasion.

Take the particular case mentioned by the meeting. They assert in substance that Mr Vallandigham was by a military commander, seized and tried 'for no other reason than words addressed to a public meeting, in criticism of the course of the administration, and in condemnation of the military orders of that general.'[1] Now, if there be no mistake about this — if this assertion is the truth and the whole truth — if there was no other reason for the arrest, then I concede that the arrest was wrong. But the arrest, as I understand, was made for a very different reason. Mr Vallandigham avows his hostility to the war on the part of the Union; and his arrest was made because he was laboring, with some effect, to prevent the raising of troops, to encourage desertions from the army, and to leave the rebellion without an adequate military force to suppress it. He was not arrested because he was damaging the political prospects of the administration, or the personal interests of the commanding general; but because he was damaging the army, upon the existence, and vigor of which, the life of the nation depends. He was warring upon the military; and this gave the military constitutional jurisdiction to lay hands upon him. If Mr Vallandigham was not damaging the military power of the country, then his arrest was made on mistake of fact, which I would be glad to correct, on reasonably satisfactory evidence.

I understand the meeting, whose resolutions I am considering, to be in favor of suppressing the rebellion by military force — by armies. Long experience has shown that armies cannot be maintained unless desertion shall be punished by the severe penalty of death. The case requires, and the law and the Constitution sanction this punishment. Must I shoot a simple-minded soldier boy who deserts, while I must not touch a hair of a wily agitator who induces him to desert? This is none the less injurious when effected by getting a father, a brother, or friend, into a public meeting, and there working upon his feelings, till he is persuaded to write the soldier boy that he is fighting in a bad cause, for a wicked administration of a contemptible government, too weak to arrest and punish him if he shall desert. I think that in such a case, to silence the agitator, and save the boy, is not only constitutional, but, withal, a great mercy.

If I be wrong on this question of constitutional power, my error lies in believing that certain proceedings are constitutional when,

---

[1] Clement L. Vallandigham, former Democratic Congressman from Ohio, had, by the spring of 1863, become the boldest northern opponent of the war. On 5 May 1863 he had been arrested at Dayton, and on the following day was convicted by a military commission for expressing treasonable sympathy with the rebellion. Lincoln banished him to the Confederacy. When Vallandigham returned to the United States a year later the government ignored him. His increasingly intemperate attacks and the turning fortunes of the war soon stripped him of influence.

in cases of rebellion or invasion, the public safety requires them, which would not be constitutional when, in absence of rebellion or invasion, the public safety does not require them – in other words, that the Constitution is not in its application in all respects the same, in cases of rebellion or invasion, involving the public safety, as it is in time of profound peace and public security. The Constitution itself makes the distinction; and I can no more be persuaded that the government can constitutionally take no strong measure in time of rebellion, because it can be shown that the same could not be lawfully taken in time of peace, than I can be persuaded that a particular drug is not good medicine for a sick man, because it can be shown to not be good food for a well one. Nor am I able to appreciate the danger, apprehended by the meeting, that the American people will, by means of military arrests during the rebellion, lose the right of public discussion, the liberty of speech and the press, the law of evidence, trial by jury, and habeas corpus, throughout the indefinite peaceful future which I trust lies before them, any more than I am able to believe that a man could contract so strong an appetite for emetics during temporary illness, as to persist in feeding upon them through the remainder of his healthful life.

In giving the resolutions that earnest consideration which you request of me, I cannot overlook the fact that the meeting speak as 'Democrats.' Nor can I, with full respect for their known intelligence, and the fairly presumed deliberation with which they prepared their resolutions, be permitted to suppose that this occurred by accident, or in any way other than that they preferred to designate themselves 'Democrats' rather than 'American citizens.' In this time of national peril I would have preferred to meet you upon a level one step higher than any party platform; because I am sure that from such more elevated position, we could do better battle for the country we all love, than we possibly can from those lower ones, where from the force of habit, the prejudices of the past, and selfish hopes of the future, we are sure to expend much of our ingenuity and strength, in finding fault with, and aiming blows at each other. But since you have denied me this, I will yet be thankful, for the country's sake, that not all Democrats have done so. He on whose discretionary judgment Mr Vallandigham was arrested and tried, is a Democrat, having no old party affinity with me; and the judge who rejected the constitutional view expressed in these resolutions, by refusing to discharge Mr V. on habeas corpus, is a Democrat of better days than these, having received his judicial mantle at the hands of President Jackson. And still more, of all those Democrats who are nobly exposing their lives and shedding their blood on the battlefield, I have learned that many approve the course taken with Mr V. while I have not heard of a single one condemning it. I cannot assert that there are none such. . .

And yet, let me say that in my own discretion, I do not know whether I would have ordered the arrest of Mr V. While I cannot shift the responsibility from myself, I hold that, as a general rule, the commander in the field is the better judge of the necessity in any particular case. Of course I must practice a general directory and revisory power in the matter.

One of the resolutions expresses the opinion of the meeting that arbitrary arrests will have the effect to divide and distract those who should be united in suppressing the rebellion; and I am specifically called on to discharge Mr Vallandigham. I regard this as, at least, a fair appeal to me, on the expediency of exercising a constitutional power which I think exists. In response to such appeal I have to say it gave me pain when I learned that Mr V. had been arrested – that is, I was pained that there should have seemed to be a necessity for arresting him – and that it will afford me great pleasure to discharge him so soon as I can, by any means, believe the public safety will not suffer by it. I further say, that as the war progresses, it appears to me, opinion, and action, which were in great confusion at first, take shape, and fall into more regular channels; so that the necessity for arbitrary dealing with them gradually decreases. I have every reason to desire that it would cease altogether; and far from the least is my regard for the opinions and wishes of those who, like the meeting at Albany, declare their purpose to sustain the government in every constitutional and lawful measure to suppress the rebellion. Still, I must continue to do so much as may seem to be required by the public safety.

Letter to General Joseph Hooker.

16 June 1863

My dear General: I send you this by the hand of Captain Dahlgren. Your dispatch of 11.30 a.m. to-day is just received. When you say I have long been aware that you do not enjoy the confidence of the major-general commanding, you state the case much too strongly.

You do not lack his confidence in any degree to do you any harm. On seeing him, after telegraphing you this morning, I found him more nearly agreeing with you than I was myself. Surely you do not mean to understand that I am withholding my confidence from you when I happen to express an opinion (certainly never discourteously) differing from one of your own.

I believe Halleck is dissatisfied with you to this extent only, that he knows that you write and telegraph ('report,' as he calls it) to me. I think he is wrong to find fault with this; but I do not think he withholds any support from you on account of it. If you and he would use the same frankness to one another, and to me, that I use to both of you, there would be no difficulty. I need and must have the professional skill of both, and yet these suspicions tend to deprive me of both.

I believe you are aware that since you took command of the army I have not believed you had any chance to effect anything till now. As it looks to me, Lee's now returning toward Harper's Ferry gives you back the chance that I thought McClellan lost last fall. Quite possibly I was wrong both then and now; but, in the great responsibility resting upon me, I cannot be entirely silent. Now, all I ask is that you will be in such mood that we can get into our action the best cordial judgment of yourself and General Halleck, with my poor mite added, if indeed he and you shall think it entitled to any consideration at all. Yours as ever

Letter to General Robert H. Milroy, who had been badly defeated at Winchester two weeks earlier.

29 June 1863

My dear Sir: Your letters to Mr Blair and to myself, are handed to me by him. I have never doubted your courage and devotion to the cause. But you have just lost a Division, and *prima facie* the fault is upon you; and while that remains unchanged, for me to put you in command again is to justly subject me to the charge of having put you there on purpose to have you lose another. If I knew facts sufficient to satisfy me that you were not in fault, or error, the case would be different. But the facts I do know, while they are not at all conclusive, and I hope they may never prove so, tend the other way.

First, I have scarcely seen anything from you at any time, that did not contain imputations against your superiors, and a chafing against acting the part they had assigned you. You have constantly urged the idea that you were persecuted because you did not come from West Point, and you repeat it in these letters. This, my dear general, is I fear, the rock on which you have split.

In the Winchester case, you were under General Schenck, and he under Gen. Halleck. I know by Gen. Halleck's order-book, that he, on the 11th of June advised Gen. Schenck to call you in from Winchester to Harper's Ferry; and I have been told, but do not know, that Gen. Schenck gave you the order accordingly, on the same day – and I have been told, but do not know, that on receiving it, instead of obeying it, you sent by mail a written protest against obeying it, which did not reach him until you were actually beleaguered at Winchester. I say I do not know this. You hate West Point generally, and General Halleck particularly; but I do know that it is not his fault that you were at Winchester on the 13th, 14th, and morning of the 15th – the days of your disaster. If Gen. Schenck gave the order on the 11th as Gen. Halleck advised, it was an easy matter for you to have been off at least on the 12th. The case is inevitably between Gen. Schenck and you. Neither Gen. Halleck, nor anyone else, so far as I know, required you to stay and fight 60,000, with 6,000 as you insinuate. I know Gen. Halleck, through Gen. Schenck, required you to get away, and that in abundant time for you to have done it. Gen. Schenck is not a West Pointer and has no prejudice against you on that score. Yours very truly

Announcement of victory at Gettysburg.

4 July 1863

The President announces to the country that news from the Army of the Potomac, up to 10 p.m. of the 3rd, is such as to cover that Army with the highest honor, to promise a great success to the cause of the Union, and to claim the condolence of all for the many gallant fallen. And that for this, he especially desires that on this day, He whose will, not ours, should ever be done, be everywhere remembered and reverenced with profoundest gratitude.

Letter to General Ulysses S. Grant, who had taken Vicksburg nine days earlier.

13 July 1863

My dear General: I do not remember that you and I ever met personally. I write this now as a grateful acknowledgment for the almost inestimable service you have done the country. I wish to say a word further. When you first reached the vicinity of Vicksburg, I thought you should do what you finally did — march the troops across the neck, run the batteries with the transports, and thus go below; and I never had any faith, except a general hope that you knew better than I, that the Yazoo Pass expedition, and the like, could succeed. When you got below and took Port Gibson, Grand Gulf, and vicinity, I thought you should go down the river and join Gen. Banks; and when you turned northward east of the Big Black, I feared it was a mistake. I now wish to make the personal acknowledgment that you were right, and I was wrong. Yours very truly

Letter, never sent, to General George G. Meade, who had commanded the Army of the Potomac since 28 June.

14 July 1863

I have just seen your dispatch to Gen. Halleck, asking to be relieved of your command, because of a supposed censure of mine. I am very — *very* — grateful to you for the magnificent success you gave the cause of the country at Gettysburg; and I am sorry now to be the author of the slightest pain to you. But I was in such deep distress myself that I could not restrain some expression of it. I have been oppressed nearly ever since the battles at Gettysburg, by what appeared to be evidences that yourself, and Gen. Couch, and Gen. Smith, were not seeking a collision with the enemy, but were trying to get him across the river without another battle. What these evidences were, if you please, I hope to tell you at some time, when we shall both feel better. The case, summarily stated, is this. You fought and beat the enemy at Gettysburg; and, of course, to say the least, his loss was as great as yours. He retreated; and you did not, as it seemed to me, pressingly pursue him; but a flood in the river detained him, till, by slow degrees, you were again upon him. You had at least twenty thousand veteran troops directly with you, and as many more raw ones within supporting distance, all in addition to those who fought with you at Gettysburg; while it was not possible that he had received a single recruit; and yet you stood and let the flood run down, bridges be built, and the enemy move away at his leisure, without attacking him. And Couch and Smith! The latter left Carlisle in time, upon all ordinary calculation, to have aided you in the last battle at Gettysburg; but he did not arrive. At the end of more than ten days, I believe twelve, under constant urging, he reached Hagerstown from Carlisle, which is not an inch over fifty-five miles, if so much. And Couch's movement was very little different.

Again, my dear general, I do not believe you appreciate the magnitude of the misfortune involved in Lee's escape. He was within your easy grasp, and to have closed upon him would, in connection with our other late successes, have ended the war. As it is, the war will be prolonged indefinitely. If you could not safely attack Lee last Monday, how can you possibly do so south of the river, when you can take with you very few more than two-thirds of the force you then had in hand? It would be unreasonable to expect, and I do not expect you can now effect much. Your golden opportunity is gone, and I am distressed immeasurably because of it.

I beg you will not consider this a prosecution, or persecution of yourself. As you had learned that I was dissatisfied, I have thought it best to kindly tell you why.

Letter to Francis P. Blair, Sr.

30 July 1863

My dear Sir: Yours of to-day with enclosure is received. Yesterday I commenced trying to get up an expedition for Texas. I shall do the best I can. Meantime I would like to know who is the great man Alexander, that talks so oracularly about 'if the president keeps his word' and Banks not having 'capacity to run an omnibus on Broadway.' How has this Alexander's immense light been obscured hitherto?[1] Yours truly

---

[1] Blair replied that William Alexander, then living in New York City, was 'a Texan of talent, a lawyer, one of the first Union men driven out and made the agent of like sufferers.'

Letter to Mary Todd Lincoln, in the White Mountains.

8 August 1863

My dear Wife: All is well as usual, and no particular trouble any way. I put the money into the Treasury at 5 per cent, with the privilege of withdrawing it any time upon thirty days' notice. I suppose you are glad to learn this. Tell dear Tad, poor 'Nanny Goat,' is lost; and Mrs Cuthbert and I are in distress about it. The day you left Nanny was found resting herself, and chewing her little cud, on the middle of Tad's bed. But now she's gone! The gardener kept complaining that she destroyed the flowers, till it was concluded to bring her down to the White House. This was done, and the second day she had disappeared, and has not been heard of since. This is the last we know of poor 'Nanny.'

The weather continues dry, and excessively warm here.

Nothing very important occurring. The election in Kentucky has gone very strongly right. Old Mr Wickliffe got ugly, as you know, ran for Governor, and is terribly beaten. Upon Mr Crittenden's death, Brutus Clay, Cassius's brother, was put on the track for Congress, and is largely elected. Mr Menzies, who, as we thought, behaved very badly last session of Congress, is largely beaten in the district opposite Cincinnati, by Green Clay Smith, Cassius Clay's nephew. But enough. Affectionately

Letter to General John A. McClernand, whom Grant had relieved during the Vicksburg campaign.

12 August 1863

My dear Sir: Our friend, William G. Greene, has just presented a kind letter in regard to yourself, addressed to me by our other friends, Yates, Hatch, and Dubois. I doubt whether your present position is more painful to you than to myself. Grateful for the patriotic stand so early taken by you in this life-and-death struggle of the nation, I have done whatever has appeared practicable to advance you and the public interest together. No charges, with a view to a trial, have been preferred against you by anyone; nor do I suppose any will be. All there is, so far as I have heard, is Gen. Grant's statement of his reasons for relieving you. And even this I have not seen or sought to see; because it is a case, as appears to me, in which I could do nothing without doing harm. Gen. Grant and yourself have been conspicuous in our most important successes; and for me to interfere, and thus magnify a breach between you, could not but be of evil effect. Better leave it where the law of the case has placed it. For me to force you back upon Gen. Grant would be forcing him to resign. I cannot give you a new command because we have no forces except such as already have commanders. I am constantly pressed by those who *scold* before they *think*, or without thinking at all, to give commands respectively to Fremont, McClellan, Butler, Sigel, Curtis, Hunter, Hooker, and perhaps others; when, all else out of the way, I have no commands to give them. This is now your case, which, as I have before said, pains me not less than it does you.

My belief is that the permanent estimate of what a general does in the field, is fixed by the 'cloud of witnesses' who have been with him in the field; and that relying on these, he who has the right needs not to fear. Your friend as ever

Letter to James H. Hackett, actor.

17 August 1863

My dear Sir: Months ago I should have acknowledged the receipt of your book, and accompanying kind note; and I now have to beg your pardon for not having done so.

For one of my age, I have seen very little of the drama. The first presentation of Falstaff I ever saw was yours here, last winter or spring. Perhaps the best compliment I can pay is to say, as I truly can, I am very anxious to see it again. Some of Shakespeare's plays I have never read; while others I have gone over perhaps as frequently as any unprofessional reader. Among the latter are *Lear*, *Richard Third*, *Henry Eighth*, *Hamlet*, and especially *Macbeth*. I think nothing equals *Macbeth*. It is wonderful. Unlike you gentlemen of the profession, I think the soliloquy in *Hamlet* commencing 'O, my offense is rank' surpasses that commencing 'To be, or not to be.' But pardon this small attempt at criticism. I should like to hear you pronounce the opening speech of Richard the Third. Will you not soon visit Washington again? If you do, please call and let me make your personal acquaintance. Yours truly

Letter to General James G. Blunt, commanding in Arkansas.
                                                    18 August 1863

Yours of 31st July is received. Governor Carney did leave some papers with me concerning you; but they made no great impression upon me; and I believe they are not altogether such as you seem to think. As I am not proposing to act upon them, I do not now take the time to re-examine them.

I regret to find you denouncing so many persons as liars, scoundrels, fools, thieves, and persecutors of yourself. Your military position looks critical, but did anybody *force* you into it? Have you been *ordered* to confront and fight ten thousand men, with three thousand men? The government cannot make men; and it is very easy, when a man has been given the highest commission, for him to turn on those who gave it and vilify them for not giving him a command according to his rank.

My appointment of you first as a Brigadier, and then as a Major General, was evidence of my appreciation of your service; and I have not since marked but one thing in connection with you, with which to be dissatisfied. The sending a military order twenty-five miles outside of your lines, and all military lines, to take men charged with no offense against the military, out of the hands of the courts, to be turned over to a mob to be hanged, can find no precedent or principle to justify it. Judge Lynch sometimes takes jurisdiction of cases which prove too strong for the courts; but this is the first case within my knowledge, wherein the court being able to maintain jurisdiction against Judge Lynch, the military has come to the assistance of the latter. I take the facts of this case as you state them yourself, and not from any report of Governor Carney, or other person.[1] Yours truly

Letter to James C. Conkling, to be read to a Union mass meeting in Lincoln's home.
                                                    26 August 1863

My dear Sir: Your letter inviting me to attend a mass-meeting of unconditional Union-men, to be held at the capital of Illinois, on the 3rd day of September, has been received.

It would be very agreeable to me, to thus meet my old friends, at

[1] Blunt was relieved of his command on 9 October 1863.

my own home; but I cannot, just now, be absent from here, so long as a visit there, would require.

The meeting is to be of all those who maintain unconditional devotion to the Union; and I am sure my old political friends will thank me for tendering, as I do, the nation's gratitude to those other noble men, whom no partisan malice, or partisan hope, can make false to the nation's life.

There are those who are dissatisfied with me. To such I would say: You desire peace; and you blame me that we do not have it. But how can we attain it? There are but three conceivable ways. First, to suppress the rebellion by force of arms. This I am trying to do. Are you for it? If you are, so far we are agreed. If you are not for it, a second way is to give up the Union. I am against this. Are you for it? If you are, you should say so plainly. If you are not for *force*, nor yet for *dissolution*, there only remains some imaginable *compromise*. I do not believe any compromise, embracing the maintenance of the Union, is now possible. All I learn leads to a directly opposite belief. The strength of the rebellion is its military – its army. That army dominates all the country, and all the people, within its range. Any offer of terms made by any man or men within that range, in opposition to that army, is simply nothing for the present; because such man or men, have no power whatever to enforce their side of a compromise, if one were made with them. To illustrate – Suppose refugees from the South, and peace men of the North, get together in convention, and frame and proclaim a compromise embracing a restoration of the Union; in what way can that compromise be used to keep Lee's army out of Pennsylvania? Meade's army can keep Lee's army out of Pennsylvania; and, I think, can ultimately drive it out of existence. But no paper compromise, to which the controllers of Lee's army are not agreed, can, at all, affect that army. In an effort at such compromise we should waste time, which the enemy would improve to our disadvantage; and that would be all. A compromise, to be effective, must be made either with those who control the rebel army, or with the people first liberated from the domination of that army, by the success of our own army. Now allow me to assure you, that no word or intimation, from that rebel army, or from any of the men controlling it, in relation to any peace compromise, has ever come to my knowledge or belief. All charges and insinuations to the contrary are deceptive and groundless. And I promise you, that if any such proposition shall hereafter come, it shall not be rejected, and kept a secret from you. I freely acknowledge myself the servant of the people, according to the bond of service — the United States Constitution; and that, as such, I am responsible to them.

But, to be plain, you are dissatisfied with me about the Negro. Quite likely there is a difference of opinion between you and myself upon that subject. I certainly wish that all men could be free, while I suppose you do not. Yet I have neither adopted nor proposed any measure which is not consistent with even your view, provided you are for the Union. I suggested compensated emancipation; to which you replied you wished not to be taxed to buy Negroes. But I had not asked you to be taxed to buy Negroes, except in such way as to save you from greater taxation to save the Union exclusively by other means.

You dislike the emancipation proclamation; and, perhaps, would have it retracted. You say it is unconstitutional — I think differently. I think the Constitution invests its Commander-in-Chief with the law of war, in time of war. The most that can be said, if so much, is, that slaves are property. Is there — has there ever been — any question that by the law of war, property, both of enemies and friends, may be taken when needed? And is it not needed whenever taking it helps us, or hurts the enemy? Armies, the world over, destroy enemies' property when they cannot use it; and even destroy their own to keep it from the enemy. Civilized belligerents do all in their power to help themselves, or hurt the enemy, except a few things regarded as barbarous or cruel. Among the exceptions are the massacre of vanquished foes and non-combatants, male and female.

But the proclamation, as law, either is valid, or is not valid. If it is not valid, it needs no retraction. If it is valid, it cannot be retracted, any more than the dead can be brought to life. Some of you profess to think its retraction would operate favorably for the Union. Why better *after* the retraction, than *before* the issue? There was more than a year and a half of trial to suppress the rebellion before the proclamation issued, the last one hundred days of which passed under an explicit notice that it was coming, unless averted by those in revolt returning to their allegiance. The war has certainly progressed as favorably for us since the issue of the proclamation as before. I know as fully as one can know the opinions of others, that some of the commanders of our armies in the field who have given us our most important successes, believe the emancipation policy, and the use of colored troops, constitute the heaviest blow yet dealt to the rebellion; and that at least one of those important successes, could not have been achieved when it was, but for the aid of black soldiers. Among the commanders holding these views are some who have never had any affinity with what is called abolitionism, or with Republican party politics; but who hold them purely as military opinions. I submit these opinions as being entitled to some weight against the objections, often urged, that emancipation, and arming the blacks, are unwise as military measures, and were not adopted, as such, in good faith.

You say you will not fight to free Negroes. Some of them seem willing to fight for you; but no matter. Fight you, then, exclusively to save the Union. I issued the proclamation on purpose to aid you in saving the Union. Whenever you shall have conquered all resistance to the Union, if I shall urge you to continue fighting, it will be an apt time, then, for you to declare you will not fight to free Negroes.

I thought that in your struggle for the Union, to whatever extent the Negroes should cease helping the enemy, to that extent it weakened the enemy in his resistance to you. Do you think differently? I thought that whatever Negroes can be got to do as soldiers, leaves just so much less for white soldiers to do, in saving the Union. Does it appear otherwise to you? But Negroes, like other people, act upon motives. Why should they do anything for us, if we will do nothing for them? If they stake their lives for us, they must be prompted by the strongest motive—even the promise of freedom. And the promise being made, must be kept.

The signs look better. The Father of Waters[1] again goes unvexed to the sea. Thanks to the great North-west for it. Nor yet wholly to them. Three hundred miles up, they met New-England, Empire, Key-stone,[2] and Jersey, hewing their way right and left. The Sunny South too, in more colors than one, also lent a hand. On the spot, their part of the history was jotted down in black and white. The job was a great national one; and let none be banned who bore an honorable part in it. And while those who have cleared the great river may well be proud, even that is not all. It is hard to say that anything has been more bravely, and well done, than at Antietam, Murfreesboro, Gettysburg, and on many fields

[1] Mississippi river.
[2] New York state; Pennsylvania.

of lesser note. Nor must Uncle Sam's web-feet be forgotten. At all the watery margins they have been present. Not only on the deep sea, the broad bay, and the rapid river, but also up the narrow muddy bayou, and wherever the ground was a little damp, they have been, and made their tracks. Thanks to all. For the great republic – for the principle it lives by, and keeps alive – for man's vast future – thanks to all.

Peace does not appear so distant as it did. I hope it will come soon, and come to stay; and so come as to be worth the keeping in all future time. It will then have been proved that among free men, there can be no successful appeal from the ballot to the bullet; and that they who take such appeal are sure to lose their case, and pay the cost. And then there will be some black men who can remember that, with silent tongue, and clenched teeth, and steady eye, and well-poised bayonet, they have helped mankind on to this great consummation; while, I fear, there will be some white ones unable to forget that, with malignant heart, and deceitful speech, they have strove to hinder it.

Still let us not be over-sanguine of a speedy final triumph. Let us be quite sober. Let us diligently apply the means, never doubting that a just God, in his own good time, will give us the rightful result. Yours very truly

Letter to Henry W. Halleck, General-in-Chief of the Army.
           19 September 1863

By Gen. Meade's dispatch to you of yesterday it appears that he desires your views and those of the government, as to whether he shall advance upon the enemy. I am not prepared to order, or even advise an advance in this case, wherein I know so little of particulars, and wherein he, in the field, thinks the risk is so great, and the promise of advantage so small. And yet the case presents matter for very serious consideration in another aspect. These two armies confront each other across a small river, substantially midway between the two capitals, each defending its own capital, and menacing the other. Gen. Meade estimates the enemy's infantry in front of him at not less than forty thousand. Suppose we add 50 per cent to this, for cavalry, artillery, and extra duty men stretching as far as Richmond, making the whole force of the enemy sixty thousand. Gen. Meade, as shown by the returns, has with him, and between him and Washington, of the same classes of well men, over ninety thousand. Neither can bring the whole of his men into a battle; but each can bring as large a percentage in as the other. For a battle, then, Gen. Meade has three men to Gen. Lee's two. Yet, it having been determined that choosing ground, and standing on the defensive, gives so great advantage that the three cannot safely attack the two, the three are left simply standing on the defensive also. If the enemy's sixty thousand are sufficient to keep our ninety thousand away from Richmond, why, by the same rule, may not forty thousand of ours keep their sixty thousand away from Washington, leaving us fifty thousand to put to some other use? Having practically come to the mere defensive, it seems to be no economy at all to employ twice as many men for that object as are needed. With no object, certainly, to mislead myself, I can perceive no fault in this statement, unless we admit we are not the equal of the enemy man for man. I hope you will consider it.

To avoid misunderstanding, let me say that to attempt to fight the enemy slowly back into his intrenchments at Richmond, and there to capture him, is an idea I have been trying to repudiate for quite a year. My judgment is so clear against it that I would scarcely allow the attempt to be made, if the general in command should desire to make it. My last attempt upon Richmond was to get McClellan, when he was nearer there than the enemy was, to run in ahead of him. Since then I have constantly desired the Army of the Potomac to make Lee's army, and not Richmond, its objective point. If our army cannot fall upon the enemy and hurt him where he is, it is plain to me it can gain nothing by attempting to follow him over a succession of intrenched lines into a fortified city. Yours truly

Proclamation of Thanksgiving.

3 October 1863

By the President of the United States of America.
A Proclamation.

The year that is drawing towards its close, has been filled with the blessings of fruitful fields and healthful skies. To these bounties, which are so constantly enjoyed that we are prone to forget the source from which they come, others have been added, which are of so extraordinary a nature, that they cannot fail to penetrate and soften even the heart which is habitually insensible to the ever watchful providence of Almighty God. In the midst of a civil war of unequaled magnitude and severity, which has sometimes seemed to foreign states to invite and to provoke their aggression, peace has been preserved with all nations, order has been maintained, the laws have been respected and obeyed, and harmony has prevailed everywhere except in the theater of military conflict; while that theater has been greatly contracted by the advancing armies and navies of the Union. Needful diversions of wealth and of strength from the fields of peaceful industry to the national defence, have not arrested the plow, the shuttle, or the ship; the axe has enlarged the borders of our settlements, and the mines, as well of iron and coal as of the precious metals, have yielded even more abundantly than heretofore. Population has steadily increased, notwithstanding the waste that has been made in the camp, the siege, and the battlefield; and the country, rejoicing in the consciousness of augmented strength and vigor, is permitted to expect continuance of years with large increase of freedom. No human counsel hath devised nor hath any mortal hand worked out these great things. They are the gracious gifts of the Most High God, who, while dealing with us in anger for our sins, hath nevertheless remembered mercy. It has seemed to me fit and proper that they should be solemnly, reverently, and grate-fully acknowledged as with one heart and one voice by the whole American People. I do therefore invite my fellow-citizens in every part of the United States, and also those who are at sea and those who are sojourning in foreign lands, to set apart and observe the last Thursday of November next, as a day of Thanksgiving and Praise to our beneficent Father who dwelleth in the Heavens. And I recommend to them that while offering up the ascriptions justly due to Him for such singular deliverances and blessings, they do also, with humble penitence for our national perverseness and disobedience, commend to His tender care all those who have become widows, orphans, mourners, or sufferers in the lament-able civil strife in which we are unavoidably engaged, and fervently implore the interposition of the Almighty Hand to heal the wounds of the nation and to restore it as soon as may be consistent with the Divine purposes to the full enjoyment of peace, harmony, tranquility, and Union.

In testimony whereof, I have hereunto set my hand and caused the Seal of the United States to be affixed.

Done at the City of Washington, this Third day of October, in the year of our Lord one thousand eight hundred and sixty-three, and of the Independence of the United States the Eighty-eighth.

By the President: ABRAHAM LINCOLN.
WILLIAM H. SEWARD, Secretary of State.

Letter to Captain James M. Cutts, Jr, who had been court-martialed for surreptitiously watching a lady undress, and for using unbecoming language to fellow-officers.

26 October 1863

Although what I am now to say is to be, in form, a reprimand, it is not intended to add a pang to what you have already suffered upon the subject to which it relates. You have too much of life yet before you, and have shown too much of promise as an officer, for your future to be lightly surrendered. You were convicted of two offenses. One of them, not of great enormity, and yet greatly to be avoided, I feel sure you are in no danger of repeating.[1] The other you are not so well assured against. The advice of a father to his son 'Beware of entrance to a quarrel, but being in, bear it that the opposed may beware of thee,' is good, and yet not the best. Quarrel not at all. No man resolved to make the most of himself, can spare time for personal contention. Still less can he afford to take all the consequences, including the vitiating of his temper, and the loss of self-control. Yield larger things to which you can show no more than equal rights; and yield lesser ones, though clearly your own. Better give your path to a dog, than be bitten by him in contesting for the right. Even killing the dog would not cure the bite.

In the mood indicated deal henceforth with your fellow men, and especially with your brother officers; and even the unpleasant events you are passing from will not have been profitless to you.

Letter to James H. Hackett, who had apologized for allowing a letter of Lincoln's to be published.

2 November 1863

My dear Sir: Yours of 22nd October is received, as also was, in

---

[1] Privately, Lincoln had quipped that Cutts should be 'elevated to the peerage' with the title of Count Peeper – a play upon the name of the Swedish Minister, Edward Count Piper.

due course, that of 3rd October. I look forward with pleasure to the fulfilment of the promise made in the former.

Give yourself no uneasiness on the subject mentioned in that of the 22nd.

My note to you I certainly did not expect to see in print; yet I have not been much shocked by the newspaper comments upon it. Those comments constitute a fair specimen of what has occurred to me through life. I have endured a great deal of ridicule without much malice; and have received a great deal of kindness not quite free from ridicule. I am used to it. Yours truly

Letter to Edwin M. Stanton, Secretary of War.

11 November 1863

My dear Sir: I personally wish Jacob R. Freese, of New Jersey, to be appointed a Colonel for a colored regiment – and this regardless of whether he can tell the exact shade of Julius Caesar's hair. Yours truly

Address at Gettysburg, Pennsylvania.

19 November 1863

Four score and seven years ago our fathers brought forth on this continent, a new nation, conceived in Liberty, and dedicated to the proposition that all men are created equal.

Now we are engaged in a great civil war, testing whether that nation, or any nation so conceived and so dedicated, can long endure. We are met on a great battle-field of that war. We have come to dedicate a portion of that field, as a final resting place for those who here gave their lives that the nation might live. It is altogether fitting and proper that we should do this.

But, in a larger sense, we cannot dedicate – we cannot consecrate – we cannot hallow – this ground. The brave men, living and dead, who struggled here, have consecrated it, far above our poor power to add or detract. The world will little note, nor long remember what we say here, but it can never forget what they did here. It is for us the living, rather, to be dedicated here to the unfinished work which they who fought here have thus far so nobly advanced. It is rather for us to be here dedicated to the great task remaining before us – that from these honored dead we take increased devotion to that cause for which they gave the last full measure of devotion – that we here highly resolve that these dead shall not have died in vain – that this nation, under God, shall have a new birth of freedom – and that government of the people, by the people, for the people, shall not perish from the earth.[1]

Letter to Edward Everett, who had made the principal address, lasting two hours, at Gettysburg.

20 November 1863

My dear Sir: Your kind note of to-day is received. In our respective parts yesterday, you could not have been excused to make a short address, nor I a long one. I am pleased to know that in your judgment, the little I did say was not entirely a failure. Of course I knew Mr Everett would not fail; and yet, while the whole discourse was eminently satisfactory, and will be of great value, there were passages in it which transcended my expectation. The point made against the theory of the general government being only an agency, whose principals are the states, was new to me, and, as I think, is one of the best arguments for the national supremacy. The tribute to our noble women for their angel-ministering to the suffering soldiers, surpasses, in its way, as do the subjects of it, whatever has gone before.

Our sick boy, for whom you kindly inquire, we hope is past the worst. Your Obt. Servt.

From the Annual Message to Congress. This was accompanied by a Proclamation of Amnesty and Reconstruction, proposing the formation of new state governments in the rebel states, on the basis of an oath of loyalty taken by at least ten per cent of the 1860 electorate.

8 December 1863

. . . When Congress assembled a year ago the war had already

[1] There are five autograph copies of the Gettysburg Address in existence. Two were written before 19 November 1863, three afterwards. On the assumption that the final copy represents the maturity of Lincoln's thought and expression, we have selected that for inclusion here. The manuscript was written some time after 4 March 1864, for reproduction in facsimile in a book entitled *Autograph Leaves of Our Country's Authors.* In this printing, the manuscript is reproduced with complete fidelity except for the omission of a heading, 'Address delivered at the dedication of a Cemetery at Gettysburg,' a date line, 'November 19, 1863,' and the signature, 'Abraham Lincoln.'

lasted nearly twenty months, and there had been many conflicts on both land and sea, with varying results.

The rebellion had been pressed back into reduced limits; yet the tone of public feeling and opinion, at home and abroad, was not satisfactory. With other signs, the popular elections, then just past, indicated uneasiness among ourselves, while amid much that was cold and menacing the kindest words coming from Europe were uttered in accents of pity, that we were too blind to surrender a hopeless cause. Our commerce was suffering greatly by a few armed vessels built upon and furnished from foreign shores, and we were threatened with such additions from the same quarter as would sweep our trade from the sea and raise our blockade. We had failed to elicit from European governments anything hopeful upon this subject. The preliminary emancipation proclamation, issued in September, was running its assigned period to the beginning of the new year. A month later the final proclamation came, including the announcement that colored men of suitable condition would be received into the war service. The policy of emancipation, and of employing black soldiers, gave to the future a new aspect, about which hope, and fear, and doubt contended in uncertain conflict. According to our political system, as a matter of civil administration, the general government had no lawful power to effect emancipation in any state, and for a long time it had been hoped that the rebellion could be suppressed without resorting to it as a military measure. It was all the while deemed possible that the necessity for it might come, and that if it should, the crisis of the contest would then be presented. It came, and as was anticipated, it was followed by dark and doubtful days. Eleven months having now passed, we are permitted to take another view. The rebel borders are pressed still further back, and by the complete opening of the Mississippi the country dominated by the rebellion is divided into distinct parts, with no practical communication between them. Tennessee and Arkansas have been substantially cleared of insurgent control, and influential citizens in each, owners of slaves and advocates of slavery at the beginning of the rebellion, now declare openly for emancipation in their respective states. Of those states not included in the emancipation proclamation, Maryland, and Missouri, neither of which three years ago would tolerate any restraint upon the extension of slavery into new territories, only dispute now as to the best mode of removing it within their own limits.

Of those who were slaves at the beginning of the rebellion, full one hundred thousand are now in the United States military service, about one-half of which number actually bear arms in the ranks; thus giving the double advantage of taking so much labor from the insurgent cause, and supplying the places which otherwise must be filled with so many white men. So far as tested, it is difficult to say they are not as good soldiers as any. No servile insurrection, or tendency to violence or cruelty, has marked the measures of emancipation and arming the blacks. These measures have been much discussed in foreign countries, and contemporary with such discussion the tone of public sentiment there is much improved. At home the same measures have been fully discussed, supported, criticized, and denounced, and the annual elections following are highly encouraging to those whose official duty it is to bear the country through this great trial. Thus we have the new reckoning. The crisis which threatened to divide the friends of the Union is past.

Looking now to the present and future, and with reference to the resumption of the national authority within the states wherein that authority has been suspended, I have thought fit to issue a proclamation . . .

It is . . . proffered that if, in any of the states named, a state government shall be, in the mode prescribed, set up, such government shall be recognized and guarantied by the United States, and that under it the state shall, on the constitutional conditions, be protected against invasion and domestic violence. The constitutional obligation of the United States to guaranty to every state in the Union a republican form of government, and to protect the state, in the cases stated, is explicit and full. But why tender the benefits of this provision only to a state government set up in this particular way? This section of the Constitution contemplates a case wherein the element within a state, favorable to republican government, in the Union, may be too feeble for an opposite and hostile element external to, or even within, the state; and such are precisely the cases with which we are now dealing.

An attempt to guaranty and protect a revived state government, constructed in whole, or in preponderating part, from the very element against whose hostility and violence it is to be protected, is simply absurd. There must be a test by which to separate the opposing elements, so as to build only from the sound; and that test is a sufficiently liberal one, which accepts as sound whoever will make a sworn recantation of his former unsoundness.

But if it be proper to require, as a test of admission to the political body, an oath of allegiance to the Constitution of the United States, and to the Union under it, why also the laws and proclamations in regard to slavery? Those laws and proclamations were enacted and put forth for the purpose of aiding in the suppression of the rebellion. To give them their fullest effect, there had to be a pledge for their maintenance. In my judgment they have aided, and will further aid, the cause for which they were intended. To now abandon them would be not only to relinquish a lever of power, but would also be a cruel and an astounding breach of faith. I may add at this point, that while I remain in my present position I shall not attempt to retract or modify the emancipation proclamation; nor shall I return to slavery any person who is free by the terms of that proclamation, or by any of the acts of Congress. For these and other reasons it is thought best that support of these measures shall be included in the oath; and it is believed the Executive may lawfully claim it in return for pardon and restoration of forfeited rights, which he has clear constitutional power to withhold altogether, or grant upon the terms which he shall deem wisest for the public interest. It should be observed, also, that this part of the oath is subject to the modifying and abrogating power of legislation and supreme judicial decision.

The proposed acquiescence of the national Executive in any reasonable temporary state arrangement for the freed people is made with the view of possibly modifying the confusion and destitution which must, at best, attend all classes by a total revolution of labor throughout whole states. It is hoped that the already deeply afflicted people in those states may be somewhat more ready to give up the cause of their affliction, if, to this extent, this vital matter be left to themselves; while no power of the national Executive to prevent an abuse is abridged by the proposition . . .

Saying that, on certain terms, certain classes will be pardoned, with rights restored, it is not said that other classes, or other terms, will never be included. Saying that reconstruction will be accepted if presented in a specified way, it is not said it will never be accepted in any other way.

The movements, by state action, for emancipation in several of the states not included in the emancipation proclamation, are matters of profound gratulation. And while I do not repeat in detail what I have heretofore so earnestly urged upon this subject, my general views and feelings remain unchanged; and I trust that Congress will omit no fair opportunity of aiding these important steps to a great consummation.

In the midst of other cares, however important, we must not lose sight of the fact that the war power is still our main reliance. To that power alone can we look, yet for a time, to give confidence to the people in the contested regions, that the insurgent power will not again overrun them. Until that confidence shall be established, little can be done anywhere for what is called reconstruction. Hence our chiefest care must still be directed to the army and navy, who have thus far borne their harder part so nobly and well. And it may be esteemed fortunate that in giving the greatest efficiency to these indispensable arms, we do also honorably recognize the gallant men, from commander to sentinel, who compose them, and to whom, more than to others, the world must stand indebted for the home of freedom disenthralled, regenerated, enlarged, and perpetuated.

Chapter 9
Triumph and Tragedy
1864–5

The North endured much frustration during 1864. It knew that it had the strength to win the war, but was unable to deliver the knock-out blow. Grant and Sherman adopted the kind of strategy, based on relentless pressure at various points, which Lincoln had long favored. But its implementation, especially in Virginia, cost many lives, and did not bring quick results.

The most remarkable event on the home front was the holding of a presidential election in the midst of a civil war. Lincoln's re-election was by no means a foregone conclusion. His party was divided, and there was even an attempt within his own party, long after the Convention, to replace him as the candidate. In late summer, with the war apparently stalled, Lincoln himself doubted whether he could be re-elected, as he made plain in his extraordinary memorandum of 23 August. The prospects changed rapidly in September, when Sherman's capture of Atlanta, and victories in the Shenandoah Valley, revived Northern (and Republican) morale. In November, Lincoln won a convincing victory. In his Second Inaugural Address, in March 1865, he expressed, in language of great beauty, his deepest feelings about the nature and purpose of the conflict.

Lincoln put his full weight behind the proposed Thirteenth Amendment to the Constitution, which would end slavery once and for all; Congress approved it early in 1865. Postwar Reconstruction had steadily moved up the political agenda, and Lincoln's pragmatic, piecemeal methods failed to satisfy more radical members of his own party. But the President's policy was steadily evolving, and in what proved to be his last major speech he hinted at further steps to come.

In the early spring of 1865, Confederate resistance finally crumbled. On 4 April Lincoln was able to walk through the streets of Richmond. On 9 April Lee's surrender at Appomattox effectively ended the war. Five days later, on Good Friday, Lincoln was shot in Ford's Theater by John Wilkes Booth, and died the following morning.

Letter to Edwin M. Stanton, Secretary of War.

1 March 1864

My dear Sir: A poor widow, by the name of Baird, has a son in the army, that for some offense has been sentenced to serve a long time without pay, or at most, with very little pay. I do not like this punishment of withholding pay — it falls so very hard upon poor families. After he has been serving in this way for several months, at the tearful appeal of the poor mother, I made a direction that he be allowed to enlist for a new turn, on the same conditions as others. She now comes, and says she cannot get it acted upon. Please do it. Yours truly

Letter to John A. J. Creswell, Congressman from Maryland.

7 March 1864

My dear Sir: I am very anxious for emancipation to be effected in Maryland in some substantial form. I think it probable that my expressions of a preference for *gradual* over *immediate* emancipation, are misunderstood. I had thought the *gradual* would produce less confusion, and destitution, and therefore would be more satisfactory; but if those who are better acquainted with the subject, and are more deeply interested in it, prefer the *immediate*, most certainly I have no objection to their judgment prevailing. My wish is that all who are for emancipation *in any form*, shall co-operate, all treating all respectfully, and all adopting and acting upon the major opinion, when fairly ascertained. What I have dreaded is the danger that by jealousies, rivalries, and consequent ill-blood — driving one another out of meetings and conventions — perchance from the polls — the friends of emancipation themselves may divide, and lose the measure altogether. I wish this letter to not be made public; but no man representing me as I herein represent myself, will be in any danger of contradiction by me. Yours truly

Speech to General Ulysses S. Grant.

9 March 1864

The nation's appreciation of what you have done, and its reliance upon you for what remains to do, in the existing great struggle, are now presented with this commission, constituting you Lieutenant-General in the Army of the United States. With this high honor devolves upon you also, a corresponding responsibility. As the country herein trusts you, so, under God, it will sustain you. I scarcely need to add that with what I here speak for the nation goes my own hearty personal concurrence.

Reply to New York Working Men's Democratic Republican Association, which includes an important statement of Lincoln's political and social philosophy.

21 March 1864

. . . None are so deeply interested to resist the present rebellion as the working people. Let them beware of prejudice, working division and hostility among themselves. The most notable feature of a disturbance in your city last summer was the hanging of some working people by other working people.[1] It should never be so. The strongest bond of human sympathy, outside of the family relation, should be one uniting all working people, of all nations, and tongues, and kindreds. Nor should this lead to a war upon property, or the owners of property. Property is the fruit of labor — property is desirable — is a positive good in the world. That some should be rich, shows that others may become rich, and hence is just encouragement to industry and enterprise. Let not him who is houseless pull down the house of another; but let him labor diligently and build one for himself, thus by example assuring that his own shall be safe from violence when built.

A Fragment on Slavery.

22 March 1864

I never knew a man who wished to be himself a slave. Consider if you know any good thing, that no man desires for himself.

---

[1] In the New York draft riots in July 1863, white rioters attacked and killed a number of free blacks.

Letter to Albert G. Hodges, editor of the Frankfort, Kentucky, Commonwealth.

4 April 1864

My dear Sir: You ask me to put in writing the substance of what I verbally said the other day, in your presence, to Governor Bramlette and Senator Dixon. It was about as follows:

'I am naturally anti-slavery. If slavery is not wrong, nothing is wrong. I cannot remember when I did not so think, and feel. And yet I have never understood that the presidency conferred upon me an unrestricted right to act officially upon this judgment and feeling. It was in the oath I took that I would, to the best of my ability, preserve, protect, and defend the Constitution of the United States. I could not take the office without taking the oath. Nor was it my view that I might take an oath to get power, and break the oath in using the power. I understood, too, that in ordinary civil administration this oath even forbade me to practically indulge my primary abstract judgment on the moral question of slavery. I had publicly declared this many times, and in many ways. And I aver that, to this day, I have done no official act in mere deference to my abstract judgment and feeling on slavery. I did understand, however, that my oath to preserve the Constitution to the best of my ability, imposed upon me the duty of preserving, by every indispensable means, that government – that nation – of which that Constitution was the organic law. Was it possible to lose the nation, and yet preserve the Constitution? By general law life *and* limb must be protected; yet often a limb must be amputated to save a life; but a life is never wisely given to save a limb. I felt that measures, otherwise unconstitutional, might become lawful, by becoming indispensable to the preservation of the Constitution, through the preservation of the nation. Right or wrong, I assumed this ground, and now avow it. I could not feel that, to the best of my ability, I had even tried to preserve the Constitution, if, to save slavery, or any minor matter, I should permit the wreck of government, country, and Constitution all together. When, early in the war, Gen. Fremont attempted military emancipation, I forbade it, because I did not then think it an indispensable necessity. When a little later, Gen. Cameron, then Secretary of War, suggested the arming of the blacks, I objected, because I did not yet think it an indispensable necessity. When, still later, Gen. Hunter attempted military emancipation, I again forbade it, because I did not yet think the indispensable necessity had come. When, in March, and May, and July 1862 I made earnest, and successive appeals to the border states to favor compensated emancipation, I believed the indispensable necessity for military emancipation and arming the blacks would come, unless averted by that measure. They declined the proposition; and I was, in my best judgment, driven to the alternative of either surrendering the Union, and with it, the Constitution, or of laying strong hand upon the colored element. I chose the latter. In choosing it, I hoped for greater gain than loss; but of this, I was not entirely confident. More than a year of trial now shows no loss by it in our foreign relations, none in our home popular sentiment, none in our white military force—no loss by it any how or any where. On the contrary, it shows a gain of quite a hundred and thirty thousand soldiers, seamen, and laborers. These are palpable facts, about which, as facts, there can be no caviling. We have the men; and we could not have had them without the measure.

'And now let any Union man who complains of the measure, test himself by writing down in one line that he is for subduing the rebellion by force of arms; and in the next, that he is for taking these hundred and thirty thousand men from the Union side, and placing them where they would be but for the measure he condemns. If he cannot face his case so stated, it is only because he cannot face the truth.'

I add a word which was not in the verbal conversation. In telling this tale I attempt no compliment to my own sagacity. I claim not to have controlled events, but confess plainly that events have controlled me. Now, at the end of three years struggle the nation's condition is not what either party, or any man devised, or expected. God alone can claim it. Whither it is tending seems plain. If God now wills the removal of a great wrong, and wills also that we of the North as well as you of the South, shall pay fairly for our complicity in that wrong, impartial history will find therein new cause to attest and revere the justice and goodness of God. Yours truly

Address at Sanitary Fair,[1] *Baltimore.*

18 April 1864

Ladies and Gentlemen: Calling to mind that we are in Baltimore,

[1] The United States Sanitary Commission was the Civil War counterpart of the Red Cross. To finance its activities it held 'sanitary fairs' in the larger cities of the country.

we cannot fail to note that the world moves. Looking upon these many people, assembled here, to serve, as they best may, the soldiers of the Union, it occurs at once that three years ago, the same soldiers could not so much as pass through Baltimore. The change from then till now is both great and gratifying. Blessings on the brave men who have wrought the change, and the fair women who strive to reward them for it.

But Baltimore suggests more than could happen within Baltimore. The change within Baltimore is part only of a far wider change. When the war began, three years ago, neither party, nor any man, expected it would last till now. Each looked for the end, in some way, long ere to-day. Neither did any anticipate that domestic slavery would be much affected by the war. But here we are; the war has not ended, and slavery has been much affected – how much needs not now to be recounted. So true is it that man proposes, and God disposes.

But we can see the past, though we may not claim to have directed it; and seeing it, in this case, we feel more hopeful and confident for the future.

The world has never had a good definition of the word liberty, and the American people, just now, are much in want of one. We all declare for liberty; but in using the same *word* we do not all mean the same *thing*. With some the word liberty may mean for each man to do as he pleases with himself, and the product of his labor; while with others the same word may mean for some men to do as they please with other men, and the product of other men's labor. Here are two, not only different, but incompatible things, called by the same name – liberty. And it follows that each of the things is, by the respective parties, called by two different and incompatible names – liberty and tyranny.

The shepherd drives the wolf from the sheep's throat, for which the sheep thanks the shepherd as a *liberator*, while the wolf denounces him for the same act as the destroyer of liberty, especially as the sheep was a black one. Plainly the sheep and the wolf are not agreed upon a definition of the word liberty; and precisely the same difference prevails to-day among us human creatures, even in the North, and all professing to love liberty. Hence we behold the processes by which thousands are daily passing from under the yoke of bondage, hailed by some as the advance of liberty, and bewailed by others as the destruction of all liberty. Recently, as it seems, the people of Maryland have been doing something to define liberty; and thanks to them that, in what they have done, the wolf's dictionary has been repudiated. . .

Letter to William Dennison and others, accepting nomination for the Presidency.

27 June 1864

Hon. William Dennison and others, a Committee of the National Union Convention.[1]

Gentlemen: Your letter of the 14th inst. formally notifying me that I have been nominated by the convention you represent for the Presidency of the United States for four years from the fourth of March next has been received. The nomination is gratefully accepted, as the resolutions of the convention, called the platform, are heartily approved.

While the resolution in regard to the supplanting of republican government upon the western continent is fully concurred in, there might be misunderstanding were I not to say that the position of the government, in relation to the action of France in Mexico, as assumed through the State Department, and approved and indorsed by the convention, among the measures and acts of the Executive, will be faithfully maintained, so long as the state of facts shall leave that position pertinent and applicable.

I am especially gratified that the soldier and the seaman were not forgotten by the convention, as they forever must and will be remembered by the grateful country for whose salvation they devote their lives.

Thanking you for the kind and complimentary terms in which you have communicated the nomination and other proceedings of the convention, I subscribe myself Your Obt. Servt.

Telegram to General Ulysses S. Grant, besieging Richmond.

17 August 1864

I have seen your dispatch expressing your unwillingness to break your hold where you are. Neither am I willing. Hold on with a bulldog grip, and chew and choke, as much as possible.

---

[1] Technically, Lincoln was nominated in 1864 by the National Union party, an amalgam of Republicans, who constituted the great majority, and Democrats who supported the war without reservations.

Speech to the 166th Ohio Regiment.

22 August 1864

I suppose you are going home to see your families and friends. For the service you have done in this great struggle in which we are engaged I present you sincere thanks for myself and the country. I almost always feel inclined, when I happen to say anything to soldiers, to impress upon them in a few brief remarks the importance of success in this contest. It is not merely for to-day, but for all time to come that we should perpetuate for our children's children this great and free government, which we have enjoyed all our lives. I beg you to remember this, not merely for my sake, but for yours. I happen temporarily to occupy this big White House. I am a living witness that any one of your children may look to come here as my father's child has. It is in order that each of you may have through this free government which we have enjoyed, an open field and a fair chance for your industry, enterprise, and intelligence; that you may all have equal privileges in the race of life, with all its desirable human aspirations. It is for this the struggle should be maintained, that we may not lose our birthright – not only for one, but for two or three years. The nation is worth fighting for, to secure such an inestimable jewel.

Memorandum on the President's duty if not re-elected.

23 August 1864

This morning, as for some days past, it seems exceedingly probable that this administration will not be re-elected. Then it will be my duty to so co-operate with the President-elect, as to save the Union between the election and the inauguration; as he will have secured his election on such ground that he cannot possibly save it afterwards.[1]

Letter to Eliza P. Gurney, member of the Society of Friends.

4 September 1864

My esteemed friend: I have not forgotten – probably never shall forget – the very impressive occasion when yourself and friends

[1] After writing this paper Lincoln folded it and asked each member of his Cabinet to write his name, by way of endorsement, on an outside fold. All complied. On 11 November 1864, three days after his re-election, Lincoln showed the members of his Cabinet what they had signed.

visited me on a Sabbath forenoon two years ago. Nor has your kind letter, written nearly a year later, ever been forgotten. In all, it has been your purpose to strengthen my reliance on God. I am much indebted to the good Christian people of the country for their constant prayers and consolations; and to no one of them, more than to yourself. The purposes of the Almighty are perfect, and must prevail, though we erring mortals may fail to accurately perceive them in advance. We hoped for a happy termination of this terrible war long before this; but God knows best, and has ruled otherwise. We shall yet acknowledge His wisdom and our own error therein. Meanwhile we must work earnestly in the best light He gives us, trusting that so working still conduces to the great ends He ordains. Surely He intends some great good to follow this mighty convulsion, which no mortal could make, and no mortal could stay.

Your people – the Friends – have had, and are having, a very great trial. On principle, and faith, opposed to both war and oppression, they can only practically oppose oppression by war. In this hard dilemma, some have chosen one horn and some the other. For those appealing to me on conscientious grounds, I have done, and shall do, the best I could and can, in my own conscience, under my oath to the law. That you believe this I doubt not; and believing it, I shall still receive, for our country and myself, your earnest prayers to our Father in Heaven. Your sincere friend

Response to a serenade, two days after the President's re-election.
10 November 1864

It has long been a grave question whether any government, not *too* strong for the liberties of its people, can be strong *enough* to maintain its own existence, in great emergencies.

On this point the present rebellion brought our republic to a severe test; and a presidential election occurring in regular course during the rebellion added not a little to the strain. If the loyal people, *united*, were put to the utmost of their strength by the rebellion, must they not fail when *divided*, and partially paralysed, by a political war among themselves?

But the election was a necessity.

We cannot have free government without elections; and if the rebellion could force us to forgo, or postpone a national election, it might fairly claim to have already conquered and ruined us. The strife of the election is but human nature practically applied to the facts of the case. What has occurred in this case, must ever recur in similar cases. Human nature will not change. In any future great national trial, compared with the men of this, we shall have as weak and as strong; as silly and as wise; as bad and good. Let us, therefore, study the incidents of this, as philosophy to learn wisdom from, and none of them as wrongs to be revenged.

But the election, along with its incidental and undesirable strife, has done good too. It has demonstrated that a people's government can sustain a national election, in the midst of a great civil war. Until now it has not been known to the world that this was a possibility. It shows also how *sound*, and how *strong* we still are. It shows that, even among candidates of the same party, he who is most devoted to the Union, and most opposed to treason, can receive most of the people's votes. It shows also, to the extent yet known, that we have more men now than we had when the war began. Gold is good in its place; but living, brave, patriotic men, are better than gold.

But the rebellion continues; and now that the election is over, may not all, having a common interest, reunite in a common effort to save our common country? For my own part I have striven, and shall strive to avoid placing any obstacle in the way. So long as I have been here I have not willingly planted a thorn in any man's bosom.

While I am deeply sensible to the high compliment of a re-election, and duly grateful, as I trust, to Almighty God for having directed my countrymen to a right conclusion, as I think, for their own good, it adds nothing to my satisfaction that any other man may be disappointed or pained by the result.

May I ask those who have not differed with me, to join with me, in this same spirit towards those who have?

And now, let me close by asking three hearty cheers for our brave soldiers and seamen and their gallant and skilful commanders.

Letter to Mrs Lydia Bixby.[1]

21 November 1864

Dear Madam: I have been shown in the files of the War

---

[1] Lincoln wrote this letter upon an inaccurate representation of fact. Only two of Mrs

Department a statement of the Adjutant General of Massachusetts, that you are the mother of five sons who have died
gloriously on the field of battle.

I feel how weak and fruitless must be any words of mine which
should attempt to beguile you from the grief of a loss so
overwhelming. But I cannot refrain from tendering to you the
consolation that may be found in the thanks of the Republic they
died to save.

I pray that our Heavenly Father may assuage the anguish of
your bereavement, and leave you only the cherished memory of
the loved and lost, and the solemn pride that must be yours, to
have laid so costly a sacrifice upon the altar of Freedom. Yours,
very sincerely and respectfully

From the Annual Message to Congress.

6 December 1864

. . . The war continues. Since the last annual message all the
important lines and positions then occupied by our forces have
been maintained, and our arms have steadily advanced; thus
liberating the regions left in rear, so that Missouri, Kentucky,
Tennessee, and parts of other states have again produced
reasonably fair crops.

The most remarkable feature in the military operations of the
year is General Sherman's attempted march of three hundred
miles directly through the insurgent region. It tends to show a
great increase of our relative strength that our General-in-Chief
should feel able to confront and hold in check every active force of
the enemy, and yet to detach a well-appointed large army to move
on such an expedition. The result not yet being known, conjecture
in regard to it is not here indulged.[1]

Important movements have also occurred during the year to the
effect of molding society for durability in the Union. Although

---

Bixby's sons were killed in action. A third is reported (1) to have deserted to the enemy,
and (2) to have died in a Confederate war prison. A fourth son was undoubtedly a
deserter. The fifth and last son was awarded an honorable discharge.

While the many facsimiles of the Bixby letter are fabrications, there is no reason to
doubt the authenticity of the text. It remains one of the noblest expressions of condolence
in the world's literature.

[1] Sherman had started from Atlanta on his famous 'march to the sea' on 16 November
1864.

short of complete success, it is much in the right direction, that twelve thousand citizens in each of the states of Arkansas and Louisiana have organized loyal state governments with free constitutions, and are earnestly struggling to maintain and administer them. The movements in the same direction, more extensive though less definite in Missouri, Kentucky, and Tennessee, should not be overlooked. But Maryland presents the example of complete success. Maryland is secure to Liberty and Union for all the future. The genius of rebellion will no more claim Maryland. Like another foul spirit, being driven out, it may seek to tear her, but it will woo her no more.

At the last session of Congress a proposed amendment of the Constitution abolishing slavery throughout the United States,[1] passed the Senate, but failed for lack of the requisite two-thirds vote in the House of Representatives. Although the present is the same Congress, and nearly the same members, and without questioning the wisdom or patriotism of those who stood in opposition, I venture to recommend the reconsideration and passage of the measure at the present session. Of course the abstract question is not changed; but an intervening election shows, almost certainly, that the next Congress will pass the measure if this does not. Hence there is only a question of *time* as to when the proposed amendment will go to the states for their action. And as it is to so go, at all events, may we not agree that the sooner the better? It is not claimed that the election has imposed a duty on members to change their views or their votes, any further than, as an additional element to be considered, their judgment may be affected by it. It is the voice of the people now, for the first time, heard upon the question. In a great national crisis like ours, unanimity of action among those seeking a common end is very desirable – almost indispensable. And yet no approach to such unanimity is attainable, unless some deference shall be paid to the will of the majority, simply because it is the will of the majority. In this case the common end is the maintenance of the Union; and among the means to secure that end, such will, through the election, is most clearly declared in favor of such constitutional amendment.

The most reliable indication of public purpose in this country is

[1] The Thirteenth Amendment to the Constitution, ratified 18 December 1865.

derived through our popular elections. Judging by the recent canvass and its result, the purpose of the people, within the loyal states, to maintain the integrity of the Union, was never more firm, nor more nearly unanimous, than now. The extraordinary calmness and good order with which the millions of voters met and mingled at the polls, give strong assurance of this. Not only all those who supported the Union ticket, so called, but a great majority of the opposing party also, may be fairly claimed to entertain, and to be actuated by, the same purpose. It is an unanswerable argument to this effect, that no candidate for any office whatever, high or low, has ventured to seek votes on the avowal that he was for giving up the Union. There have been much impugning of motives, and much heated controversy as to the proper means and best mode of advancing the Union cause; but on the distinct issue of Union or no Union, the politicians have shown their instinctive knowledge that there is no diversity among the people. In affording the people the fair opportunity of showing, one to another and to the world, this firmness and unanimity of purpose, the election has been of vast value to the national cause.

The election has exhibited another fact not less valuable to be known – the fact that we do not approach exhaustion in the most important branch of national resources – that of living men. While it is melancholy to reflect that the war has filled so many graves, and carried mourning to so many hearts, it is some relief to know that, compared with the surviving, the fallen have been so few. While corps, and divisions, and brigades, and regiments have formed, and fought, and dwindled, and gone out of existence, a great majority of the men who composed them are still living. The same is true of the naval service. The election returns prove this. So many voters could not else be found. The states regularly holding elections, both now and four years ago, to wit, California, Connecticut, Delaware, Illinois, Indiana, Iowa, Kentucky, Maine, Maryland, Massachusetts, Michigan, Minnesota, Missouri, New Hampshire, New Jersey, New York, Ohio, Oregon, Pennsylvania, Rhode Island, Vermont, West Virginia, and Wisconsin cast 3,982,011 votes now, against 3,870,222 cast then, showing an aggregate now of 3,982,011. To this is to be added 33,762 cast now in the new states of Kansas and Nevada, which states did not vote in 1860, thus swelling the aggregate to 4,015,773 and the net increase during the three years and a half of war to 145,551. A table is appended showing particulars. To this again should be added the number of all soldiers in the field from Massachusetts, Rhode Island, New Jersey, Delaware, Indiana, Illinois, and California, who, by the laws of those states, could not vote away from their homes, and which number cannot be less than 90,000. Nor yet is this all. The number in organized territories is triple now what it was four years ago, while thousands, white and black, join us as the national arms press back the insurgent lines. So much is shown, affirmatively and negatively, by the election. It is not material to inquire *how* the increase has been produced, or to show that it would have been *greater* but for the war, which is probably true. The important fact remains demonstrated, that we have *more* men *now* than we had when the war *began*; that we are not exhausted, nor in process of exhaustion; that we are *gaining* strength, and may, if need be, maintain the contest indefinitely. This as to men. Material resources are now more complete and abundant than ever.

The national resources, then, are unexhausted, and, as we believe, inexhaustible. The public purpose to re-establish and maintain the national authority is unchanged, and, as we believe, unchangeable. The manner of continuing the effort remains to choose. On careful consideration of all the evidence accessible it seems to me that no attempt at negotiation with the insurgent leader could result in any good. He would accept nothing short of severance of the Union – precisely what we will not and cannot give. His declarations to this effect are explicit and oft-repeated. He does not attempt to deceive us. He affords us no excuse to deceive ourselves. He cannot voluntarily reaccept the Union; we cannot voluntarily yield it. Between him and us the issue is distinct, simple, and inflexible. It is an issue which can only be tried by war and decided by victory. If we yield, we are beaten; if the southern people fail him, he is beaten. Either way, it would be the victory and defeat following war. What is true, however, of him who heads the insurgent cause, is not necessarily true of those who follow. Although he cannot reaccept the Union, they can. Some of them, we know, already desire peace and reunion. The number of such may increase. They can, at any moment, have peace simply by laying down their arms and submitting to the national authority under the Constitution. After so much, the government could not, if it would, maintain war against them. The loyal people would not sustain or allow it. If questions should remain, we would adjust them by the peaceful means of legislation, conference, courts, and votes, operating only in constitutional and lawful channels. Some certain, and other possible, questions are, and would be, beyond the executive power to adjust; as, for instance, the admission of members into Congress, and whatever might require the appropriation of money. The executive power itself would be greatly diminished by the cessation of actual war. Pardons and remissions of forfeitures, however, would still be within executive control. In what spirit and temper this control would be exercised can be fairly judged of by the past.

A year ago general pardon and amnesty, upon specified terms, were offered to all, except certain designated classes; and it was, at the same time, made known that the excepted classes were still within contemplation of special clemency. During the year many availed themselves of the general provision, and many more would, only that the signs of bad faith in some led to such precautionary measures as rendered the practical process less easy and certain. During the same time also special pardons have been granted to individuals of the excepted classes, and no voluntary application has been denied. Thus practically, the door has been, for a full year, open to all, except such as were not in condition to make free choice — that is, such as were in custody or under constraint. It is still so open to all. But the time may come — probably will come — when public duty shall demand that it be closed; and that, in lieu, more rigorous measures than heretofore shall be adopted.

In presenting the abandonment of armed resistance to the national authority on the part of the insurgents, as the only indispensable condition to ending the war on the part of the government, I retract nothing heretofore said as to slavery. I repeat the declaration made a year ago, that 'while I remain in my present position I shall not attempt to retract or modify the emancipation proclamation, nor shall I return to slavery any person who is free by the terms of that proclamation, or by any of the Acts of Congress.' If the people should, by whatever mode or means, make it an executive duty to re-enslave such persons, another, and not I, must be their instrument to perform it.

In stating a single condition of peace, I mean simply to say that the war will cease on the part of the government, whenever it shall have ceased on the part of those who began it.

Story written for Noah Brooks, correspondent of the Sacramento, California, Union.

[6 December 1864]

THE PRESIDENT'S LAST, SHORTEST, AND BEST SPEECH

On Thursday of last week two ladies from Tennessee came before the President asking the release of their husbands held as prisoners of war at Johnson's Island. They were put off till Friday, when they came again; and were again put off to Saturday. At each of the interviews one of the ladies urged that her husband was a religious man. On Saturday the President ordered the release of the prisoners, and then said to this lady: 'You say your husband is a religious man; tell him when you meet him, that I say I am not much of a judge of religion, but that, in my opinion, the religion that sets men to rebel and fight against their government, because, as they think, that government does not sufficiently help *some* men to eat their bread on the sweat of *other* men's faces, is not the sort of religion upon which people can get to heaven!'

Letter to General William T. Sherman, who had just announced the capture of Savannah, Georgia.

26 December 1864

My dear General Sherman: Many, many, thanks for your Christmas gift – the capture of Savannah.

When you were about leaving Atlanta for the Atlantic coast, I was *anxious*, if not fearful; but feeling that you were the better judge, and remembering that 'nothing risked, nothing gained' I did not interfere. Now, the undertaking being a success, the honor is all yours; for I believe none of us went farther than to acquiesce. And, taking the work of Gen. Thomas into the count,[1] as it should be taken, it is indeed a great success. Not only does it afford the obvious and immediate military advantages; but, in showing to the world that your army could be divided, putting the stronger part to an important new service, and yet leaving enough to vanquish the old opposing force of the whole – Hood's army – it brings those who sat in darkness, to see a great light. But what

[1] Virginia-born George H. Thomas had literally smashed the last Confederate resistance in the West at the Battle of Nashville (Tennessee) on 15th–16th December 1864.

next? I suppose it will be safer if I leave Gen. Grant and yourself to decide.

Please make my grateful acknowledgments to your whole army, officers and men. Yours truly

The Second Inaugural Address.

4 March 1865

At this second appearing to take the oath of the presidential office, there is less occasion for an extended address than there was at the first. Then a statement, somewhat in detail, of a course to be pursued, seemed fitting and proper. Now, at the expiration of four years, during which public declarations have been constantly called forth on every point and phase of the great contest which still absorbs the attention, and engrosses the energies of the nation, little that is new could be presented. The progress of our arms, upon which all else chiefly depends, is as well known to the public as to myself; and it is, I trust, reasonably satisfactory and encouraging to all. With high hope for the future, no prediction in regard to it is ventured.

On the occasion corresponding to this four years ago, all thoughts were anxiously directed to an impending civil war. All dreaded it – all sought to avert it. While the inaugural address was being delivered from this place, devoted altogether to *saving* the Union without war, insurgent agents were in the city seeking to *destroy* it without war – seeking to dissolve the Union, and divide effects, by negotiation. Both parties deprecated war; but one of them would *make* war rather than let the nation survive; and the other would *accept* war rather than let it perish. And the war came.

One-eighth of the whole population were colored slaves, not distributed generally over the Union, but localized in the southern part of it. These slaves constituted a peculiar and powerful interest. All knew that this interest was, somehow, the cause of the war. To strengthen, perpetuate, and extend this interest was the object for which the insurgents would rend the Union, even by war; while the government claimed no right to do more than to restrict the territorial enlargement of it. Neither party expected for the war, the magnitude, or the duration, which it has already attained. Neither anticipated that the *cause* of the conflict might cease with, or even before, the conflict itself should cease. Each looked for an easier triumph, and a result less fundamental and astounding. Both read the same Bible, and pray to the same God; and each invokes His aid against the other. It may seem strange that any men should dare to ask a just God's assistance in wringing their bread from the sweat of other men's faces; but let us judge not that we be not judged. The prayers of both could not be answered; that of neither has been answered fully. The Almighty has His own purposes. 'Woe unto the world because of offenses! for it must needs be that offenses come; but woe to that man by whom the offense cometh!' If we shall suppose that American slavery is one of those offenses which, in the providence of God, must needs come, but which, having continued through His appointed time, He now wills to remove, and that He gives to both North and South, this terrible war, as the woe due to those by whom the offense came, shall we discern therein any departure from those divine attributes which the believers in a Living God always ascribe to Him? Fondly do we hope – fervently do we pray – that this mighty scourge of war may speedily pass away. Yet, if God wills that it continue, until all the wealth piled by the bondman's two hundred and fifty years of unrequited toil shall be sunk, and until every drop of blood drawn with the lash, shall be paid by another drawn with the sword, as was said three thousand years ago, so still it must be said 'the judgments of the Lord, are true and righteous altogether.'

With malice toward none; with charity for all; with firmness in the right, as God gives us to see the right, let us strive on to finish the work we are in; to bind up the nation's wounds; to care for him who shall have borne the battle, and for his widow, and his orphan – to do all which may achieve and cherish a just, and a lasting peace, among ourselves, and with all nations.

Letter to Thurlow Weed, New York State Republican leader.
15 March 1865

My dear Sir: Everyone likes a compliment. Thank you for yours on my little notification speech, and on the recent Inaugural Address. I expect the latter to wear as well as – perhaps better than – anything I have produced; but I believe it is not immediately popular. Men are not flattered by being shown that there has been a difference of purpose between the Almighty and them. To deny it, however, in this case, is to deny that there is a God governing the world. It is a truth which I thought needed to be told; and as whatever of humiliation there is in it, falls most directly on myself, I thought others might afford for me to tell it. Yours truly

Reply to a serenade the day after Lee's surrender.

10 April 1865

Fellow-citizens: I am very greatly rejoiced to find that an occasion has occurred so pleasurable that the people cannot restrain themselves. I suppose that arrangements are being made for some sort of a formal demonstration, this, or perhaps, to-morrow night. If there should be such a demonstration, I, of course, will be called upon to respond, and I shall have nothing to say if you dribble it all out of me before. I see you have a band of music with you. I propose closing up this interview by the band performing a particular tune which I will name. Before this is done, however, I wish to mention one or two little circumstances connected with it. I have always thought 'Dixie' one of the best tunes I have ever heard.[1] Our adversaries over the way attempted to appropriate it, but I insisted yesterday that we fairly captured it. I presented the question to the Attorney General, and he gave it as his legal opinion that it is our lawful prize. I now request the band to favor me with its performance.

Lincoln's last speech, discussing the evolution of policy on reconstruction in Louisiana, and in the South generally.

11 April 1865

We meet this evening, not in sorrow, but in gladness of heart. The evacuation of Petersburg and Richmond, and the surrender of the principal insurgent army, give hope of a righteous and speedy peace whose joyous expression cannot be restrained. In the midst of this, however, He, from Whom all blessings flow, must not be forgotten. A call for a national thanksgiving is being prepared, and will be duly promulgated. Nor must those whose harder part gives us the cause of rejoicing be overlooked. Their honors must

---

[1] Lincoln first heard 'Dixie,' a minstrel tune written by Daniel D. Emmett of Mt Vernon, Ohio, in Chicago in March 1860. 'Lincoln was perfectly "taken" with it,' wrote Henry C. Whitney in *Life on the Circuit with Lincoln*, 'and clapped his great hands, demanding an encore, louder than anyone. I never saw him so enthusiastic.'

not be parceled out with others. I myself, was near the front, and had the high pleasure of transmitting much of the good news to you; but no part of the honor, for plan or execution, is mine. To Gen. Grant, his skilful officers, and brave men, all belongs. The gallant navy stood ready, but was not in reach to take active part.

By these recent successes the reinauguration of the national authority — reconstruction — which has had a large share of thought from the first, is pressed much more closely upon our attention. It is fraught with great difficulty. Unlike the case of a war between independent nations, there is no authorized organ for us to treat with. No one man has authority to give up the rebellion for any other man. We simply must begin with, and mold from, disorganized and discordant elements. Nor is it a small additional embarrassment that we, the loyal people, differ among ourselves as to the mode, manner, and means of recon-struction.

As a general rule, I abstain from reading the reports of attacks upon myself, wishing not to be provoked by that to which I cannot properly offer an answer. In spite of this precaution, however, it comes to my knowledge that I am much censured for some supposed agency in setting up, and seeking to sustain, the new state government of Louisiana. In this I have done just so much as, and no more than, the public knows. In the Annual Message of December 1863 and accompanying proclamation, I presented *a* plan of reconstruction (as the phrase goes) which, I promised, if adopted by any state, should be acceptable to, and sustained by, the executive government of the nation. I distinctly stated that this was not the only plan which might possibly be acceptable; and I also distinctly protested that the Executive claimed no right to say when, or whether members should be admitted to seats in Congress from such states. This plan was, in advance, submitted to the then Cabinet, and distinctly approved by every member of it. One of them suggested that I should then, and in that connection, apply the Emancipation Proclamation to the theretofore excepted parts of Virginia and Louisiana; that I should drop the suggestion about apprenticeship for freed-people, and that I should omit the protest against my own power, in regard to the admission of members to Congress; but even he approved every part and parcel of the plan which has since been employed or touched by the action of Louisiana. The new constitution of Louisiana, declaring emancipation for the whole state, practically applies the Proclamation to the part previously excepted. It does not adopt apprenticeship for freed-people; and it is silent, as it could not well be otherwise, about the admission of members to Congress. So that, as it applies to Louisiana, every member of the Cabinet fully approved the plan. The message went to Congress, and I received many commendations of the plan, written and verbal; and not a single objection to it, from any professed emancipationist, came to my knowledge, until after the news reached Washington that the people of Louisiana had begun to move in accordance with it. From about July 1862, I had corresponded with different persons, supposed to be interested, seeking a reconstruction of a state government for Louisiana. When the message of 1863, with the plan before mentioned, reached New Orleans, Gen. Banks wrote me that he was confident the people, with his military co-operation, would reconstruct, substantially on that plan. I wrote him and some of them to try it; they tried it, and the result is known. Such only has been my agency in getting up the Louisiana government. As to sustaining it, my promise is out, as before stated. But, as bad promises are better broken than kept, I shall treat this as a bad promise, and break it, whenever I shall be convinced that keeping it is adverse to the public interest. But I have not yet been so convinced.

I have been shown a letter on this subject, supposed to be an able one, in which the writer expresses regret that my mind has not seemed to be definitely fixed on the question whether the seceded states, so called, are in the Union or out of it. It would perhaps add astonishment to his regret, were he to learn that since I have found professed Union men endeavoring to make that question, I have *purposely* forborne any public expression upon it. As appears to me that question has not been, nor yet is, a practically material one, and that any discussion of it, while it thus remains practically immaterial, could have no effect other than the mischievous one of dividing our friends. As yet, whatever it may hereafter become, that question is bad, as the basis of a controversy, and good for nothing at all – a merely pernicious abstraction.

We all agree that the seceded states, so called, are out of their proper practical relation with the Union; and that the sole object of the government, civil and military, in regard to those states is to again get them into that proper practical relation. I believe it is not only possible, but in fact, easier, to do this, without deciding, or even considering, whether these states have ever been out of the Union, than with it. Finding themselves safely at home, it would be utterly immaterial whether they had ever been abroad. Let us all join in doing the acts necessary to restoring the proper practical relations between these states and the Union; and each for ever after, innocently indulge his own opinion whether, in doing the acts, he brought the states from without, into the Union, or only gave them proper assistance, they never having been out of it.

The amount of constituency, so to speak, on which the new Louisiana government rests, would be more satisfactory to all, if it contained fifty, thirty, or even twenty thousand, instead of only about twelve thousand, as it does. It is also unsatisfactory to some that the elective franchise is not given to the colored man. I would myself prefer that it were now conferred on the very intelligent, and on those who serve our cause as soldiers. Still the question is not whether the Louisiana government, as it stands, is quite all that is desirable. The question is 'Will it be wiser to take it as it is, and help to improve it; or to reject, and disperse it?' 'Can Louisiana be brought into proper practical relation with the Union sooner by sustaining, or by discarding, her new state government?'

Some twelve thousand voters in the heretofore slave-state of Louisiana have sworn allegiance to the Union, assumed to be the rightful political power of the state, held elections, organized a state government, adopted a free-state constitution, giving the benefit of public schools equally to black and white, and empowering the legislature to confer the elective franchise upon the colored man. Their legislature has already voted to ratify the constitutional amendment recently passed by Congress, abolishing slavery throughout the nation. These twelve thousand persons are thus fully committed to the Union, and to perpetual freedom in the state – committed to the very things, and nearly all the things the nation wants – and they ask the nation's recognition, and its assistance to make good their committal. Now, if we reject, and spurn them, we do our utmost to disorganize and disperse them. We in effect say to the white men 'You are worthless, or worse – we will neither help you, nor be helped by you.' To the blacks we say 'This cup of liberty which these, your old masters, hold to your lips, we will dash from you, and leave you to the chances of gathering the spilled and scattered contents in some vague and undefined when, where and how.' If this course, discouraging and paralyzing both white and black, has any tendency to bring Louisiana into proper practical relations with the Union, I have, so far, been unable to perceive it. If, on the contrary, we recognize, and sustain the new government of Louisiana the converse of all this is made true. We encourage the hearts, and nerve the arms of the twelve thousand to adhere to their work, and argue for it, and proselyte for it, and fight for it, and feed it, and grow it, and ripen it to a complete success. The colored man, too, in seeing all united for him, is inspired with vigilance, and energy, and daring, to the same end. Grant that he desires the elective franchise, will he not attain it sooner by saving the already advanced steps toward it, than by running backward over them? Conceding that the new government of Louisiana is only to what it should be as the egg is to the fowl, we shall sooner have the fowl by hatching the egg than by smashing it? Again, if we reject Louisiana, we also reject one vote in favor of the proposed amendment to the national constitution . . .

I repeat the question. 'Can Louisiana be brought into proper practical relation with the Union sooner by sustaining or by discarding her new state government?'

What has been said of Louisiana will apply generally to other states. And yet so great peculiarities pertain to each state; and such important and sudden changes occur in the same state; and withal, so new and unprecedented is the whole case, that no exclusive and inflexible plan can safely be prescribed as to details and colaterals. Such exclusive and inflexible plan would surely become a new entanglement. Important principles may, and must, be inflexible.

In the present 'situation' as the phrase goes, it may be my duty to make some new announcement to the people of the South. I am considering, and shall not fail to act, when satisfied that action will be proper.

An informal proclamation of peace, written on the last full day of the President's life.

14 April 1865

No pass is necessary now to authorize anyone to go to and return from Petersburg and Richmond. People go and return just as they did before the war.

Chronology of Lincoln's Life

1809, February 12.   Abraham Lincoln, first son and second child of Thomas and Nancy Hanks Lincoln, is born near Hodgen's Mill, now Hodgenville, Kentucky.

1811, Spring.   Thomas Lincoln moves his family to a farm of 230 acres on Knob Creek, about twelve miles north-east of the farm on which his son was born.

1816, December. Thomas Lincoln and his family leave Kentucky to settle in Spencer County in south-western Indiana.

1818, October 5.   Nancy Hanks Lincoln dies of the milk sickness, an ailment common on the American frontier.

1819, December 2.   Thomas Lincoln marries Sarah Bush Johnston, a widow of Elizabethtown, Kentucky, and brings her to the cabin in Indiana.

1828, January 20.   Sarah Lincoln Grigsby, older sister of Abraham Lincoln, dies in childbirth.

1828, Spring.   Young Lincoln, with Allen Gentry, takes a flatboat with farm produce to New Orleans.

1830, March.   The Lincoln family moves to Macon County, Illinois.

1831, April–July.   Abraham Lincoln makes his second flatboat trip to New Orleans.

1831, July.   Lincoln settles at New Salem, Illinois, twenty miles north-west of Springfield, and earns his living as a clerk and mill hand.

1832, April 21.   Lincoln volunteers for service in the Black Hawk War and is elected captain of the local company.

1832, July 18.   Lincoln returns, unharmed, from the campaign.

1832, August 6.   Lincoln fails of election to the Illinois legislature, but receives 277 of the 300 votes cast in his own precinct.

1833, Spring. Lincoln is appointed deputy surveyor of Sangamon County.

1833, May 7. President Andrew Jackson appoints Lincoln postmaster of New Salem.

1834, August 4. Lincoln is elected a member of the Illinois House of Representatives.

1836, August 1. Lincoln is re-elected to the Illinois House.

1837, February 28. Under Lincoln's management, the Illinois legislature transfers the state capital from Vandalia to Springfield.

1837, March 1. Lincoln is granted a license to practice law.

1837, April 15. Lincoln moves from New Salem to Springfield and becomes the junior law partner of John T. Stuart.

1838, August 6. Lincoln is elected to the Illinois legislature for the third time.

1840, August 3. Lincoln is again elected to the legislature, but this will be his final term.

1841, January 1. The engagement between Lincoln and Mary Todd is broken.

1841, April. The partnership of Stuart and Lincoln is dissolved, and Lincoln becomes the junior partner of Stephen T. Logan.

1842, September 19. James Shields challenges Lincoln to a duel. Three days later, on the dueling ground, the two men settle their differences amicably.

1842, November 4. Lincoln and Mary Todd are married.

1843, August 1. The first child of the Lincolns is born and named Robert Todd.

1844, December. The Lincoln-Logan partnership is dissolved. Lincoln forms his own firm with William H. Herndon as his partner.

1846, March 10. Edward Baker Lincoln, second son, is born.

1846, August 3. Lincoln, a Whig, is elected to the US House of Representatives from the Seventh District of Illinois.

1847, December 3. Lincoln takes his seat in the House at Washington.

1849, March 4. Lincoln's one term as a member of Congress comes to an end. Disillusioned with politics, he returns to Springfield determined to practice law more assiduously than ever.

1850, February 1. Edward Baker Lincoln, aged three years and ten months, dies after an illness of two weeks' duration.

1850, December 21. William Wallace Lincoln, third son, is born.

1853, April 4.   Thomas Lincoln, fourth son and last child, is born.

1854, May 30.   President Franklin Pierce signs the Kansas-Nebraska Bill. Lincoln, aroused as never before, determines to re-enter politics.

1854, November 7.   Lincoln is elected to the Illinois House of Representatives.

1854, November 27.   Lincoln files notice that he will not accept election to the legislature.

1855, February 8.   The Illinois legislature comes within a few votes of electing Lincoln to the US Senate to succeed James Shields.

1856, May 10.   By signing the call for a state convention, Lincoln formally joins the Republican party.

1856, June 23.   At Urbana, Illinois, Lincoln makes the first of many speeches in behalf of John C. Fremont, first Republican presidential candidate.

1858, June 16.   The Republican State Convention names Lincoln as its 'first and only choice' for the US Senate in opposition to Stephen A. Douglas.

1858, August 12.   At Beardstown, Illinois, Lincoln begins his campaign to elect Republican members of the legislature, who in turn will elect the Senator. In the next two and a half months he will speak almost daily and engage in seven joint debates with Douglas.

1858, November 2.   In this day's election the Democrats win control of the legislature, thus assuring the re-election of Douglas.

1860, May 18.   The Republican National Convention, meeting in Chicago, nominates Lincoln for the Presidency.

1860, November 6.   Though lacking a popular majority, Lincoln is elected with 180 electoral votes as against a total of 123 for his three opponents.

1860, December 20.   South Carolina passes the Ordinance of Secession declaring herself out of the Union.

1861, March 4.   Lincoln is inaugurated the sixteenth President of the United States. By this time seven states have declared themselves in secession.

1861, April 12.   When Confederate forces open fire on Fort Sumter in Charleston harbor, the Civil War begins.

1861, July 21.   In the first Battle of Bull Run, Union forces under

General Irvin McDowell are badly defeated by Confederates under Joseph E. Johnston and P. G. T. Beauregard.

1861, November 1.   Lincoln gives command of the US Army to General George B. McClellan, who succeeds General Winfield Scott, retired.

1862, February 6.   General U. S. Grant takes Fort Henry on the Tennessee River, and gives the Union its first important success.

1862, February 16.   Fort Donelson on the Cumberland River surrenders to Grant – a far greater victory than Fort Henry.

1862, February 20.   William Wallace Lincoln, aged eleven years, dies after a brief illness.

1862, March 9.   The *Monitor*, Federal, and the *Merrimac*, Confederate, fight to a draw in Hampton Roads, near Norfolk, Virginia. The engagement, the first between ironclads, inaugurates a new era in naval warfare.

1862, April 6–7.   Union troops under General U. S. Grant win a costly victory in the Battle of Shiloh, one of the bloodiest of the war.

1862, May 31–June 1.   The Army of the Potomac, moving on Richmond under General B. McClellan, fights an inconclusive battle at Fair Oaks (Seven Pines).

1862, June 25–July 1.   In the Seven Days Battles, Confederate General Robert E. Lee turns back McClellan and saves Richmond.

1862, June 27.   Lincoln places General John Pope in command of a new army, the Army of Virginia.

1862, July 22.   Lincoln submits a proclamation of emancipation to his Cabinet, but decides not to issue it until the Union has won a major victory.

1862, August 29–30. The Union forces under Pope are disastrously defeated in the Second Battle of Bull Run.

1862, September 17.   McClellan, again in command of the Union army, stops Lee's invasion of Maryland in the Battle of Antietam.

1862, September 22.   Lincoln issues the first, or preliminary, Proclamation of Emancipation.

1862, November 5.   Lincoln relieves McClellan and names General Ambrose E. Burnside as commander of the Army of the Potomac.

1862, December 13.   In the Battle of Fredericksburg, Burnside is badly defeated by Lee.

1863, January 1. By the final or definitive Proclamation of Emancipation the President proclaims freedom for all slaves in states or parts of states in rebellion.

1863, January 25. General Joseph Hooker succeeds Burnside at the head of the Army of the Potomac.

1863, May 1–4. Lee defeats Hooker in the Battle of Chancellorsville but loses his most effective subordinate, Thomas J. ('Stonewall') Jackson.

1863, May 18. General Grant places the Confederate stronghold of Vicksburg, Mississippi, under siege.

1863, June 28. Lincoln replaces Hooker as commander of the Army of the Potomac with General George Gordon Meade.

1863, July 1–3. Meade defeats Lee in a three-day battle at Gettysburg, Pennsylvania, that marks the turning point of the war.

1863, July 4. Vicksburg surrenders to Grant, thus giving the Union complete control of the Mississippi River.

1863, September 19–20. Union forces under General W. S. Rosecrans are defeated in a heavy battle at Chickamauga, Georgia.

1863, October 16. General U. S. Grant is placed in command of all western armies of the Union.

1863, November 19. At a memorial ceremony on the Pennsylvania battlefield, Lincoln delivers his immortal Gettysburg Address.

1863, November 23–25. In a series of battles around Chattanooga, Tennessee, the Union army wins an important victory.

1864, March 10. Grant, now a lieutenant-general, is assigned to the command of all Union armies.

1864, May 5. Grant, with Meade's Army of the Potomac, starts an advance on Richmond. For the next six weeks almost continuous fighting will result in unprecedented casualties.

1864, May 6. General William Tecumseh Sherman, commanding the armies of the West, starts his advance towards Atlanta.

1864, June 19. Grant begins the siege of Petersburg, key to Richmond.

1864, September 2. Atlanta falls to Sherman.

1864, November 8. Lincoln is re-elected President, receiving 212 electoral votes to 21 for George B. McClellan.

1864, November 16. Sherman starts from Atlanta on 'the march to the sea.'

1864, December 15–16. In the Battle of Nashville, General George B. Thomas smashes the last important Confederate army in the west.

1864, December 22. Sherman occupies Savannah, Georgia.

1865, February 1. Sherman leaves Savannah to march north through the Carolinas, laying the country waste as he proceeds.

1865, March 4. Lincoln is inaugurated the second time.

1865, April 2. The Confederate army and government evacuate Richmond.

1865, April 9. At Appomattox Courthouse, Virginia, Lee surrenders the Army of Northern Virginia to Grant, practically ending the war.

1865, April 14. John Wilkes Booth shoots Lincoln as he watches a play at Ford's Theater in Washington.

1865, April 15. Lincoln dies at 7.22 a.m.